THE LITERATE MIND

The Literate Mind

A Study of Its Scope and Limitations

Andrew Wells
Institute of Social Psychology,
London School of Economics, UK

First published 2012 by
PALGRAVE MACMILLAN

Palgrave Macmillan in the UK is an imprint of Macmillan Publishers Limited, registered in England, company number 785998, of Houndmills, Basingstoke, Hampshire RG21 6XS.

Palgrave Macmillan in the US is a division of St Martin's Press LLC, 175 Fifth Avenue, New York, NY 10010.

Palgrave Macmillan is the global academic imprint of the above companies and has companies and representatives throughout the world.

Palgrave® and Macmillan® are registered trademarks in the United States, the United Kingdom, Europe and other countries.

ISBN: 978–1–137–02550–0 hardback
ISBN: 978–0–230–20119–4 paperback

This book is printed on paper suitable for recycling and made from fully managed and sustained forest sources. Logging, pulping and manufacturing processes are expected to conform to the environmental regulations of the country of origin.

A catalogue record for this book is available from the British Library.

A catalog record for this book is available from the Library of Congress.

10 9 8 7 6 5 4 3 2 1
21 20 19 18 17 16 15 14 13 12

Printed and bound in Great Britain by
CPI Antony Rowe, Chippenham and Eastbourne

For Joan and Arthur

Contents

Tables

Acknowledgements

Many people have contributed to the book. I am grateful to Jaime Marshall at Palgrave Macmillan for his continuing support of my projects and to Aléta Bezuidenhout for her careful shepherding of this one through its various phases. Vidhya Jayaprakash of Newgen Knowledgeworks has again headed the production team and I am grateful to her and her colleagues for their meticulous care and professionalism. The evolutionary orientation of the book owes a great deal to past and present members of the Darwinian work-in-progress group which has met weekly during term time at LSE for more than 15 years. The group has been kind enough to discuss parts of the book on several occasions. I have benefited particularly from discussions with Christopher Badcock, Tom Dickins, Fatima Felisberti, David Hardman, Dieneke Hubbeling, Nick Humphrey, Rob King, David Lawson, Rebecca Sear, Paula Sheppard, John Skoyles, Peter Sozou, Max Steuer, Paul Taylor, Sandra Virgo and Richard Webb. I have also drawn on their writings, both published and unpublished. Steven Pinker has done a great deal to bring evolutionary theory to a wider audience through his books and lectures. He kindly gave me permission to use the list of human universals from *The Blank Slate* and I am very grateful to him. Poets and poetry grace a number of pages of the book. I am very pleased to record my thanks to Kathleen Jamie and Picador for permission to use *The Blue Boat*, to Paul Taylor for permission to use *Night Shift* and to Joe Winter and Anvil Press for permission to use *At Khelaghar*. I would also like to thank Faber and Faber Ltd, and Farrar, Strauss and Giroux, LLC, for permission to reprint *At Fossoli* by Primo Levi. The first draft of the book was read by an anonymous reviewer who provided me with helpful comments, for which I am grateful. It was also reviewed by David Wray, who should have remained anonymous but whose identity inadvertently became known to me. I am very pleased to have the opportunity to thank him for his thoughtful reading and for his wise comments and suggestions. The book is greatly improved as a result of his input. I have used some of the material in the book in seminars and lectures at LSE and elsewhere. Several cohorts of students have contributed to my education with their sharp questions and helpful comments. They are too numerous to mention individually but I am grateful to them all. Some of the work on the book was done while I was on sabbatical leave. I am grateful to LSE for granting me the leave and to my colleagues in the Institute of Social Psychology for taking over my responsibilities while I was away. My wife, Mia, has been, as always, a staunch supporter. I have gotten my book into print ahead of hers but the flow of papers and chapters that has delayed her own long-awaited book is indicative of a productivity that far outstrips my own. She was the dedicatee of my previous book and would have been of this one too had I not wanted to thank my parents, without whom neither I, nor this book, would have happened. Finally, it is important to say that none of the people mentioned above can be held responsible in any way for the errors that remain in the book. I have had a great deal of good advice and much warm-hearted support. The support I have accepted unconditionally but the advice I have not always heeded and thus the mistakes are all my own.

Chapter 1

Literacy in the World Today

1.1 Introduction

Literacy is a fundamental part of contemporary human life. With the possible exception of systematic agriculture, literacy is the most important technology that humans have invented. It is undoubtedly the most important *intellectual* technology, particularly when it is defined broadly to include numeracy and other kinds of mathematical symbol processing such as algebra, as well as alphabetic reading and writing. The origins of the first writing systems remain mysterious to a degree. Early work proposed a single site in the Middle East but more recent scholarship suggests that there were multiple, independent sites of origin, the earliest being some 5000 years ago (Houston, 2004). The reasons for the development of the early writing systems are also somewhat uncertain but coping with the societal pressures of living in the large settled groups that were made possible by systematic agriculture and the need to account for the production and distribution of foodstuffs seem to have been among the stimuli that provided the motivation. Thus it appears that both social and technological imperatives accompanied the emergence of literacy in at least some of its earliest sites. Social practices and technology are even more important sources of change and development now. The invention of printing with movable type in the middle of the fifteenth century enabled much more widespread dissemination of texts and contributed to a growth in reading and a wider selection of texts (Eisenstein, 1979; Hellinga, 2009). In the twentieth century the development of the computer led to new tools for literacy, most notably perhaps, the word processor and desktop publishing. In the twenty-first century the internet and World Wide Web will dominate further development in the study and uses of literacy. Over its short history the internet has transformed many existing literacy practices and has led to the invention of completely new ones. Email was once revolutionary but is now old hat and we have blogs, wikis, tweets, instant messaging, and many other possibilities for communication. Social networking has changed our understanding of what the internet is for and how and why people use it. Education in schools, colleges, and universities is changing to absorb and adapt to the new possibilities. Access to the internet via mobile phone infrastructure makes it possible to use the net wherever a phone signal is available. The

1

keyboard/keypad, not the pen or pencil, is the primary tool for many literacy practices, and the electronic symbol is rapidly replacing human calligraphy and penmanship.

Do we have adequate theory to understand these potent changes and to help us think about where they may be leading? Since about the middle of the twentieth century there has been a great deal of theoretical development in the study of literacy but there is no well-established consensus. For some theorists literacy can best be understood in terms of skills which are relatively context free, that is they work wherever you use them. For others, literacy needs to be understood in terms of the social practices in which it is embedded and in terms of the ideologies which sustain those practices. Some theorists of this persuasion deny the value or significance of thinking about literacy in terms of skills.

Perhaps we should not be surprised that there is no theoretical consensus. Literate practices are found in an immense range of contexts involving most, if not all, of the activities that humans engage in. Indeed, so wide is this range and so diverse the contexts that one of the relatively recent turns of theory has been to think of literacies in the plural, rather than of literacy as a singular phenomenon (Street, 1993; Pahl and Rowsell, 2005). Moreover, computers and the internet have led to a surge of interest in 'new literacies' and 'multiliteracies' (Cope and Kalantzis, 2000; Coiro et al., 2008). In all this ferment of activity, it is easy to think that there is nothing holding it all together. Perhaps 'literacy' is a family concept in the same way that 'game' is a family concept. The thinking here goes back to the philosopher Ludwig Wittgenstein and his famous book *Philosophical Investigations*, which was first published in 1953. Kenny (2006) provides an interesting and accessible introduction to Wittgenstein's philosophy. Games are such varied things that there is nothing they all share in common but they can, nonetheless, be recognised as games. Literacies may be the same.

The framework outlined in this book, while paying heed to the diversity, plurality, and multiplicity of literate life, takes the view that there are two important things that all literate activities do have in common: They are human and they use external symbol systems. They are human because they involve human minds, meanings, feelings, and purposes, and they are externally symbolic because they use symbols and materials, numerals, alphabets, and paper and pencils, which are outside the mind, to represent other things. External symbol systems underpin the skills involved in reading and writing and human minds and purposes underlie the social practices in which literacy activities are embedded. The important point is to think about both of these things simultaneously because it is the combination of them that generates literate meanings and gives humans a uniquely powerful means of representing the world to themselves and to others.

The combination of humanness and external symbol use, when taken as definitive of literacy, implies that there are two fundamental ways of being non-literate: by not being human and by not using external symbols.

Computers are non-literate for the first reason, although they process external symbols, because they do not think, they have no feelings, and they have no purposes. What computers do does not mean anything to them. By contrast, humans who do not read and write are non-literate for the second reason, because they do not use external symbol systems. All humans engage in symbolic thought and reasoning and their lives are suffused with meaning but the systematic use and understanding of external symbols distinguishes those who are literate from those who are not.

To develop the many implications of this point of view, I use two important bodies of theory which are not commonly put together and have not, as far as I know, previously been used to study literacy. I use evolutionary theory to explore the humanness of literacy and I use computational theory to explore the possibilities of external symbol use. A substantial part of the book is given over to covering enough of the basics of these theories to make their application to the study of literacy comprehensible and, I hope, plausible. Much of the literacy literature is understandably concerned with practical issues and questions: How should children best be taught to read and write? How early in life should children begin to experience texts? What aspects of early environments are conducive to success or failure in reading and writing? Can the problems of adult illiteracy be overcome? Recent studies are charting the effects of digital media and their pervasive presence in everyday life. This book stands back from these crucial issues and explores literacy as a unique form of human activity, as an unprecedented achievement for an unusual kind of primate.

The principal questions the book addresses are why literacy is such a powerful tool, what scope it offers, and what limitations it might have. To anticipate the main lines of argument, I propose that there are four principal reasons why literacy is powerful: First, literacy makes available a potentially infinite universe of texts. Second, literacy provides durable representations which make extended chains of reasoning possible and which provide space for reflection away from the cut and thrust of social interaction. Third, literacy amplifies the distinctively human capacities of the non-literate mind, both cooperative and competitive, including the capacity for culture. Fourth, external symbol systems have objective properties which provide the foundations for mathematics and science. Clearly the scope of literate life is enormous, but computational theory suggests that literate reasoning may have some formal limitations and evolutionary theory helps us to reflect on limitations arising from aspects of human nature which dispose us to act in ways which may be harmful to ourselves and to the planet in the long run.

The power of literacy can, and I believe should, be understood in terms of a fundamental distinction between syntax and semantics or equivalently between form and meaning. The syntax of a text includes basic matters such as the alphabet used to record it and the range of structural components such as words, sentences, paragraphs and so on which it contains.

The semantics of a text concerns what it means. Literate humans have command of both syntax and semantics. Computers are non-literate because their operations are purely syntactic and humans who cannot read and write are non-literate because they cannot exploit the syntactic possibilities of external symbol systems. There is a powerful potential synergy between the high speed syntactic capabilities of computers and the semantic capabilities of human minds, the beginnings of which we are starting to see made manifest in the internet and other aspects of digital technology.

1.2   Benefits of literacy

The most obvious thing that literate people do which the non-literate cannot is to make written records which have many uses. The relative permanence of written records means that they can serve as aids to human memory. The unaided memory has limited capacity and functions with systematic biases such as the 'effort after meaning', (Bartlett, 1932) which privileges rational reconstruction over verbatim recall. Humans have a strong tendency to remember things the way they would like them to have been or to remember what they think is likely to have happened. We're not very good at remembering plain, unadorned facts, the things that actually did happen. Without written records the past is likely to be systematically reshaped to meet current needs. An early, influential, and contentious paper by Goody and Watt (1963) made just this point, among others.

The permanence of written records increases the power of what Tomasello et al. (1993) have called the 'ratchet effect', a process by which cumulative cultural evolution is made possible. A ratchet is a device, typically used in mechanical clocks, to stop springs unwinding or weights descending precipitately as soon as they are released by the winder. Tomasello et al argue that humans, uniquely in the animal world, have the capacity to stop their cultural inventions from unwinding by remembering them long enough to be able to improve them; writing things down clearly helps this process. The possibility of making copies of a written text facilitates its dissemination so that more people can read it and think about what it says, and writing enables what we now call 'virtual' communication between individuals at different times and in different places. Before telephones and email became widely available letters were the principal means of private communication between distant people. Records of all sorts such as commercial transactions and legal judgements are maintained for information and to support contracts and arguments. Verbatim transcripts of speech such as Hansard, the record of proceedings in the British parliament, are intended to be neutral and objective, and straightforward factual reporting is one clear use for written records. Whether neutrality and objectivity are actually achieved is, of course, a different matter.

1.3   Negative effects of literacy

Written records also offer almost unlimited opportunities for strategic manipulation, or, putting it in a less academic fashion, for various forms of cheating. Writing makes it possible for people to favour themselves in a fashion which may be hard to spot. It gives a huge range of opportunities for what Trivers (1971) called 'subtle' cheating. If someone writes a document which is biased in their favour and claims 'It is written that...' rather than 'I wrote that...' a degree of distance and objectivity seems to have been achieved and attention may be diverted from the selfish purposes of the writer. Religious texts which claim that the gods have spoken in favour of the chosen few remove the operation of favouritism from the perpetrators and locate it in the voices of the gods whose will it is then assumed to reflect. 'It is the will of the people' is another statement that could have the same kind of effect. Dictators are fond of appealing to the will of the people as the source of their authority. Positive emphases can also be created in this way. 'All men are created equal' has a different tone from 'I claim that all men are created equal' or 'One can argue that all men are created equal'. The United Nations' declaration making a commitment to universal human rights has this kind of positive emphasis.

Objectification, either positive or negative, implies a loss of innocence and a heightening of strategic awareness. Maybe the first scribes were precisely those who were the best schemers, those who were well suited to take advantage of the levers of power that literacy offered. Scribes would have been in a position to offer each other privileges and bribes at the expense of those who were producing the goods that they distributed (Damerow, 1996). The scribal class as a whole would have had good reasons for developing relations of reciprocity among themselves. Writing may very well have led to increased verbal sophistication as well as manipulative enhancement, strengthening the advantages that the scribes already enjoyed.

For much of the time since it was invented, literacy has been largely restricted to elite groups who have, by and large, used it to maintain and increase their power and wealth. Widespread, school-based literacy was a nineteenth and twentieth century phenomenon, and universal, global education to at least primary level was a late twentieth-century aspiration which may be achieved in the present century although some current initiatives are well behind target (Unesco, 2008, 2010, 2011). For individuals in contemporary societies, fluent reading and writing are necessary pre-requisites for active citizenship (Stromquist, 2006): They also offer opportunities for learning and entertainment. Literacy is generally, but not inevitably, understood as being beneficial for individuals. A literate person with adequate access to reading materials has potentially unlimited scope for intellectual enquiry. However, the effects of literacy at the institutional, societal, and cultural levels are not always positive. Apart from the possibilities of strategic manipulation described above, surveillance, oppression, and indoctrination are all facilitated by literacy when schooling is overseen and controlled by undemocratic and tyrannical regimes. Gordon (2010), for example, writes about his dismal experiences as a teacher and teacher trainer in Eritrea. He describes how an education system can be used to control the lives of young people and to channel them into military service. Even in democratic societies literacy may be managed through schooling in ways that tend to subordinate individual needs and desires to national economic or political imperatives (Zjada and Zjada, 2003; Levintova, 2010). The 2010 Unesco report, 'Education under Attack', and the 2011 Education for All Global Monitoring Report (Unesco, 2011), describe how educational institutions, teachers, and students are sometimes deliberately targeted in conflict zones. Chapter 12 discusses some of the problems in greater detail.

1.4   The objectivity of mathematics

Cheating, other than the falsification of results, seems less possible in mathematics and associated quantitative disciplines than in purely alphabetic literacy. There is greater objectivity and independence from human wishes and purposes in mathematics than in everyday writing. For example, although the concept of a prime number is a human invention which describes a specific property (a number is prime if it is divisible without remainder by itself and by one but by no other number), the sequence of prime numbers which plays a fundamental role in number theory seems so far removed from human creation that some have thought numbers to constitute a separate and independent realm of abstract objects. The classical exponent of this view was Plato, and the philosophical approach to mathematics called Platonism continues to have adherents among mathematicians, physicists, and philosophers of science (Penrose, 2004), although many other points of view can also be found in the mathematical literature (Kitcher, 1984; Maddy, 1990,1997; George, 1994; Tymoczko, 1998). Since mathematics is a part of literacy, broadly construed, it would be desirable, as part of a general theory, to understand why there appears to be a fundamental difference between mathematical and alphabetic forms of literacy although the two often go together (Barwell, 2009). One of the goals of the book is to explore this issue.

1.5   The multidisciplinary study of literacy

Literacy has been studied by scholars from a wide range of disciplines. This breadth of interest reflects its importance for all of us. The study of literacy in general, as distinct from the study of particular literate disciplines, is in a curious position with respect to the accumulated written records and archives that have been produced over the 5000 or so years of literate endeavour. There is a sense in which anything recorded using external symbolic media is relevant to the study of literacy and yet this is an embarrassment of riches since it would be both impossible and absurd for a scholar of literacy to attempt to survey the whole of the cumulative written record. Quite apart from the quantity of material, there is no one equipped to tackle more than a tiny fraction of the specialised information that exists in the world's literature when that term is understood in the broadest possible fashion. Who could hope to have expert knowledge of the earliest epic poems, of the emerging science of genomics, and of the physics of quantum gravity, for example? There have been attempts to survey literate knowledge and to list the world's most influential books, see for example Seymour-Smith (1998), but any such attempt will inevitably do little more than reflect the particularities of time and place and the judgment of the selector. The introduction to Seymour-Smith's book, somewhat pompous, a touch arrogant, and rather dismissive by turns, is a good illustration.

There is specialised literature on how literacy affects individual human minds and wider human society and culture which must be considered by anyone who wishes to contribute to the theoretical development of literacy studies. In view of the vast range of literate outputs, however, it is important for scholars to indicate the grounds on which they base their arguments about the effects of literacy and which aspects of literacy they take into account. If, for example, one considers mathematics as well as alphabetic forms of literacy it is not clear that they can necessarily be understood in terms of the same theoretical categories. Take the case of social practices. There are, of course, social practices associated with the teaching, learning, and practice of mathematics, but the meaning of a particular theorem or proof is not contingent on those practices in the way in which the meaning of a literary text might be.

Different disciplines approach the study of literacy using a range of methods which emphasise specific aspects of literacy practices and outputs. Anthropologists and psychologists, for example, have been prominent in the study of literacy (Goody and Watt, 1963; Goody, 1968, 1977, 1986, 2000; Scribner and Cole, 1981; Street, 1984, 1991; Kellogg, 1994; Olson, 1994; Kintsch, 1998; Astington, 2000; Collins and Blot, 2003; Snowling and Hulme, 2005). Ethnographies and experiments, the favoured tools of anthropologists and psychologists respectively, almost inevitably produce rather different types of findings. Linguists with an interest in literacy also tend to have a particular focus (Householder, 1971; Harris, 2000, 2009), and educators at all levels, from pre-school to university and beyond, have their own distinctive concerns (Goodman and Martens, 2007; Alexander, 2010; Janks, 2010; Laidlaw, 2005; Wagner, 2008; Pring et al, 2009). In earlier generations there were classicists who left their mark on the study of literacy based on their understanding of the significance of the founding literatures of the classical world (Snell, 1953). Some philosophers have made seminal contributions to the study of written forms (Wittgenstein, 1953; Derrida, 1997). Philosophy, logic, and meta-mathematics may in some ways be thought to blend into each other with regard to attempts to understand what the possibilities of symbolic forms might be. The pioneers of theoretical computer science and some of its current practitioners are also included in this book, in the roll call of those whose expertise helps us to understand the scope and limitations of literate enquiry (Gödel, 1931; Turing, 1936; von Neumann, 1948; Chaitin, 1987; Li and Vitányi, 2008). There is also a relatively new branch of study which situates literature, rather than literacy as a whole, within a Darwinian context (Carroll, 1995, 2004; Gottschall and Wilson, 2005; Gottschall, 2008). Equally important has been the work of historians whose enquiries into rates of literacy and their associations with issues such as economic and technological development provide an essential background for contemporary theorists and practitioners (Eisenstein, 1979; Ginzburg, 1980; Graff, 1991, 1995, 2007).

1.6   Realism and constructivism

Have the varied interests and approaches of those who study literacy yielded concordant and consistent findings? The simple answer is that they have not. This is due, in part, to the relativist philosophy underpinning some of the literature. There is a vein of radical social constructivism and relativism in the literacy literature. To the extent that constructivism emphasises the multiplicity of literate practices it is to be welcomed, but some constructivist writers question the independence of external reality from human concerns and purposes. There are important institutions which exist solely because humans have constructed them, but the suggestion that the physical world is a construction of this kind is wrong and self-defeating. The viewpoint taken in this book is realist. There is an external world, independent of human thoughts and desires which grounds our understanding and provides a basis for the unity of knowledge. Chapter 2 discusses social construction from a realist, evolutionary standpoint.

The book emphasises the dynamic links between minds and texts. To understand these links properly, the prior existence of the world and the long evolutionary history of the pre-literate mind must be explored. Minds are the active partners in literacy but they interact with texts in processes of meaning making. Different minds may be particularly attuned to specific kinds of syntactic and semantic properties. Some people are good at maths from an early age while others are great story tellers. It may be, as the study of expertise in mathematics shows, that minds closer to the mechanistic end of what has been called a mentalist/mechanist spectrum (Badcock, 2009) have a special affinity for abstract thinking and can see patterns in symbol structures which are less obvious to other minds. Extreme qualities at the mentalist end of the spectrum may also be apparent in other genres, perhaps particularly in the authors of famous literary classics. Shakespeare continues to be valued for his profound insights into human nature as well as for the beauty of his language.

1.7   Science, society, and language

The study of literacy is related to, but not identical with, a number of disciplines which are important for it. It covers more than just reading and writing. It draws on grammatology, a term coined by Gelb (1952) to describe the science of the structural properties of writing systems. Literacy has been studied from the standpoint of individuals, from the standpoint of societal concerns, and from the standpoint of linguistics. The contrasts are interesting, as Coulmas points out (1996, p. 304). In individual terms, literacy may be contrasted with illiteracy; in social terms, literacy may be contrasted with orality; and in linguistic terms, literacy is contrasted with spoken language and the medium of expression is the major focus of concern. This book is multi-focal. It is concerned with the power of literacy as a technology and with ideological and political power. Both individual and societal levels of analysis are needed to give an adequate picture. It is also clear, however, that dichotomies such as literate/illiterate and literacy/orality may hinder enquiry as much as help it. One of the contributions that computer theory makes to the book is its emphasis on processes. Different kinds of literate processes and the capacities they support can be described without the use of terms such as 'illiterate'.

Much of the work by prominent scholars of literacy has assumed that the development of alphabetic writing was of primary importance because it made it possible to write down anything which could be said. The invention of alphabets was hugely important but is not the whole story. Mathematical symbolism shows that the technological power of literacy cannot be understood solely in terms of the alphabetic principle and that writing is more than a static record of speech. Mathematical structures seem to provide guidance to the minds that explore them in a way that alphabetic literacy does not. This guidance is based on the objective properties of mathematical concepts, structures, and spaces but it may lead to erroneous empirical conclusions if the structure being explored does not map onto the world in precisely the way that the theorist supposes. Euclidean geometry is an interesting case in point (see Chapter 8).

1.8   Skills and social practices

What kind of a phenomenon is literacy? Most non-specialists would say that literacy involves individual cognitive skills whose learning and exercise are embedded in social institutions and practices. The skills perspective on literacy is simple and rather obvious. Humans are not born able to read or write and almost all require some formal tuition in order to learn to do so. Alphabets are social constructions (although they tend to have structural principles in common, Dehaene, 2009): the links between the spoken and written forms of words are conventional and have to be learned. Reading and writing are teachable, learnable, skills. Some people learn quickly, others find literacy more challenging. The need for skills is even more obvious when considering arithmetic and mathematics. Modern techniques involving Arabic numerals and positional notation (units, tens, hundreds, etc.) make the basic arithmetical operations of addition, subtraction, multiplication, and division reasonably straightforward but everyone has to be taught them and they are not intuitively obvious. The Romans, for example, did not develop any significant mathematics, probably because they used a cumbersome, non-positional, system for representing numbers. Addition using Roman numerals is challenging enough, multiplying or dividing them is just about impossible, mentally somewhat like riding a bike on a high-wire over Niagara falls while juggling.

The abstraction involved in elementary algebra which is a prerequisite for further development towards higher mathematics must also, in most cases, be taught formally. There are occasional exceptional individuals who can learn advanced techniques from books or develop methods of their own but they are very much the exceptions. In the cases of both alphabetic writing and arithmetic, therefore, it is appropriate to talk about the learning of skills. Writing good academic English is a skill, as is the ability to find the roots of a quadratic equation. Fluent reading of English is a learnable skill, which some acquire much more readily than others.

A type of literate skill, with both alphabetic and numerical components, which has become economically and socially important over the past 50 years, is computer programming. Thousands of computer languages have been invented to cope with the multiple challenges of the contemporary digital age (Landin, 1966). Mastery of any of these languages is a distinct skill. Programming skills are second order because they require and build on the first order skills of reading and writing with alphabetic and numerical symbols.

In all cases, literate skills involve the use of some kind of syntax which has to be learned to create or comprehend meaningful structures. The distinction between syntax and semantics is often not readily apparent because one of the key literate skills is to become able to understand meaning without a struggle with the form. Whereas novice readers may have to spell out words letter by letter, the expert reader appears to extract the meaning of a text without any obvious effort. However, the sharper the separation we can achieve theoretically between syntax and semantics the better able we will be to appreciate the fundamental role of syntactic skills in literacy. Computational theory provides exactly the tools needed to make the separation. Poets are also expert at exploiting syntax for specific semantic purposes. John Hollander's book *Rhyme's Reason* (2001, p. 16) is a source of witty and inventive examples which are often self-referential:

> The *ballad stanza's* four short lines
>   Are very often heard;
> The second and the fourth lines rhyme
>   But not the first and third.

The idea that literacy involves social practices is equally obvious. Literacy learning, for most people, is embedded in the social practices associated with schooling and with the societies of which they happen to be members. Aspects of textual presentation such as whether words go from left to right, from right to left, or up and down on the page are determined by social practices, as are alphabets and other symbol systems. Social practices also determine who gets to go to school and who does not. In societies across the world, girls and women are deprived of access to education and literacy training or given a lower level of provision because of social practices which deem them less worthy of education or less capable of benefiting from it (Jayaweera, 1987; Skelton and Francis, 2009). Lower perceived economic returns on investment in education for girls may also serve as a barrier to their inclusion. Social practices in the form of stereotypes influence who learns what in school. Some literate skills are considered more valuable than others and some social groups are considered more educable than others.

1.9   Literacy is a contested domain

It might appear that the skills and social practice perspectives on literacy would be viewed by theorists as complementary and that a broad, consensual, framework for the study of literacy would have been developed along the following lines. Individuals need to acquire specific skills in order to be able to read, write, and calculate. Many of these skills, which are essential for modern life, can be described independently of the contexts in which they are learned and used; but for a full picture, the cultural contexts and social practices in which literacy skills are embedded must also be understood. Many contexts, some local, some more global, impinge on literacy events and practices. Unfortunately, there is little sign of such a consensus; indeed, rather than a consensus there is a contest. The skills and social practice perspectives on literacy are often opposed to each other and are seen as alternatives rather than as complementary. For a notable exception to this tendency, see Purcell-Gates, Jacobson and Degener (2004)[1]. One of

---

1. The text was largely complete before I became aware of the book by Purcell-Gates et al. They argue that the skills and social practices approaches can be reconciled. Their approach is rather different from that taken in this book, but is, I think, compatible with it.

the striking features of the literacy literature is the extent of disagreement and debate about fundamentals among its scholars. In a background paper for the 2006 Education For All Global Monitoring Report, Brian Street, a leading ethnographer of literacy, says that

> The meaning of 'literacy' as an object of enquiry and of action – whether for research purposes or in practical programmes – is highly contested and we cannot understand the term and its uses unless we penetrate these contested spaces. (Street, 2005, p. 3)

More recently, the editors of *The Cambridge Handbook of Literacy* have described the theoretical linkage between literacy and social change as

> an area of considerable dispute as scholars try to work out precise relationships between the cognitive processes specifically recruited in learning to deal with a writing system...and those recruited by the social uses of writing and reading in diverse social contexts...Contacts among workers in these areas are seriously limited and sometimes marked by disciplinary rivalry. (Olson and Torrance, 2009, pp. xix-xx)

One of the effects of disputes and lack of contact is that researchers from different perspectives fail to engage with each other. This leads to a fragmentation of the literature and a tendency for those from opposed positions to underestimate the value of their opponents' perspectives. This book proposes a framework in which both the skills and social practice perspectives are indispensable. The framework makes a firm and principled distinction between individual and social levels of analysis and between syntax and semantics. The analysis of individual literacy capabilities is grounded in a model drawn from the theory of computation. The analysis of social practices is grounded in the theory of evolution. The theory of computation provides tools which can be used to develop ideas about the scope and limitations of literacy, and the theory of evolution provides an underpinning for the exploration and understanding of social practices and ideology both in literacy contexts and more generally. The linkage between the two is derived from ecological understandings of the relationships between texts and minds and between individuals and wider social groupings. In the remainder of this chapter the major contours of the framework are laid out to provide a sense of how the approach will be developed in later chapters.

1.10   Literacy and computation

The mathematical theory of computation provides the theoretical underpinning for digital computers and the internet, both of which are having a profound influence on how texts are produced, thought about, and used. It may surprise some readers to learn that the fundamental ideas of computation theory are also directly applicable to literacy because they were derived from an analysis of the process of calculation with paper and pencil, carried out in the 1930s by the mathematician Alan Turing, probably better known, in Britain at least, for his code breaking work during the Second World War. Turing was trying to answer a rather abstruse question about the foundations of mathematics, and in tackling this question he asked himself what numerical processes it was possible for an individual human calculator working with paper and pencil to carry out. In particular he was interested in trying to work out what limits, if any, there were on the processes involved in paper and pencil calculation. General questions of this kind are not easy to think about but a good way to approach this one is to ask yourself which numbers you could write down given unlimited time, as much paper and as many pencils as you need, but nothing else. You have to rely on brain power alone.

You might begin by considering the series of natural numbers, sometimes called the 'counting' numbers, 1, 2, 3, 4, and so on. It's easy enough to see that anyone who can count and who has learned to write numerals could, in principle, write down an endless stream of numbers because one of the things that we learn early on is that it's always possible to add 1 to any number, no matter how big. So, if you had an infinite amount of time you could write down an infinite number of numbers. It would be very boring, but it could be done. The theory of computation is thus linked to questions about what it is possible for individuals to calculate when they are restricted to working with paper and pencil only. Talk about calculation may suggest that the analysis is limited to mathematical questions only but it should be easy for a contemporary reader to see that similar principles apply to writing down letters, words, or sentences as well. In fact, numbers can always be written as words and vice versa. The sequence of counting numbers can be written down as a sequence of words. Rather than writing, 1, 2, 3, and so on, we could write 'one, two, three,...' Any numeral can, in principle, be written down in words. Most people also know that letters and punctuation are represented in computers as binary numerals. Any text of any length, not just number words, can be represented by a binary numeral. Many texts from more and more of the world's literatures already exist somewhere in a computer memory as huge binary numerals. If you have an e-book reader you are a consumer of binary representations of texts. If you use a word processor you are a producer and a consumer of binary representations of texts even though you probably never see the underlying binary codes. Binary coding shows that questions about what alphabetic texts it is possible for the unaided mind to write are equivalent in principle, given suitable translation, to questions about what numbers it is possible for the unaided mind to calculate. We normally think of calculation and alphabetic writing as based on different kinds of mental processes, but for theoretical purposes, if we treat those processes in a sufficiently abstract way (as described in Chapter 7), we can think of them as syntactically equivalent. This equivalence is important for the study of literacy because it makes it possible to use some formal results from the theory of computation to illuminate questions about the scope and limitations of alphabetic literacy. The most striking result shows that in a precisely definable sense, a literate mind is infinitely more powerful than a non-literate mind (see Chapter 8). This result speaks indirectly to the complex debate about the consequences of literacy which was sparked almost 50 years ago by the publication of the famous paper by Goody and Watt (1963). The result is indirect because Goody and Watt were primarily concerned with the societal effects of literacy, whereas Turing's theory of computation is concerned with the capacities of individuals.

1.11   Autonomy versus social practices?

Turing worked out his theory of computation using a mathematical model now called a Turing machine. The machine has two components: one represents the set of states of a human mind engaged in a calculation, the other represents a text. There is thus an absolutely sharp distinction between minds and texts in the model, although both are represented purely syntactically using symbol structures. The processes of reading and writing that can be constructed in terms of the model rely equally on structure in the mind and text components, but on nothing else. This shows that an 'autonomous' treatment of literacy at the level of the individual is possible despite strong arguments to the contrary from a number of distinguished theorists. Brian Street, for example, claimed in an influential book that

> literacy can only be known to us in forms which already have political and ideological significance and it cannot, therefore, be helpfully separated from that significance and treated as though it were an 'autonomous' thing; (Street, 1984, p. 8)

In a similar vein, in another highly regarded book, James Gee has made an equally strong claim:

> Literacy practices are almost always fully integrated with, interwoven into, constituted part of, the very texture of wider practices... You can no more cut the literacy out of the overall social practice, or cut away the non-literacy parts from the literacy parts of the overall practice, than you can subtract the white squares from a chessboard and still have a chessboard. (Gee, 2008, p. 45)

The approach taken in this book shows that these claims are too strong. They amount to the claim that the syntactic and semantic aspects of literacy cannot be examined independently of each other. The Turing machine model lets us examine a number of different types of relationship between mind and text in a way that is completely independent of politics or ideology. The model is also informative about the theoretical links between orality and literacy. Such 'autonomous' modelling of literacy may be seen as contentious because the debate has a normative character and is morally charged. This is clear in the work of both Street and Gee. Street's 1984 book proposes that autonomous modelling 'tends implicitly to privilege and to generalise the writer's own conceptions and practices' (p. 2) and that such models are constructed for specific political purposes. Gee argues that literacy cannot be separated from the 'Discourses' within which it is embedded and that these Discourses are morally weighted.

> A Discourse with a capital "D" is composed of distinctive ways of speaking/listening and often, too, writing/reading *coupled* with distinctive ways of acting, interacting, valuing, feeling, dressing, thinking, believing, with other people and with various objects, tools, and technologies, so as to enact specific socially recognizable identities engaged in specific socially recognizable activities. (Gee, 2008, p. 155)

Further on, Gee describes Discourses as theories about the world and argues that each of us has a moral obligation to reflect on our theories, particularly with regard to the possibility that 'a Discourse of which we are a member advantages us or our group over other people or other groups.' (p. 221). In Gee's view this is a Kantian imperative, one with which everyone should agree. He goes on to say,

> Should you choose not to adopt this moral stance, then I, and others, like the non-mainstream people we have studied in this book, reserve the right to actively resist you and the ways in which your unreflective performances limit our humanity. (Gee, 2008, p. 221)

Gee and Street are right to assert the moral significance of intellectual work and the need for each of us to reflect critically on our professional practice. They also rightly point to the profound significance of social practices and to the ideologically charged nature of much of the literacy literature. However, I disagree with them when they imply that the disinterested, scientific study of literacy is not possible and that anyone who claims that it is has ulterior motives of dubious moral probity. Turing machine theory provides a genuinely neutral framework within which the key syntactic properties of literacy can be explored. One fundamental property of texts is that they provide stable, relatively permanent, durable representations of their subject matter. Stable and durable texts facilitate reflection, revision, extension, and long-term study. In these respects literate processes using texts are markedly different from transient spoken utterances and they are, as a result, partly independent of circumstances and may be considered autonomous. The contents of texts are often politically motivated and ideologically significant but that does not alter their formal properties.

Models related to the Turing machine have been used to clarify the goals of a cognitive neuroscientific perspective (Petersson et al., 2009), but Turing's theory is insufficient, by itself, as a basis for the study of literacy. The theory is abstract and syntactic in the same way that calculi in formal logic are abstract and syntactic. This characteristic locates the Turing machine model firmly in the autonomous, context free, skills-based domain. The theory is also quite specifically concerned with the interactions between an individual mind and a single text.

In addition to this focus on the individual it is essential, as Street, Gee, and others have shown, to understand the institutions, contexts, and practices in which literacy events and practices are embedded. First, it is important to have a theory of social institutions and the facts that arise from them. Numerous questions arise. What does it mean to call something a social construction? How are social constructions distinguished from the rest of reality? What does literacy contribute to the development and maintenance of social institutions? My approach to these questions has been inspired by the work of the philosopher John Searle, in particular his book *The Construction of Social Reality* (1995). Second, it is important to understand the range of institutions, contexts, environments, ideologies, and political structures which impinge on actual literacy practices. The New Literacy Studies (NLS) movement (Street, 1993; Street and Lefstein, 2007; Barton, 2007) has been at the forefront of an extensive programme of research to document the multiplicity of literacy practices and to construct theories to explain them. Critical extensions of the NLS approach have also been proposed (Brandt and Clinton, 2002; Collins and Blot, 2003; Reder and Davila, 2005; Lewis et al., 2007). I have drawn on this body of work to inform an account of the distinctions which are needed to underpin a taxonomy of social practices, although I am also critical of some of its reasonings and conclusions.

1.12   Literacy and evolution

The use of Turing machine theory is a new departure in the study of literacy. A strong commitment to evolutionary theory is another new departure. Literacy is set, in this book, in the context of an understanding of the human being, and the human mind in particular, as the products of an immensely long evolutionary history. The principal reasons for a focus on evolution as part of the study of literacy are the light it sheds on human sociality and the expectations it leads to with regard to differences between literate and non-literate minds and societies. Whereas Turing machine theory helps us to understand the syntactic skills associated with literacy, evolutionary theory helps us to understand the social institutions in which those skills are formed and practised. Humanity is unique in the animal kingdom for the range and complexity of social relationships with other individuals. A number of features of human life contribute to this complexity. The existence of language is perhaps the most obvious but there are many others. Humans are born physically immature by comparison with the neonates of most other species and require a long period of care before they become independent. The relationships formed with care givers in infancy and with peers slightly later have important consequences for social integration and confidence about dealing with others, for example in school (Ainsworth, 1978; Harris, 1998). The human life span is relatively long and social relationship needs are different at different stages of life history. Human males invest more in their offspring than do the males of any other primate species, but their minimal obligatory investment is lower than that of human females. This investment asymmetry, coupled with the concealed ovulation of human females and the cessation of female reproduction relatively early in life, leads to complex patterns of human sociality in which issues to do with power, status, and dominance are fundamentally important and contested both within and between the sexes. There is more than one battle of the sexes and all of them are important for understanding human social life.

Evolutionary thinking leads to the expectation that literacy will be used as a strategic tool. Since humans have both selfish and pro-social forms of motivation we should expect to find evidence for both in the history of literacy and in current literacy practices. We should expect to find some users of literacy whose efforts have been devoted to their own dominance and status, but we should also expect to find others whose efforts have been devoted, at least in part, to the betterment of humanity more generally. Many people think of evolution in terms of nature red in tooth and claw, of early humans doing battle with sabre toothed tigers, mammoths, and other large and challenging creatures, but there is an important strand of evolutionary theory which considers other humans as the most serious challenges faced by individuals trying to make their way in the world. From this perspective the complex problems of social life are the primary drivers of human intellectual capacities (Jolly, 1966; Humphrey, 1976). Chapter 6 considers social evolution and its importance for the study of literacy.

I am not advocating an evolutionary approach to written language of the kind criticised by Barton (2007, pp.120ff.). I do not argue that there has been an evolution 'from pictographs, through logographs, to syllabic systems and on to the alphabet' (p. 120) nor do I claim that alphabetic writing is superior to other forms. Thus far we agree. I differ from Barton, though, when he suggests that evolutionary theorising inevitably includes ideas of progress from earlier, less valuable, to later, more valuable, forms. He says that use of the term 'evolution'

> implies a certain sort of change: it brings along a whole set of notions, ideas such as that change is unidirectional, natural and inevitable. Passive and impersonal adaptation is implied and it also carries with it notions of improvement, superiority and progress. (p. 121)

While it is undoubtedly true that some forms of evolutionary theorising have had notions of progress built into them, it is not true of the theory of evolution developed by Charles Darwin which is based on the processes of natural and sexual selection. Our contemporary understanding is buttressed by knowledge of genetics which was not available to Darwin and by further developments of evolutionary theory built on the foundations he laid, but most of his central insights remain in place. Darwinian evolutionary change is indeed natural and inevitable when there is competition for resources and heritable variability in the members of a species, but it is certainly not unidirectional as Barton suggests. A characteristic which undergoes positive selection in one environment may become negative in another. As a result, one cannot say that any particular adaptation, or indeed any particular species, is superior to any other. Natural selection changes gene frequencies from one generation to the next and, if the environment remains stable long enough, selection will lead to the accumulation of changes in a particular direction, but that is all that can be said. *Homo sapiens* is the only surviving hominid species but that does not mean that we are superior in all respects to the other hominid species which became extinct. They may have been gentler, less aggressive creatures than our ancestors and ultimately unable to compete with them. It is true, in a sense, that we have inherited the earth, but we may prove unable to manage the complex challenges which are posed by our numerical success. In November of 2009 the US Census Bureau website estimated that the global human population was 6,798,699,772. By December of 2010 the figure had reached 6,887,311,284, in 2011 the figure passed seven billions, and further growth to more than nine billions is forecast to occur by mid-century. Current estimates can be found at http://www.census.gov/main/www/popclock.html. Evolutionary history records many instances of animal populations which have outstripped the resources available to them and have suffered catastrophic collapses as a result of starvation, disease, and conflict. Humanity is not protected against such an outcome.

Although progress is not a feature of contemporary Darwinian theory properly understood, there are interesting indicators, linked to literacy, which bear on the global situation. It is clear, although still a matter of contention in some quarters, that fertility levels are associated with literacy levels, particularly with female literacy. Higher levels of female literacy are associated with lower fertility. This is known as the demographic transition. It is not known for certain whether the transition is causal or not, but it may well be (Caldwell, 1976, 2006; Kirk, 1996). Educated women are better able to take control of their reproductive lives than are uneducated women and there is evidence that educated women frequently choose to limit their fertility. That may well be thought socially progressive but it does not imply that evolution is a progressive force.

A second interesting point is that literacy and evolution have led to a situation which is unparalleled in the history of life on the planet. There is now, for the first time ever, a species, *Homo sapiens*, which has begun to understand the mechanisms by which populations change and by which complex organisms are formed. It is inconceivable that a non-literate species could have achieved this understanding. The volume of data and range of observations needed to secure the evolutionary understanding we now have are simply too great for the unaided mind. This is not to say that literacy had to be invented; it is simply to say that had it not been we would not now understand how evolution works. Reflexive self-understanding is a particularly well developed characteristic of literate individuals (Olson, 1994), but it is not uniquely associated with literacy. It is also not obvious from an evolutionary perspective that humans will be good at understanding their own mental structures or have clear insights into their own motivations. Evolution has structured human minds to be particularly skilled (not necessarily in a conscious way) at solving problems to do with resource acquisition and reproduction in competitive social contexts; other native forms of understanding are by-products of these basic functions and we should not expect human minds to be equally good at all kinds of problem solving. The enormous scope for knowledge and intellectual enquiry opened up by literacy may make it hard for us to understand that human minds have particular proclivities and that some mental activities are more natural and intuitive than others that have been made possible by literacy. Reflective practices are considered further in Chapter 12.

1.13   The ecological study of literacy

The theory of computation and the theory of evolution are not immediately obvious partners, although Dennett (1995) linked them by describing evolution as an algorithmic process. In this book the bridging concepts are ecological, and one inspiration for the approach is the pioneering work of the psychologist J.J. Gibson (1966, 1979). The fundamental idea of Gibson's ecological approach to psychology is that perception and thinking involve the interaction of two sources of structure, one in the person, and the other in the environment. Gibson coined the term 'affordance' to describe what environmental structures offer the individual.

An ecological understanding of the theory of computation is based on the fundamental distinction between the agent or engine that carries out a computation and the medium which stores data and results. In modern computers this is realised in the familiar distinction between memory and central processor; in Turing machine theory there is an analogous distinction between the 'finite automaton' and the 'tape', and in the literate human there is the distinction between mind and text. The agent and the medium interact to produce the sequence of symbols that is the output of a computation. In previous work (Wells, 2002, 2006) I have examined the ecological nature of computational processes in detail.

An ecological approach to evolution is equally appropriate. The process of evolution by natural selection involves constant interactions between individuals and their environments. The outcomes of those interactions determine the number of offspring that each individual leaves, and hence that individual's contribution to the population gene pool. Individuals are relatively short lived whereas environments have at least some characteristics which are very long lasting. The 24-hour day/night cycle, for example, is a constant feature of most human environments and it has given rise to numerous adaptations. Stable environmental features exert selection pressures on human characteristics and determine whether mutations are positive, neutral, or negative.

An ecological approach to the study of literacy has been proposed by Barton (2007). From Barton's perspective the strength of the ecological approach is

> that it changes the whole endeavour of trying to understand the nature of reading and writing. Rather than isolating literacy activities from everything else in order to understand them, an ecological approach aims to understand how literacy is embedded in other human activity, its embeddedness in social life and in thought, and its position in history, in language and in learning. (Barton, 2007, p.32)

Barton's espousal of a social ecology of literacy is valuable for the emphasis it puts on the embedding of literacy practices in other kinds of human activity, but his approach involves a subtle change of definition which seems to me to run counter to common understanding. If you ask the proverbial man or woman in the street what they think literacy is most will say (correctly, I believe) that it is the ability to read and write. But a little further down the page from the previous quote Barton writes as follows:

> If at this point a succinct statement of what is meant by an ecological approach is needed, I would say that it is one which examines the social

and mental embeddedness of human activities in a way which allows change. Instead of studying the separate skills which underlie reading and writing, it involves a shift to studying literacy, a set of social practices associated with particular symbol systems and their related technologies. (Barton, 2007, p.32)

The final sentence is the game changer. Instead of studying reading and writing, says Barton, we're going to shift to studying literacy, which has unobtrusively but quite clearly been redefined as a set of social practices. This strikes me as an unhelpful move and it can be confusing because the new definition is not used consistently thereafter in the book. What is puzzling about Barton's (and other) approaches which emphasise the importance of social practices is the idea that they are alternatives to more traditional conceptualisations. Is it not better to think of them as additions to, and extensions of, the traditional understanding of literacy as the ability to read and write, rather than as wholesale replacements which treat traditional ideas as outmoded ways of thinking?

The proposal I explore in this book is that literacy can and should be analyzed as an ecological activity at a range of different levels. My principal focus is on what might be called the 'micro-ecology' of the processes engaged in by an individual mind interacting with a single text. It is this level of analysis to which the Turing machine model specifically applies, but the focus on the individual is not in any sense intended to deny the importance of the social ecology with which Barton and others are concerned. To the contrary, I refer in later chapters to a literate individual as the 'functional core' of a system whose full complexity can only be grasped by considering a potentially endless array of surrounding institutions and practices. I want, though, to insist on the importance of the individual in this social matrix and I think this is very much in the spirit of the social practice approach. To lose sight of the individual is as bad as losing sight of social practices, and we need to keep shifting our focus from the individual to the social and back in order to understand our subject matter fully.

Reading and writing, at the micro-ecological level of analysis, involve two sources of structure, minds and texts. (The word 'text' is being used here in a very general sense to include any kind of written material of any length). The process of reading uses the external symbols of a text to cause a sequence of state changes in the mind and the process of writing uses the mind to produce an external sequence of symbols which constitutes a text. The conceptual resources of both evolutionary theory and the theory of computation help to give a full account of these processes. The computational account of the mind is highly abstract and geared towards the description of rule-governed processes. The principal elements in the theory are states of mind which are identified solely by syntactic labels. States of mind have transition relations among themselves and input and output relations to external symbols. There is nothing else in the theory but its slender resources are capable of describing processes of great complexity. We look in vain, though, for anything to do with the pleasures and pains of reading and writing or for the manifold human aims and goals that literacy serves. The point of the computational account is that it makes it possible to say some quite general things about different levels of literacy. If you can read but not write we would be inclined to say that there are some parts of literacy which are beyond you. If you can read and write but you are not able to re-read what you have written or revise it, you would again seem to be more limited in scope than someone who can re-read and revise. Using your imagination alone to create a written text seems rather different from using an existing template to create a story. All of these examples relate to different things that individuals can do with texts and all of them can be expressed precisely in the theory of Turing machines. That is part of why I think it is a worthwhile addition to the toolkit of literacy theorists.

Evolutionary theory and an account of social institutions are used to add a human dimension to the abstract skeleton of computational theory. The influential historian of literacy, Harvey Graff, has endorsed the value of setting literacy in the larger time scale of evolutionary chronology:

> The numerical exercise may appear frivolous to many fearful persons today; still, I contend that a reflection upon this time sequence and its implications can be both liberating – from the chains of the present moment or the recent past – and stimulating to new points of view. It assists us in placing literacy and the primacy with which we hold it in a larger, proper, context. (Graff, 1995, p.14)

When we look at humanity from an evolutionary perspective we see a hyper-social primate which has had language for a very long time but which invented literacy very recently. This suggests that contemporary non-literate and literate humans are much more alike than they are different. Most of the structure of human minds has been put in place by evolutionary processes acting over immense time spans. The period involved is not simply the five million years or so since our ancestors and the ancestors of chimpanzees (our closest relatives) diverged from their common parentage. Part of our basic mental equipment stems from our mammalian heritage which is more ancient still and some aspects have their roots even further back in phylogeny (Foley, 1995). Consequently, the suggestion that there is a fundamental divide between literate and non-literate minds is implausible. Nevertheless, literacy has had a profound impact on the conditions of life for most people on the planet. The proposal explored in this book is that literacy amplifies and extends the capacities of non-literate minds as well as facilitating some new capacities. There is no 'great divide' between oral and literate societies or between literate and non-literate individuals.

Literate societies all retain significant aspects of oral culture as one would expect, while literate individuals are able to explore and exploit new ways of thinking and living. Individual human desires and motivations have not changed with the invention of literacy but the ways in which they can be satisfied have been greatly expanded. Literacy does provide entirely new kinds of processes for human minds to engage in but these exist along with the manifold non-literate things that humans have always been able to do.

1.14   Literacy and human nature

An assessment of the possible effects of literacy on individuals and societies has to start with a perspective on human nature. Without an understanding of what non-literate humans are like it is impossible to say what effects literacy is likely to have. We need to know what kinds of intellectual and emotional processes non-literate minds can engage in, in order to tell whether becoming literate changes the ways our minds and feelings work. Some social theorists argue that there is no such thing as human nature, that there are simply social and cultural ideas about people which are geographically and temporally local and, in principle, indefinitely variable. According to such a view the human mind is a blank slate or *tabula rasa* on which culture inscribes its conventions and patterns of thought and behaviour. Human nature, from this perspective, is a cultural and social construction, and literacy might have a range of effects on it but none which could be systematic. Darwinian thinking rejects this point of view (Darwin, 1871; Brown, 1991; Barkow et al., 1992; Pinker, 2002). From a Darwinian standpoint human thought patterns and behaviour are not indefinitely malleable although they are extremely flexible. Brown (1991) listed a range of characteristics found in all human societies which have been explored by contemporary investigators, or for which there are historical or ethnographic records. These characteristics are called human universals. The discussion of the possible effects of literacy in this book is based on consideration of these universals. Brown's list of universals with some updates was republished by Pinker (2002), and Pinker's updated list forms the basis for discussion in this book. Literacy might reflect or have effects on none, some, or all of these universals. Let us take just one example. What do people read for pleasure? If I were to suggest that most people read government documents for pleasure you would rightly think I was mad or mistaken. If instead I said that most people choose to read stories with a strong plot and interesting characters you would think that much more plausible, as indeed it is. Moreover, it's plausible wherever you go and whoever you ask. A preference for stories is a human universal. It reflects a built-in liking for narratives and, in particular, a liking for narratives which are about people doing interesting things. If the human mind were a blank slate we would expect to see significant cultural variability in what people read for pleasure. It might be that one culture would like stories and another would like minutes of committee meetings but that's not how things are. People like stories about other people because our minds are strongly tuned to social experiences. Knowing about human nature will help us to understand what kinds of literacy skills are most natural and relatively easy to acquire and what kinds, although highly valuable, may be harder to acquire because they are less intuitive for human minds. Among the latter may be purely logical reasoning, independently of our own interests, and abstract thought of the kind represented by higher mathematics. Knowledge of human nature will help us to understand what makes an attractive and stimulating curriculum for learners at different stages of their education and in different places.

1.15   Literacy and the imagination

It is possible that the greatest effects of literacy have been to stimulate and liberate the imagination. R.A. Fisher, one of the most important Darwinian theorists of the twentieth century, argued for the importance of the imagination in a discussion of the differences of approach between biologists and mathematicians:

> The types of mind which result from training in mathematics and in biology certainly differ profoundly; but the difference does not seem to lie in the intellectual faculty...What is profoundly susceptible of training is the imagination, and mathematicians and biologists seem to differ enormously in the manner in which their imaginations are employed...I can imagine no more beneficial change in scientific education than that which would allow each to appreciate something of the imaginative grandeur of the realms of thought explored by the other. (Fisher 1999, pp. viii–ix)

Fisher focused on the contributions of mathematical and biological training to the extension of the imagination because his purpose was to bring a mathematical perspective to bear on evolutionary biology, but his ideas are much more widely applicable and the importance of the imagination is stressed by others too (Kotsopoulos and Cordy, 2008). Training in the arts, humanities, and social sciences as well as in the natural sciences can be argued to produce particular ways in which the imagination is deployed and the exchange of ideas between disciplines opens up new 'realms of thought'. More broadly still, if stimulation and liberation of the imagination are typical products of literacy then the extension and elaboration of one's interests, whatever they are, becomes possible. Fisher's view is thus consonant with, among others, the approach to critical consciousness of Freire (1993), which stresses the importance of the imagination and the exchange of ideas in the process by which individual minds become literate and freed from the yoke of mental oppression. Shiohata (2009) describes reading for pleasure as an escape into the realms of the imagination from the harshness of everyday life in Senegal.

Discussion of the role of the imagination in natural science leads rather naturally to related questions about the possible roles of rational thought and logical deduction in imaginative literate pursuits such as poetry and prose fiction which are often considered 'creative' and 'irrational'. If Fisher was right to suggest that different forms of scientific training affect the imagination rather than the intellect it is plausible that this is true of training in prose fiction and poetry as well, that is, that they are imaginatively different forms of intellectual endeavour rather than irrational outbursts of a creative impulse. The literary critic Helen Vendler (2004) has argued that lyric poetry demonstrates thinking in the service of aesthetics:

> In poems, thinking is made visible not only to instruct but also to delight; it must enter somehow into the imaginative and linguistic fusion engaged in by the poem. While retaining its fierce intelligence, poetic think-ing must not unbalance the poem in the direction of "thought". Yeats said (in "The Phases of the Moon") that at the aesthetic moment "all thought becomes an image," reminding us that poetry abstracts "real-ity" – including the reality of human thinking – into symbolic forms. (Vendler, 2004, p. 9)

Fisher's postulation of the critical role of the imagination in the service of systematic thought, plus the converse notion that systematic thought has a critical role to play in the products of the creative imagination, together provide an idea of the breadth of theoretical approach which is required if literacy as a whole is to be tackled. For those who have not had the opportunity to study theoretical computer science or evolutionary theory, the scope that together they provide for the study of literacy may be hard to appreciate. The point of the book is to make the case that putting them together is deeply illuminating.

1.16   Summary

Literacy is undeniably complex but Turing's theory shows that the logical structure of the micro-ecology of reading and writing is straightforward. What this suggests. and everyday experience confirms, is that although it takes time to acquire the necessary capabilities and to become confident in their use, almost everyone will be able to learn to read and write given a suitable environment of instruction and access to appropriate materi-als. Expertise takes longer but that does not detract from the essentially universal nature of literacy. It is, therefore, all the more scandalous that not everyone has the chance to become literate and, even among those who do, some are unable or unwilling to become proficient to a degree that makes literacy both enjoyable and useful.

However, although there is the constant shadow of inequality of access and provision, it is the positive aspects of the theory that are imaginatively inspirational. Turing's theory is mathematical and one of its characteristics is that it explores what is possible 'in the limit' for an individual who can read and write. 'In the limit' means that considerations of time and space are set aside and it is possible to consider issues like how many texts could, in principle, be written and read. The word 'text' is used here in the broadest possible sense to cover anything written at all no matter how long (or how short!). The single letter 'A' could be the sole content of a text. Turing's theory shows that if questions of time and of supplies of materials such as paper and ink are set aside, there is no limit to the number of texts that could be written or read. There are, in principle, infinitely many of them. Harry Potter enthusiasts who have had to make do with only seven books from the fertile imagination of J.K. Rowling can console themselves with the idea that there could be infinitely many more, although Ms Rowling would have to live forever in order to write them all and readers would also have to live forever in order to read them all. A sense of the size of the space of possible books can be had from *The Library of Babel*, a short story by the Argentinean writer Jorge Luis Borges, which is published in an English translation in his collected fictions (1999). The story is revisited in Chapter 8. For those of a more mathematical turn of mind, a recent book, *The Unimaginable Mathematics of Borges' Library of Babel*, has explored the mathematics implicit in the ideas of the story and reprinted the story as well (Bloch, 2008).

A striking feature of Turing's theory is the clarity with which it demonstrates the contrast between the relatively modest investment of time, resources, and effort that literacy requires and the indefinitely large payback that it offers. A determined reader with access to a good library (or increasingly, the internet) can discover and explore for herself vast domains of knowledge. I am not implying that everyone does have such access nor, even if they do, that they have the skills and determination needed to master the complex material that can be found. The world is a grossly unfair place both in terms of individual abilities and in the opportunities available, but the theory implies that the huge dividend of literacy for individuals is the fundamental reason why it is worthwhile. Turing's theory is about the literate individual. It is not primarily concerned with the uses and abuses of literacy in the contested spaces of the social world but with the infinite range of possibilities that the simple processes of reading and writing down symbols from a finite alphabet offer to the exploring mind.

Turing's theory provides a grip on literacy at the level of the individual. The theory is syntactic but applies quite generally to all creatures or machines that use external symbol systems. The syntactic precision of the theory makes possible the proof of theorems about symbol use which have profound semantic consequences. Darwinian theory provides resources for thinking about why human minds and societies are structured as they are, and why inequality is a pervasive feature of human life. Although Darwinian thinking may lead to some pessimistic conclusions about the prospects of a universally literate world, it also has a more positive side. It provides resources for thinking about humanity and human nature without any appeal to a deity or other designer. It brings the explanation of humanity and human nature within the scope of scientific enquiry. Science is the most powerful means that humans have invented to investigate the nature of the world we find ourselves in and its application to ourselves is illuminating.

Chapter 2

Social Construction and Independent Reality

Many important insights into the nature of literacy have come from theorists and practitioners who consider it to be the result of processes of social construction. This chapter explores what it means to say that literacy is a social construction, and it enquires into the scope of the notion. Such an enquiry is particularly important in the context of this book because of its Darwinian perspective. A workable notion of social construction which is compatible with a Darwinian understanding of human life and its origins needs to be achieved in the context of theory which typically takes biological and social influences to be opposed.

2.1 The social construction of reality

One of the most influential works in the social constructivist canon is *The Social Construction of Reality* by Peter Berger and Thomas Luckmann, published in 1966. Their perspective was sociological and they studied the nature of reality and knowledge, starting from the basic assumption that reality is different for different societies and is socially constructed. Sociologists, they said, had 'systematic awareness of the fact that men in the street take quite different 'realities' for granted as between one society and another' (Berger and Luckmann, 1966, p. 14). Is that right? Is it really a fact as they claim? Do people in different societies take quite different realities for granted? It is important to note that the concept of multiple, different, realities is an assumption, not something demonstrated, and that one might with equal or greater plausibility argue that men in the street interpret a single reality in different ways from one society to another. There is clearly a marked difference between the two positions. I shall argue that the assumption of a single reality is altogether more coherent and more plausible, but for the present we can explore where the assumption of multiple realities leads. It leads, initially, to the idea that knowledge and reality are socially relative and that what counts as known and real in one society might not be known or real in another. Relativism in the work of Berger and Luckmann leads very quickly to the idea that the taken for granted nature of the everyday world results not because it is independent of the members of a society but from their constructive actions.

> The world of everyday life is not only taken for granted as reality by the ordinary members of society in the subjectively meaningful conduct of their lives. It is a world that originates in their thoughts and actions, and is maintained as real by these. (ibid., p. 33).

Assertions of this kind have become so common in social science that it can be hard to see how extraordinary they are. What could it mean to say that the everyday world originates in my thoughts and actions or in yours? The world was there before I was born and before you were born. It was there for vast time spans before the ancestors of humans appeared. How can these facts be squared with the idea that you and I create the everyday world? The simple answer is that they can't be and Berger and Luckmann did not try to do so. They bypassed the issue by restricting themselves to a phenomenological analysis.

> The phenomenological analysis of everyday life, or rather of the subjective experience of everyday life, refrains from any causal or genetic hypotheses, as well as from assertions about the ontological status of the phenomena analysed. (ibid., p. 34)

Putting things crudely, phenomenological analysis takes the 'objects' of consciousness as its reality rather than the world as it is known through scientific theories and practice. This manoeuvre is intellectually questionable because it sets aside the potential objectivity of scientific knowledge in favour of individual, subjective intuitions. What exactly is an object of consciousness? Continuing with the posit of multiple realities, Berger and Luckmann propose that different objects 'present themselves to consciousness as constituents of different spheres of reality' and that consciousness is capable of moving through these different spheres experiencing the transition from one to another as 'a kind of shock' (p. 35). They then make the following statement:

> Among the multiple realities there is one that presents itself as the reality *par excellence*. This is the reality of everyday life. Its privileged position entitles it to the designation of paramount reality. The tension of consciousness is highest in everyday life, that is, the latter imposes itself upon consciousness in the most massive, urgent and intense manner. (ibid., p. 35)

The obvious question to ask is why, if the multiple realities are all social constructions, one of them presents itself with such force as to become entitled to the designation of 'paramount' reality? Berger and Luckmann do not answer this question; their phenomenological stance, concerned only with consciousness and refraining as it does from 'causal or genetic hypotheses', allows them simply to state that consciousness of everyday life is like this without having to offer an explanation. The obvious explanation, of course, is that the reality of everyday life imposes itself on us because the world is independently real and explicable in terms of causes and effects. It's not just one among many social constructions, but Berger and Luckmann can avoid having to face this obvious contradiction of their theory by virtue of their exclusive focus on consciousness.

The effects of the posit of multiple realities and the claim that they are social constructions spill over into Berger and Luckmann's analysis of humans and their being in the world. While they accept that there are some biological determinants of the relations humans have with the environment, these are categorised as largely to do with sensory and motor equipment. When it comes to 'different ways of becoming man' (p. 66) there is 'immense plasticity':

> It is an ethnological commonplace that the ways of becoming and being human are as numerous as man's cultures. Humanness is socio-culturally variable. In other words, there is no human nature in the sense of a biologically fixed substratum determining the variability of socio-cultural formations... While it is possible to say that man has a nature, it is more significant to say that man constructs his own nature, or more simply, that man produces himself. (ibid., pp. 66–7)

A little further on, it is argued that the self-production referred to is a social enterprise which owes very little to biology:

> Man's self-production is always, and of necessity, a social enterprise. Men *together* produce a human environment, with the totality of its socio-cultural and psychological formations. None of these formations may be understood as products of man's biological constitution, which, as indicated, provides only the outer limits for human productive activity... Man's specific humanity and his sociality are inextricably intertwined. *Homo sapiens* is always, and in the same measure, *homo socius*. (ibid., p. 69)

One might wonder, given Berger and Luckmann's abstention from causal or genetic hypotheses, how they thought they could argue that none of the socio-cultural or psychological patterns that we see can be related to biology. Phenomenological analysis does not have the tools to support such claims. As a matter of fact, as Chapter 3 shows, there are many human universals which have been found in all known societies. That being so, it is appropriate to ask why the immense plasticity of human being and becoming always provides the same fundamental characteristics, contrary to the claim that humanness is socio-culturally variable. The answer takes the same form as the explanation of the force of everyday reality. There is a universal human nature, it is rooted in biology, and it is not a social construction, although it gives rise to many thoughts, feelings, and construals of humanity of varying degrees of plausibility. The proposal made in this book is that we can accept the evidence of a universal human nature, rooted in our evolved biology, while also accepting that humans construct their own meanings and social practices. These are complementary, not opposed ideas. We do not need to subscribe to a relativist philosophy or to deny the existence of human nature in order to acknowledge and explore the domain of social constructions. I shall consider one further, more recent, example of radical constructivism, this time from psychology, before turning to the task of outlining a construal of social construction which does not violate both common sense and scientific understanding.

2.2   Constructivism and language games

In its most extreme form, social constructivism denies that there is a reality independent of human thought and language. Consider the following passage from the work of Kenneth Gergen, a social psychologist, describing the conclusions that are said to follow from the assumption that the terms by which we understand the world are not grounded in an independent reality:

> First, we must suppose that everything we have learned about our world and ourselves – that gravity holds us to the earth, people cannot fly like birds, cancer kills, or that punishment deters bad behavior – could be otherwise. There is nothing about "what there is" that demands these particular accounts; we could use our language to construct alternative worlds in which there is no gravity or cancer, or in which persons and birds are equivalent, and punishment adored. (Gergen, 1999, p. 47)

How is it possible to claim coherently that 'we could use our language to construct alternative worlds in which there is no gravity or cancer' or that there could be a world in which people and birds are equivalent? It is hard to understand what such claims could mean and it is tempting simply to reject the proposal as utter nonsense, but it is a proposal which, albeit sometimes in rather less extreme form, has found many adherents. It may, indeed, be the dominant understanding, numerically at least, among social scientists. If it were true, it would give to literacy the remarkable power of world making, since literacy clearly can be used to construct alternative worlds.

An approach, which may help us to understand how such a counterintuitive idea can be proposed seriously, is to look at the whole network of beliefs and assumptions from which the claim emerges. A clue can be found in the prologue to Gergen's book in which he suggests that the ideas to be discussed 'invite us into new spaces of understanding from which a more promising world can emerge.' (p. vi) Gergen wants the world to be a place in which humans accept responsibility for their actions and try to make choices which will improve the prospects for humanity as a whole. A similar moral stance has already been seen in Chapter 1 in the writings of Street and Gee. The possibility that real choices can be made is a fundamental requirement from Gergen's perspective. However, he finds fault with the major theories from the Enlightenment philosophical tradition, Cartesian dualism, idealism and materialism which provide the background to contemporary debate. Gergen is prepared to take on the philosophical literature in a way that Berger and Luckmann were not. He does not try to avoid the issue of reality via phenomenology but attempts to find a philosophical grounding for his account of constructivism. Cartesian dualism, Gergen says, founders on the problem of interaction between mind and matter, idealism founders on the problem of solipsism, and materialism appears to him to rule out free choice.

> We generally understand the material world as a world of cause and effect...There is no room in this conception of the material world for "freely selected decisions"...If we are only machines then whatever we think is already determined in advance. (p. 9)

Do we have to accept this conclusion? The big difference between ourselves and all the things we normally describe as machines is that we are conscious and they are not. So, as a first step we need to consider whether the idea of a conscious machine embodies a contradiction. It's not clear that it does. It might be that a profitable way of thinking about humans as biological machines is that it enlarges our concept of what machines can be like. If humans are machines then conscious machines are obviously possible. Second, if we consider conscious machines, is it the case that 'freely selected decisions' are ruled out? Again, it's not clear that this must be so. Suppose we could prove conclusively that we are conscious, biological machines. Would that necessarily imply that we are no longer responsible for what we do? It would not. Attributions of responsibility for actions are based on common experience, which shows that we can and do make choices in certain contexts. I can and do decide whether to give money to a beggar; I can and do decide whether to tell the truth in an embarrassing situation. If, as I expect, we eventually know for sure that the brain is a purely physical system that will not mean that my choices were illusory.

Gergen lists three supposed further shortcomings of the philosophical tradition in the course of his first chapter: the failure of what he calls the correspondence theory of language to ensure that words and the world match appropriately; the claim that all statements are irretrievably biased and self-seeking; and, finally, the proposal that there is no way out of the web of language. 'We treat propositions about the world and the self as reflections of what is the case. As we now find, such propositions depend for their intelligibility on their place in a history of language use.' (p. 26). The conclusion to which we are driven, says Gergen, is the following:

> Semiotic and deconstructionist critique pointed the way to unravelling all propositions, descriptions, and rational arguments. We were left, then, without any significant grounds for the configuration of modernist beliefs. We confront, then, what is said to be a *legitimation crisis*: all claims to knowledge of self and world lose their authority. (p. 29)

Even if we accept the structure of the argument presented, it creates an epistemic not an ontological problem; a problem, that is, about how knowledge is obtained, not about what there is to be known. We may, if the argument is sound, have an insecure base for our knowledge of the world, but that insecurity offers no support for scepticism about realism. If it is true that we cannot know what the world is like it also follows that we cannot know that the world is not there independently of us. The rejection of realism is not warranted by Gergen's argument. Suppose, though, we assume his argument to have been valid. What of the proposed solution to the crisis of relativism apparently unleashed by the critique of traditional assumptions?

Gergen's solution is founded on Wittgenstein's concept of a language game. Words are said to gain their meanings through their uses in particular situations, and specific forms of words make sense and have a clear function in some language games but not in others. Gergen uses this idea to tie the concept of truth to specific language games and to deny that 'true' and 'false' describe relations between propositions and what there is. The 'game of truth' is described as 'a kind of cultural ritual' (p. 36), a proposal with which Berger and Luckmann might agree. This is taken to mean that there are rules governing what can be said, with respect, for example, to what has happened:

> After I announce, "Let me tell you what happened this morning," I cannot say just anything, shout, or jump up and down. There are implicit

rules – just as in games – for what counts as a proper description. In contrast, if I tell you, "Let me show you how I *felt* about what happened to me this morning" I enter another kind of game; in this case shouting and jumping might be perfectly acceptable. (p. 36)

There is an important extra-linguistic factor governing the language game of 'telling what happened' which Gergen does not mention. It is certainly true that there are linguistic conventions governing how to report what has happened and how to report what one feels about what has happened. But, in the case of reports of events rather than feelings, there is the essential added requirement that the report of what happened should correspond with what actually did happen. This is one of the 'implicit rules' for proper description. The language game for factual reporting includes the assumption that there is something independent of the reporter against which the report can be checked and evaluated. It is not just another linguistic or social convention. Gergen, however, treats factual reporting as though it were purely conventional:

The proposition that "the world is round and not flat" is neither true nor false in terms of pictorial value, that is, correspondence with "what there is". However, by current standards, it is more acceptable to play the game of "round-world-truth" when flying from Kansas to Cologne; and more useful to "play it flat" when touring the state of Kansas itself. (p. 37)

Quite apart from the fact that a picture theory of correspondence is not a good option for understanding how words and the world are linked, it is simply not true that a belief that the earth is flat is acceptable when touring on the ground but not when flying from place to place. It is never 'useful' to believe that the earth is flat because we know that it isn't.

The point, for Gergen, of making truth and correspondence depend on language games is to make meaning the property of communities rather than of individuals or of relations between language and an unknowable reality:

[T]exts only come into meaning through their function within relationships. It is the community that is prior to textual meaning and we must see texts in terms of their function within human relationships. (p. 42)

This approach emphasises the possibility of choice which, as reported earlier, is a fundamental requirement of Gergen's perspective. Although his approach is rather different in some ways from Berger and Luckmann's the emphasis on community parallels their emphasis on the social enterprise involved in constructing reality. Gergen's emphasis on community under-pins the claim that truth making is dialogical and it gives a voice to minor-ity opinions. However, the suggestion that community is prior to textual meaning is inconsistent with the earlier claim that words gain their mean-ings solely from their uses in language games; it is also inconsistent with the claim that we can never find a way out of the web of language.

The explicit relativism of Gergen's position is muddied by the fact that on the page including his claim that communities determine meaning we also find the suggestion that 'We need not conclude that there is nothing outside of text.' This suggests that Gergen might, after all, be a realist. Support for this view can be found in various places in his book. On the page following the suggestion that we could construct a world in which there is no gravity he enters a significant caveat:

> Relations among people are ultimately inseparable from the relations of people to what we call their natural environment. Our communication cannot exist without all that sustains us – oxygen, plant life, the sun, and so on. In a broad sense, we are not independent of our surrounds; our surrounds inhabit us and vice versa. Nor can we determine, as human beings, the nature of these surrounds and our relation with them beyond the languages we develop together. (p. 48)

Further qualified support for a form of realism can be found in the final chapter of the book in which, among other things, Gergen tries to counter the apparent anti-realism of his stance:

> [C]onstructionism doesn't try to rule on what is or is not fundamentally real. Whatever is, simply is. However, the moment we begin to articulate what there is – what is truly or objectively the case – we enter a world of discourse – and thus a tradition, a way of life, and a set of value prefer-ences. (p. 222)

'Whatever is, simply is' makes a clear commitment to a form of realism but for Gergen the commitment is always heavily qualified. In the pas-sage quoted, the qualification is very odd given Gergen's insistence on the creative potential of language. What he seems to be suggesting is that non-linguistic apprehension might disclose whatever is really there but 'the moment we begin to articulate' our understanding we become mired in tradition and special pleading. This seems to suggest that animals with-out language have a better grip on what is real than we do. That doesn't square with the achievements of science and technology. It seems far bet-ter to think of language as a tool for the exploration of external reality rather than as a veil which obscures what is there behind a social fabric woven from community ideologies.

Shortly after the acknowledgement that we cannot determine the nature of our surroundings, Gergen goes on to say that 'Whatever there is places no demands on our modes of understanding.' (p. 49) Quite apart from the fact that his own position ought to lead him to the conclusion that he cannot know whether the real places constraints on our understanding, it remains puzzling why he should be so insistent on the point that it does not and cannot. The postulation of gravity as a fundamental, inescapable part of our surroundings which constrains behaviour is hardly illiberal or anti-democratic.

I think an answer to the puzzle may be found in Gergen's apparent antipathy towards natural science, scientists, and scientific institutions and to his view that scientific understanding creates elite power structures which eliminate plausible world views and foreclose the possibility of meaningful dialogue. To allow that science has a better grasp of the real than other approaches is, for Gergen, a restriction on the possibility that new, more egalitarian forms of language, new 'generative discourses' as he describes them, can be created. This can be seen very clearly in the pages of his book following the ostensible commitment to realism. He makes a number of claims of rather similar character, each of which suggests the restrictive character of scientific realism:

> Whenever we hold firm to a particular account of the real, we seal ourselves off from other possibilities. (pp. 222–3)
>
> Each commitment to the real eliminates a rich sea of alternatives, and by quieting alternative discourses we limit possibilities of action. (p. 223)
>
> When committed to a language of materiality we lose a precious voice of enchantment. The same erasure takes place as the sciences tell us that love is merely hormonal arousal, desire a conditioned response, religion a neurosis, and a mother's care for her children a genetic disposition. (p. 223)

Many people think that an understanding of the real opens up new possibilities rather than closing them off. Scientific realism has given us computers and the internet for virtual communication and aircraft for swifter physical communication. Satellite technology and space telescopes provide a clear view of the depths of the universe and precision mapping of the surface of the planet. These expand our possibilities for action. Many natural scientists are politically aware, committed, 'enchanted' people who have no desire at all to restrict anyone's discourse. There are scientists with deep religious commitments, scientists who are poets, scientists who are seers and mystics, scientists who are social and political activists, as well as those who are power hungry megalomaniacs. 'The sciences' do not tell us that love is merely hormonal arousal; science provides us with some insight into the physical and physiological structures that enable us to experience love (cf. Fisher, 1999, p. 172). Science does not eliminate rich seas of alternatives; it opens up profoundly important new areas for debate and dialogue and contributes to a better everyday life for most of us. Who would wish to turn back the clock, for example, to the times when surgery and dentistry had to be practiced without anaesthesia? Moreover, it is hard to see why natural scientists should be picked out for excoriation and opprobrium. Religious institutions have been notorious for restricting discourse and enforcing specific accounts of the real. The Roman Catholic Church has gone so far as to pronounce its own infallibility with respect to certain matters of doctrine, while religious fundamentalism and zealotry in many sects and denominations are major challenges to peace, tolerance, and societal stability in the contemporary world.

If there were nothing independently real which structures the range of possibilities faced by human decision makers there would be no value in making choices. For choices to be important it has to be possible that some are made well and some are made badly. This requires a real world which can provide consequences and feedback about the quality of the judgments we make. To argue that choice is simply a matter of commitment to a particular language game empties choices both of their moral content and of the physical parameters attendant on them. Fortunately, Gergen has not provided good reasons for rejecting realism nor for adopting his regressive attitude towards natural science. Readers who are interested in following the debate about social constructionism further will find Dickins (2004) and Boghossian (2006) thought provoking and informative.

2.3   Social construction and biology

A good start for an approach to social construction which is consistent with realism and evolutionary theory is to reject the supposed dichotomy between biological and social influences which is found in the writings of Berger and Luckmann, Gergen, and many other theorists. We do not have to think of social construction and biology as distinct or opposed sources of influence on human affairs (Franks, 2011). Social construction is not a process which transcends human biology; it is the exercise of a specifically human biological capacity. In Chapter 3, evidence for this proposition is drawn from examination of the social universals which constitute the core of human nature. Human sociality is biological through and through, not something separate from or added on to our biology. Culture does not transcend biology if only for the reason that we cannot think or feel without our brains. A realist approach to social construction also does very well without the assumption that there are multiple realities.

We live in a single world whose fundamental characteristics, some of them very strange indeed, are described by the laws of physics which are, as yet, incompletely known. Physics deals with the fundamental particles and forces. Chemistry deals with larger scale units, the elements and their combinations. A significant distinction can be made between inorganic and organic chemistry. Organic chemistry is the study of the compounds of the element carbon (McMurry, 1994). Carbon atoms have a unique ability to bond together in chains and rings to make an immense diversity of compounds ranging from methane, which has a single carbon atom, to DNA, which may have tens of billions of them. Carbon is the basis of all life on the planet. As a result of the age of the Earth and the operation of the process of evolution by natural selection there are millions of different kinds of living things, all based on carbon, whose existences are interwoven with those of other creatures and with the inorganic constitution of the planet on which we all live. Among the carbon-based creatures some, perhaps most, although to varying degrees, have conscious minds and can think. Humans are unique in the range of things they can think about and, perhaps also, in the degree to which they have conscious access to their thought processes. Humans are also unique in having evolved language. Many other species have communication systems but the complex, recursive syntactic structures of human languages make it possible to express ideas with a freedom that is unavailable to any other creature. Perhaps as a result of this, or as a correlated capacity, human engagement with the environment is more complex and varied than that of any other species and human engagement with other humans is equally complex and varied.

2.4   Intentionality

One of the principal features of human thought and language is intentionality, that property whereby a thought or a speech act refers to things other than itself. A brick has no thoughts, it is not about anything, but I can have a thought about a brick and therefore I am an intentional being. The thought is not a brick but has a brick as its content; it represents a brick. Notice that a thought about a brick does not 'construct' the brick as a physical object nor does it maintain its reality. I may, of course, think of the brick in a variety of ways, as a building block, as a weapon, as a paperweight, and so forth. These ways of thinking about and using the brick may be said to 'construct' it as an object of a certain kind but there is probably less chance of misunderstanding if we talk of 'construals' rather than 'constructions'. Apart from thinking about bricks I also have thoughts about other people and they can have thoughts about me. A remarkable, profoundly important capacity, which appears to be unique to humans, is the ability to think as 'we' rather than as 'you and me'. This ability is called collective intentionality (Searle, 1995; Tomasello, 2008, 2009) and it underpins human social life. It makes it possible for us to have collective goals and purposes rather than just aggregates of individual goals and purposes. Collective intentionality is a feature of human biology, not a means of transcending it.

Humans have evolved to use tools for individual and collective purposes. *Homo sapiens* is not the only tool-using creature but the range of our tools and the power they have given us go far beyond anything that any other species has yet managed to achieve. One of the most powerful types of human tool is the use of external marks as symbols. Symbols have what can be called derived intentionality. They are, indirectly, about things. Human thought and speech, by contrast, are intrinsically intentional. The philosopher John Searle has developed a theory of intentionality on which I rely in this book. Symbolic marks, like carbon atoms, can be combined in lengthy strings and can express a vast range of meanings. They are the basic elements of all forms of literacy. A collection of symbols such as the Roman alphabet is a symbol system. Symbol systems can be hierarchical. The words of the English language constitute a second-order symbol system based on the first-order system of the Roman alphabet. Many symbol systems are used to construct written representations of spoken languages but some of the most powerful, mathematical, and logical notations do not represent spoken language. They are, nonetheless, also intentional systems because they embody and communicate meanings to those who understand them.

2.5   Biological naturalism

In the 5,000 or so years since the first written symbol systems were invented, human culture has grown explosively, as has the global human population, and technological developments have changed the conditions of life for all of us. In more recent times still, science has developed tools to study the nature of the universe and to begin to understand it. Intellectual development has reached the point at which we have begun to investigate the basic stuff of the universe and our own constitution and place in the scheme of things. Humans sense and perceive the world in ways which are not all based on thinking, but our conscious thought processes are such dominant parts of our orientation to the world that we have a tendency to privilege ideas and to think of them as entirely separate from the rest of what there is. This has led some to postulate a fundamental division between ideas and matter or, more familiarly, between mind and matter. Philosophical attempts have been made, over hundreds of years, to work out a satisfactory account of how the division between mind and matter might work, and how it might be made consistent with what we know through the deployment of scientific methods. These attempts are widely thought to have failed but the putative division between mind and matter continues to exert a powerful influence because it seems to set the terms of the debate.

If there is no fundamental division between mind and matter, it appears that everything must be either one or the other. The proposal that everything is mind leads to the philosophy of idealism and the proposal that everything is matter leads to the philosophy of materialism. Idealism has always had its proponents, but materialism is the mainstream contemporary philosophy. The view taken in this book is that neither materialism nor idealism is a satisfactory grounding theory. Instead, the book takes the approach proposed by John Searle which he calls 'biological naturalism'. According to biological naturalism mental processes 'are as much part of our biological natural history as digestion, mitosis, meiosis, or enzyme secretion.' (Searle, 1992, p. 1) Biological naturalism is a form of physicalism, but it is not a form of materialism because it does not try to reduce mental phenomena to material phenomena and because it recognises subjective as well as objective aspects of reality. Consciousness and intentionality are high level properties of brain function. One of the great strengths of Searle's approach is that it makes possible an account of social institutions and other social constructions which exist only because people believe them to exist– governments, money, and literacy being good examples. Searle's account recognises the objectivity of such social institutions without making the obviously false claim to which Gergen among others appears to have succumbed, that all reality is a social construction. In order to understand this, a number of important distinctions have to be made clear. The discussion here is based on Searle's book *The Construction of Social Reality* (Searle, 1995, chapter 1).

2.5.1   Objectivity and subjectivity

First there is a distinction between objectivity and subjectivity. Two senses of this distinction are crucial: an epistemic sense and an ontological sense. Epistemology is the study of knowledge, ontology the study of what there is. Unlike Berger and Luckmann's phenomenology, Searle's approach deals with both epistemology and ontology. The epistemic sense of the objective-subjective distinction separates objective knowledge from subjective knowledge, whereas the ontological distinction is made between entities that exist independently of perceivers and those that exist only because they are perceived. The fact that Shakespeare wrote Hamlet is epistemically objective because it is true independently of what anyone thinks about Shakespeare or about Hamlet, whereas the judgement that Shakespeare was a dreadful playwright is epistemically subjective because it depends on the attitudes and feelings of the individual who makes the judgement. The ontological sense of the objective-subjective distinction concerns entities which are, or are not, dependent on ourselves. Stars, galaxies, mountains, rivers, human beings, and other animals are ontologically objective. They exist independently of us. Pains, feelings of pleasure, thoughts, and mental phenomena generally are ontologically subjective. They are real but exist only because they are felt or thought by individual subjects. The force and utility of the distinction between the epistemic and ontological senses of the objective-subjective distinction can be seen by noting that we can make epistemically objective judgments about ontologically subjective entities and vice versa. If I say that I had a pain in my left leg after running on Thursday, that is an epistemically objective account of an ontologically subjective entity. Whereas, if I say that my wife is a wonderful woman, that is an epistemically subjective account of an ontologically objective entity.

2.5.2   Intrinsic and observer-relative properties

A second distinction, which Searle says is more fundamental than the objective-subjective distinction, is that distinction between features of the world that exist independently of us, and those which exist relative to the intentionality of observers and users. Berger and Luckmann simply ignore this distinction in their treatment of everyday reality. Searle calls independently existing features of the world 'intrinsic' and those that rely on the intentionality of observers 'observer relative'. Since this is a work about literacy let us take the example of books. On the shelf facing my desk there are various volumes. Some of them are paperbacks, some hardbacks. They are of different sizes and weights. One of the larger ones weighs about 70 ounces, as measured on my kitchen scales, and one of the smaller ones less than four ounces. Their pages are made of paper of various kinds and the contents are printed in inks of various kinds. The papers and inks have distinct chemical compositions. All of these features are intrinsic; they exist independently of me, or the authors or publishers. It is noteworthy that for most of us these intrinsic features are of rather minor interest. We get into the most interesting characteristics of books by asking what they are about and then we are in the realm of observer-relative features because books, intrinsically, are not about anything. They derive their intentionality, the ability to represent, entirely from the goals and purposes of their authors and readers and, hence, the fact that a book is about something is an observer-relative feature and thus ontologically subjective. Observer-relative features add no new physical objects to reality but may add epistemically objective features, as we shall see. At this point matters start to get a little complicated and we need to proceed carefully in thinking through some of the consequences of these distinctions because they will prove to be of significant importance for the study of literacy.

The 70-ounce volume that I mentioned earlier is a copy of *The Chambers Dictionary*. The fact that it is a dictionary is not an intrinsic feature of the book, although it is hard to see this initially because it is so obvious to a literate person that it is a dictionary that we tend to suppose its being so must be an intrinsic feature. However, we add absolutely nothing to its physical characteristics by calling it a dictionary and, indeed, it can serve as a dictionary only for someone who has language and knows what a dictionary is. Thus the fact that the book in question is a copy of *The Chambers Dictionary* is ontologically subjective and hence observer-relative not intrinsic. I am not saying, incidentally, that one has to be literate in English to know that the book is a dictionary. It is enough to know what a dictionary is and to be told or to infer that it is the case for the volume in question. The observer-relativity of the fact that my copy of *The Chambers Dictionary* is a dictionary, does not, however, make the judgement that it is a dictionary epistemically subjective. It is an epistemically objective fact that the book is a dictionary because it is not just my opinion but an independently discernible fact. We can see this by considering that there are firm criteria which we use to judge whether something should count as a dictionary or not. These criteria are socially determined and hard to state clearly and completely but, roughly speaking, something is a dictionary if and only if it consists of an ordered list of terms and their associated definitions; the ordering facilitates the finding of a required term and the definitions inform users of the meanings of the terms. If I presented you with a copy of *Harry Potter and the Philosopher's Stone* and told you it was a dictionary you would be right to say that I was mistaken even though there are some definitions in the book. Dictionaries are social constructions because there is collective agreement about what they are and what they are for. In this sense dictionaries are on a par with other social institutions like governments and money. It is because dictionaries are social constructions that it is an epistemically objective judgement that *The Chambers Dictionary* is a dictionary. By way of contrast, it is an epistemically subjective judgement that *The Chambers Dictionary* is better than *The Oxford English Dictionary*. Social institutions are of primary importance for the study of literacy, not just because all literary contents are ontologically subjective, but also because the institutions within which literacy is developed and practiced are social institutions with distinct characteristics which influence how literacy is thought about, taught, and managed.

One other important point for the account of literacy developed in this book is that although the feature of being a dictionary is observer relative, the feature of thinking that something is a dictionary is an intrinsic feature of the thinker or user. The thought that something is a dictionary is an intentional mental content, a property of the brain that thinks the thought and therefore an intrinsic, albeit ontologically subjective, feature. Let me try to summarise. There are intrinsic features of the book on my shelf which is called *The Chambers Dictionary*; among these features are the facts that it has a certain mass and its parts are of varied chemical composition. The intrinsic, physical features of the book interact with the intrinsic, physical systems of my brain and body when I read it. Among my intrinsic features are the intentional states of mind, ontologically subjective but real states, by virtue of which I treat the book as a dictionary. The intrinsic features of both brain and book are necessary for my reading; without the physical copy there would be nothing for me to read and without me there would be no reader. Book and reader together constitute an instance of the micro-ecology of literacy described in Chapter 1. The intentional contents of the book considered as a dictionary are products of the intrinsic intentional states of the lexicographers who wrote it. When I read it, the representations in the text cause intentional states in me which are intrinsic features of my conscious mind. The contents of my representations may or may not match the representations intended by the authors. To the extent that they do match, I have understood what the authors wanted me to understand. Finally, we should note that although my intentional states as I read the dictionary, the fact of its being a dictionary and all its contents are ontologically subjective features, the objects referred to by the dictionary can perfectly well be intrinsic features of the world, although of course they need not be. The fact, for example, that the dictionary definition of a mountain is part of its intentional content and thus observer relative does not mean that mountains themselves are observer relative. Language does not determine what is real. Language lets us describe real things in lots of different ways but that, of course, is a different matter.

2.6   The literate ecology has objective and subjective aspects

In the light of realism and biological naturalism, the essential components of an account of social construction can be seen to have both material and mental aspects and to include both objective and subjective elements of physical reality. In later chapters the system of individual literate minds, functioning in particular environments, is described as *the literate ecology* which can be studied at both individual and societal levels. The literate ecology is a *bio-social* system. The terminology is intended to draw attention to the fact that a literate mind is simultaneously biological and social. Let me repeat that the terms *biological* and *social* do not imply a fundamental, ontological difference. It is not that there are biological aspects of literacy and social aspects which can be distinguished and treated separately. Humans are social animals. Our sociality is as it is because of our biology and our biology is as it is because we are social creatures.

The realist understanding that there is a world which is independent of our thoughts about it does not require us to suppose that natural scientists and others who wish to understand it are simply disinterested seekers after truth. There are no doubt some such but the understanding that we have of our own origins in the evolutionary struggle leaves us in no doubt that scientists, like all other humans, are social strategists with goals and motivations of their own, not to mention political and ideological commitments. There appears to be a view in some quarters, Gergen is a case in point, that personal motivations and commitments make it impossible for science to be objective. Charles Darwin, for example, has been criticised for being a Victorian gentleman as though that somehow invalidates the theory of evolution by natural selection. Darwin was indeed a Victorian gentleman with many of the cultural values and presuppositions of his class, some of which obscured for him aspects of the evolutionary process which he might otherwise have seen more clearly. To suggest, though, that Darwin's social position somehow made it impossible for him to gain any objective understanding of evolution by natural selection is like claiming that seeing with one eye rather than two makes it impossible to have objective perceptions of any kind.

2.7   Multiple interpretations

All written materials can be given intentional interpretations and this makes them social forms. Without the possibility of intentional interpretation, literacy and literate products would be valueless. The communicative power of literate artefacts is not intrinsic to their physical aspects but derives from the agreement of their users that they should be interpreted (socially constructed) in one way or another, or that they may be interpreted in multiple ways. Consider the following poem by the Scottish poet Kathleen Jamie (from *The Tree House, 2004*).

> *The Blue Boat*
>
> How late the daylight edges
> toward the northern night
> as though journeying
> in a blue boat, gilded in mussel shell
>
> with, slung from its mast, a lantern
> like our old idea of the soul

This poem, like any other written in English, rests on collective acceptance by English speakers that the individual words mean what they do. The word 'boat', for example, means, among other things, 'a small rowing, sailing or motor vessel' (The Chambers Dictionary, 1993) not because of the shape of the letters or the fact that there are four of them but because that is one of the meanings of 'boat' in English. The poem as a whole, like all interesting poems, is open to multiple interpretations and associations. There is not just one thing that it means, but there are lots of things that it might be taken to be about. For those who are familiar with the long twilights that result from highland Scotland's northerly latitude, the poem may be profoundly evocative of summer evenings spent watching the sun set. The reference to an 'old' idea of the soul may revive memories of childhood piety or nostalgia for a lapsed Christian belief. For me the reference to the blue of the mussel shell sparks an association with another poem by the American poet Anthony Hecht called *See Naples and Die* (from *Collected Later Poems*, 2003) in which he describes

> The mussel's pearl-blue niches, as unearthly
> as Brazilian butterflies, ...

My network of associations and other readings of the poem, depend, not just on the physical forms of the words, but also, and mainly, on the mental worlds that they help to create. A poem or any other literate work derives its intentionality from the minds of its readers whose interpretations may be many and varied. Typically, poets wish to liberate the creative imaginations of their readers but multiple interpretations of a text may be problematic for an author who is attempting to convey a specific, unambiguous meaning.

2.8   The syntactic foundations of meaning

The meanings that readers find in poems depend to a great extent on their life histories but the forms of the words themselves also have a role to play. Syntax is the study of forms, semantics the study of meanings. Syntax is concerned with the grammatical structure of sentences but it also includes the way that letters are arranged to form words. When we are dealing with syntax, meanings are secondary; the primary concern is with what can be done with a given set of basic parts or components. I use computational theory in the book mainly to explore some of the syntactic properties of literacy.

An example which illustrates the distinction between syntax and semantics is the use of bricks to construct buildings. A brick is the fundamental chunk of matter from which brick buildings and other structures are made. Bricks are cemented together to make walls and walls are arranged to make rooms. Techniques for building arches make it possible for walls to have openings for doors and windows. Different ways of overlapping the bricks in a structure are known as bonds. Bonds have particular structural and aesthetic properties and bricklayers have a specialised vocabulary for describing bonds and their uses. In terms of the distinction between syntax and semantics, bricks are the basic syntactic elements, the fundamental bits of structure. They correspond to symbols in a written language. The semantics of brick structures are concerned with the purposes for which they are built and the uses to which they are put. A brick structure which carries a road over a stream or river has a different meaning from one which is used to treat people who are sick or injured. The first type of structure we call a bridge, the second a hospital. In both cases the syntactic elements are the same; bridges and hospitals can both be built of bricks, but the semantics, what the buildings are used for and mean to their users, are different. In written language the same letters and words are used in texts that have many different kinds of meanings.

Much of what is described in this section is elementary but it forms an important part of the syntactic foundation on which literacy is built and helps us to understand why it is powerful. It will also be of value for understanding the spectacular power of computers and the internet. We can start by noticing that a change of one letter, a syntactic change, usually changes the meaning of a word and the sentences it appears in. Kathleen Jamie's poem would strike us rather differently if its title were 'The Blue Boot', the 'The Blue Coat', or 'The Blue Goat'. Some words have multiple meanings; 'boot' and 'coat' for example, are both nouns and verbs but in general, different meanings are associated with different syntactic word forms. 'Boat' and 'goat' have distinct meanings associated with their different syntactic forms. The links between form and meaning, between syntax and semantics, are social constructions. 'Boat' means a small vessel and 'goat' a type of animal because that is how we use them. It could have been different– maybe the other way round. We could now be talking about sailing goats and speedgoats, or about nanny boats and billy boats if the conventions had worked out differently.

So far, so obvious. Underlying conventional word forms, though, are some less obvious but equally important properties. How many four letter words are there in English? That is a difficult question to answer and answers would probably vary according to the dictionary consulted but we can easily answer the related question, 'How many four letter words could there be in English?' To keep things simple I'm going to assume that words written in lower case and words written in capitals or in mixed case are to be counted only once. 'Boat', BOAT', 'boat', and even 'bOaT' are the same word for counting purposes. It's clear that the first letter could be any of 'a' to 'z' which gives 26 possibilities and the same is true for the second, third, and fourth letters. This means that there are exactly $26 \times 26 \times 26 \times 26 = 456,976$ possible four letter word forms. Most of these, things like 'xrzg', are not English words but the result of the calculation is interesting for a number of reasons.

First, it sets what is called an upper bound on the number of four letter words. There couldn't be more than 456,976 of them. If we wanted more we would have to add letters to the alphabet. The upper bound is an objective, syntactic, property of written English and any other language which uses a 26-letter alphabet. What this shows is that social constructions can have entirely objective properties. The English alphabet is a social construction but that does not mean that we can freely choose all its properties. Once we decide on the size of the alphabet, upper bounds on the numbers of word forms are fixed. There's an important general truth here which anchors a lot of what I want to propose about literacy. Arbitrary social constructions can have fixed and entirely objective properties.

Second, even though many, perhaps most, four letter alphabetic forms are not English words, that still leaves lots that are. The system has plenty of representational power and that's just the four letter words, never mind words of other lengths or the fact that we combine words in sentences! The reasoning can be extended to thinking about sentences and higher level structures. How many four-word English sentences could there be? We can apply the same technique and think about how many words could be the first word of a sentence, how many the second word, and so on. There's an obvious difficulty which makes an exact calculation impossible. We don't know how many English words there are. However, let's suppose that there are 50 English words which can serve as the first word of a grammatically acceptable sentence, and that for each of those first words there are 50 second words, and similarly for the third and fourth words. In each case it's plausible to think that 50 is an underestimate. If that's right there must be at least $50 \times 50 \times 50 \times 50 = 6,250,000$ four-word sentences in English. An estimate of this kind is called a lower bound. This particular lower bound is almost certainly too low but it serves to reinforce the point that written English has massive representational capacity as a result of its syntax.

I've moved fairly quickly from talking about the meanings of poems like *The Blue Boat* to underlying syntactic matters like bounds on the numbers of word forms. I want now to dig right down to the syntactic foundations of written language. English uses a 26-letter alphabet, other languages use different alphabets, and some languages like Chinese are constructed on non-alphabetic principles. Is there a minimal symbol system, one in which all other writing systems can be represented? There is. It is the binary alphabet with which we are all increasingly familiar in the computer age. The binary alphabet is conventionally written down using the symbols 0 and 1 but any other pair of symbols could be used. Like the English alphabet, the binary alphabet is a social construction which has objective properties. We can form 'words' with it in just the same way that we form words in English. There are two one-letter word forms in binary, 0 and 1; there are four two-letter words, 00, 01, 10, and 11; eight three-letter words; and so on for words of increasing length. The individual letters are called 'bits'. 'Bit' is an abbreviation of 'binary digit'. Bits are the bricks of the binary system. We normally think of letters as somehow different from numerals or digits because of the different meanings they have for us, but from the syntactic point of view, where we are not concerned about meanings, letters and digits are the same; they are basic symbols. Because there are only two letters in the alphabet, there are fewer word forms of a given size in binary than there are in English: only sixteen four-letter binary word forms by contrast with the nearly half a million four-letter word forms in English. But that doesn't matter. It doesn't mean that the binary alphabet has less representational power than written English. It simply means that we have to use longer words to get the same effect. If, for example, we want 456,976 word forms in binary we have to use nineteen-letter words, which actually gives us a few to spare since there are 524,288 nineteen-letter binary word forms.

Eight-letter words have a privileged status in the binary alphabet. An eight-letter binary word is called a 'byte' and bytes form the basis for the megabytes and gigabytes of memory that our computers, ebooks, phones, and other electronic devices have these days. The concept of the byte is a social construction, agreed by the community of computer scientists, electronics engineers, and others involved in the development of computer hardware and software, but it is a social construction which has real, physical effects on the design of computers and programming languages. Hardware data paths in computers, for example, are usually constructed in multiples of byte widths.

The byte has 256 different word forms which makes it a convenient unit for representations of different kinds. It's neither too large, nor too small, prompting possible comparisons with Goldilocks and the three bears, which I shall resist. The 256 syntactic forms of the byte have no intrinsic meanings but they can be interpreted in various ways as the result of particular conventions. One convention which links the binary alphabet to the English alphabet is called ASCII, the American Standard Code for Information Interchange. Letters of the alphabet, numerals, and punctuation marks all have ASCII codes. When the code was first invented it was restricted to the Roman alphabet, but it has since been extended to include most of the world's written languages with their various alphabets and diacritical marks. Lower case 'a' is 01100001 in binary or 97 in decimal. Capital 'A' is 01000001 in binary or 65 in decimal. ASCII is a social construction which has real world consequences. If you were able to look in the part of the memory of my computer which is keeping track of what I'm doing as I write this sentence, you would see lots of 0s and 1s, but no letters of the alphabet. It's because the hardware of my computer is programmed to use the ASCII encoding that the letter 'a' appears on the screen when I press the appropriate key on the keyboard.

Let's take an example which illustrates the conventional nature of the links between syntax and semantics and the multiple interpretations that are made possible by different conventions. We will explore some possible interpretations of the binary string 011000110110000101110100. This string of 24 symbols can be interpreted to mean a variety of different things.

2.8.1   011000110110000101110100 as a numeral

Most of us don't have a feel for how big a number 011000110110000101 110100 is because most of us don't think in binary. One of the things we can do to make it more meaningful is to convert it into a number in a different base. Doing this implies that we know quite a lot about how number representations work. For example, we know that numerals are usually interpreted as having the least significant digit in the right-most position. Decimal 32, for example, means three tens plus two units, whereas 23 means two tens plus three units. This is purely conventional. There's nothing in the syntax which says that numerals have to be interpreted in this way, but we learn in school that this is the 'correct' way to interpret and use numerical forms. We can put this into practice with 011000110110000101110100 which we are going to convert into the equivalent decimal representation. Because we're starting with a binary numeral we have units, twos, fours, etc., rather than the units, tens, hundreds etc., of the decimal system. Working from right to left we have 0 units, 0 twos, 1 four, 0 eights, 1 sixteen, 1 thirty-two, and so on. Putting it all together we get $0 + 0 + 4 + 0 + 16 + 32 + 64 + 0 + 256 + 0 + 0 + 0 + 0 + 8192 + 16384 + 0 + 65536 + 131072 + 0 + 0 + 0 + 2097152 + 4194304 + 0 = 6{,}513{,}012$. In other words, our original binary number is just over six and a half million in decimal. That's a number which is much more intuitively meaningful to most of us because we use decimal quantities in all sorts of ways in our daily life and communications.

2.8.2   011000110110000101110100 as a set of ASCII codes

To understand the string as an ASCII code we have to think of it in a different way. First we need to split it into three byte-sized chunks, each of which is interpreted as a number:

01100011   01100001   01110100

The left chunk is decimal 99, which is 'c' in ASCII; the middle chunk is decimal 97, which is 'a' in ASCII; and the right chunk is decimal 116, which is 't' in ASCII. Thus the string as a whole is the ASCII encoding of the English word 'cat'. Every English text can be represented as a single, binary numeral by concatenating all the byte-sized representations of the symbols in the text, including spaces and punctuation marks. Conversely, we can also interpret any binary numeral by dividing it up into byte-sized chunks and interpreting each of them as an ASCII encoding. More often than not, if we do this we will end up with nonsense, but that doesn't affect the fact that it can be done.

2.8.3   011000110110000101110100 as a random sequence

Another possible interpretation of the binary string is as a random sequence of the kind we would get if we tossed a fair coin 24 times and recorded each head as a 1 and each tail as a 0. Once we have such a record it is fairly easy to work out related things like how probable it is that we would get exactly the same pattern again if we were to make another 24 coin tosses. It turns out that the probability is one chance in 16,777,216, which is a somewhat smaller probability than winning the jackpot in the U.K. national lottery.

2.8.4   011000110110000101110100 as a pixel colour code

Yet another possible interpretation which is of great significance in modern computers is in terms of pixel colour codes. A pixel (picture element) is the smallest unit on a computer screen which can be independently manipulated, for example, by changing its colour. A pixel is like a tile of a mosaic but much smaller. Colours on computer screens are normally achieved by mixing elements of red, green, and blue. In a very high colour resolution system a single pixel is coded by 24 bits, such as we have in the example, with eight bits coding for red, eight for green and eight for blue. In systems with lower colour resolution, there might be only eight bits per pixel, in which case 24 bits can code the colours of three pixels.

2.8.5   011000110110000101110100 as a digital audio signal

Another interpretation, also of great significance in the computer age, is to think of binary strings as digitized audio signals. This is achieved by sampling a sound wave. A sound wave is a series of continuous variations in pressure, generally deviations from an equilibrium such as the ambient atmospheric pressure. The difference between the equilibrium pressure and the actual pressure at a specific moment can be represented by a binary numeral. If the sound wave is sampled sufficiently often and stored using numbers large enough to record a wide range of pressure changes, a very accurate representation of the wave can be achieved. Standard digital techniques sample sound waves some 44,000 times per second. A 24-bit sample gives a very high quality record.

2.8.6   011000110110000101110100 as an address

A further example, which is also relevant to thinking about computers and the internet, is to treat the binary string as an address. If you have ever wondered how the files that are stored in your computer's memory are managed or how your computer communicates with other computers via the internet, the answer is in terms of addresses. Each location in a computer's memory has a unique address and each computer on the internet has a unique address. These addresses are represented as binary numerals. When you click on a screen icon to open a file, or click on a link to visit a webpage, in the background, behind the icons and the links, are binary numerals which are interpreted as addresses where the item can be found or as links in a chain of addresses.

2.8.7   0110001101100000101110100 as a computer program

A final example is to treat the binary string as a computer program. All the previous examples have been data of one kind or another. A computer program is a set of instructions which directs the CPU to behave in particular ways, including where to find data and what to do with it. Data are passive, programs are active. The insight that binary strings can be read and interpreted both as programs and data was a key discovery for the design of modern computers. It is the principal feature that makes computers so flexible and it feeds into our understanding of the power of literacy. The ideas are intricate and are discussed at greater length in Chapters 7 and 8.

2.9   Syntax and semantics

Numerous, perhaps infinitely many, other interpretations of the binary string are also possible. Two points are of fundamental importance. First, the question of what the string is 'really' about has no answer. All the given interpretations are equally real and the one chosen at a particular time depends on the purposes of the user. Second, because there is no primary or privileged interpretation, we can, in principle, use different interpretations in mutually informative ways, and as we shall see, it is possible to work systematically with multiple interpretations simultaneously. This possibility is important for the theory developed in this book. It makes possible the investigation of some deep and interesting issues about literate capacities. It also makes clear why computers and the internet are such powerful tools for extending the possibilities of literate life. Digital media are entirely dependent on the possibility of interpreting binary strings in a variety of ways. Written language depends on both syntax and semantics and so, therefore, does literacy. In order for texts to have meanings for us we need to understand the conventions which are used to interpret them. For experienced readers and writers of English prose the link from the syntactic organisation of a text to what it means is generally so rapid and automatic that we don't notice it happening. It's a different matter for novice readers and writers or for those faced with a text written in an unfamiliar language. It is also clear that the high-speed syntactic virtuosity of computers and their communicative flexibility open up new opportunities in ways that theorists of digital literacy are starting to explore.

2.10   The social construction of literacy

What, then, does it mean to say that literacy is a social construction? In a thoughtful introduction to a collection of papers dealing with this question, Jenny Cook-Gumperz suggests that

> Literacy needs to be seen as providing not just technical skills but also a set of prescriptions about using knowledge. In this sense literacy is a socially constructed phenomenon, not simply the ability to read and write. As this book demonstrates, by performing the tasks that make up literacy, we exercise socially approved and approvable talents. Literacy as socially constructed is both a historically based ideology and a collection of context-bound communicative practices. (Cook-Gumperz, 2006, p. 1)

This characterisation includes both skills and the contexts and social practices within which they are embedded. It is consistent with biological naturalism and with the existence of a reality which is independent of us. It is consistent with the idea that literacy rests on a foundation of socially constructed syntactic conventions which have objective, independent properties. It also makes clear that there are normative aspects to literate communicative practices which depend solely on human goals and purposes, and thus they are ontologically subjective. Chapter 3 introduces a perspective on human nature which suggests that normative social practices are rooted in our evolved biology.

Chapter 3

Universal Human Nature and the Study of Literacy

This book makes the assumption that mental phenomena 'are caused by neurophysiological processes in the brain and are themselves features of the brain' (Searle, 1992, p. 1). Biological naturalism, as Searle calls the approach, is a plausible philosophical underpinning for attempts to understand the mind and thought processes. It is not a complete account, partly because the processes that produce mental phenomena from brain activity are not fully understood and partly because there is still uncertainty about exactly what matter is and what its fundamental properties are. The world as revealed by quantum physics is extraordinarily strange and has properties that do not sit at all comfortably with our everyday ideas of solid, physical objects. Some theorists think that quantum phenomena may be involved in consciousness and that new physics will be needed for a satisfactory understanding of how it works, while others think that existing theory provides a sufficient basis for a sound understanding of minds in general, including the phenomena of consciousness (Penrose, 1989, 1994; Dennett, 1991). For the purposes of this book, what is important about the commitment to biological naturalism is not that we know exactly what physical objects are or how mental phenomena are caused by the brain, but that we are committed to the same standards of reasoning and evidence as the natural sciences and to the idea that theories of the mental must be compatible with theories of the physical. Hockett (1973, p. 2) describes human rootedness in the physical world as an 'ironclad constraint'.

3.1   The case for evolutionary theory

Evolutionary theory is an essential aspect of the commitment to biological naturalism. It is important for a book about literacy because a literate person is a human being who interacts systematically and meaningfully with one or more external symbol system. A great deal can be said about symbol systems and the representational capacities of their syntax, independent of any consideration of the specifically human characteristics of the reader or writer. A certain amount can also be said about the basic capacities that readers and writers need to have in order to be able to interact with texts.

However, the literate human is first and foremost a human being and only secondarily a literate being. If we are to understand the power and scope of literacy we need to understand human beings, independently of texts to the extent that it is possible to do so, in order to learn why humans have been able to invent and use literacy while other creatures have not. Given a commitment to biological naturalism, this understanding must be founded on the processes that have led to the complex, highly social, language-using animal known to its literate self as *Homo sapiens*, and our best means for doing so is found in evolutionary theory and the associated biology. One fundamental question we would like to be able to answer is 'What are human beings like in the wild?' If all the institutions of civilised life had never been invented, in particular all those made possible by literacy, what would humans be like? In some ways this is a strange question to ask. When we think about creatures other than ourselves, 'wild' is usually contrasted with 'tame' or 'domesticated'. Wild animals are those over which we do not have control, whereas the tame and domesticated ones are those which we manage for our own purposes. Thinking of ourselves as a species which was once wild raises the question of what it could mean for humans to be tame or domesticated. In particular, it raises the question of who benefits from the institutions of civilization? Are they for the good of everyone or are the majority domesticated for the purposes of an elite minority? The institution of slavery gives one clear answer to the question; its abolition and the development of the idea of the individual as someone with absolute rights to freedom and self-determination gives a different answer.

Every human life, even that of the most cultured intellectual given over entirely to abstract speculation, begins as a fertilised egg in which the genes of two parents are combined. Those two parents had parents of their own and the chain of ancestors of each of us goes back in an unbroken sequence to the origins of life on the planet some 3.5 billion years ago. We have a truly immense non-literate prehistory compared with our tiny literate history of some 5,000 years. Even if we consider only the short period of time that has elapsed since the most recent common ancestor we share with the chimpanzees was alive, we are still dealing with a period that is more than a thousand times longer than the literate epoch. The evidence accumulating from research in comparative genomics shows that many of the genes we have are conserved in a wide range of other species. Genetically we are more similar to the chimpanzees than to any other species, but we have a substantial genetic heritage in common with species as different from ourselves as mice and fruit flies.

A sceptic might argue at this point that the substantial genetic similarity between humans and other creatures shows, contrary to my suggestion, just how unimportant the genetic heritage is for understanding the literate mind. We share most of our genes with chimpanzees, but we are literate and they are not, so genetics cannot be more than a small part of the story. What one sees looking back in time, the argument might go, is a lengthy period of stasis during which non-literate humans lived in nomadic, hunter-gatherer, societies of limited size. This lifestyle changed only when systematic agriculture and, somewhat later, literacy, were invented and significant cultural and societal development became possible. Then an explosive period of rapid change in human affairs took off, which led to the large scale sophisticated societies we see today. The speed with which this fundamental cultural change has occurred, markedly different from the slow, gradual change brought about by genetic evolution, is exactly what demonstrates that human affairs are now governed by new principles. Language, literacy, science, technology, and complex social institutions are precisely what distinguish the life of *Homo sapiens* from those of all other creatures no matter what their genetic similarities to, or differences from, ourselves might be. Literacy and other social institutions are the means by which we transcend our biological heritage and see ourselves for what we have become: a highly intelligent species capable of controlling its conditions of life to a significant extent and of constructing the social institutions of civilization. Functional and comparative genomic research, far from demonstrating our subjugation to evolutionary processes, shows that by probing our origins we are increasingly able to transcend them. Our mammalian and primate heritages are important because they provide the physical means to support the social and cultural activities we freely engage in, but that is the limit of their influence. Obviously, we need physical systems to read and write with, but even these are highly variable. Eyes and hands are the default options, but other possibilities are available for those who cannot see or use their hands. Science and technology, the arts and humanities, the construction of cities and transport infrastructure, urban living and globalization are all evidence for the profound changes to human life which have occurred since literacy was invented.

There is no doubt that literacy has led to unprecedented changes in human life and to new, fundamental understandings of a range of aspects of the world we live in. To argue, however, that we have transcended our biological heritage and that we now freely construct our conditions of life and social institutions is to go well beyond the evidence and to introduce an entirely artificial distinction between biology and culture. If humans had stopped being interested in sex, ceased to need food, felt no physical pain, and were uninterested in kinship and status relations, to pick just a few important instances, we might have grounds for the transcendence argument. As it is, of course, none of these things has happened or will happen in the foreseeable future. Contemporary human life is still part of the immense process of biological evolution and it is profoundly revealing to see how many of the institutions and practices that exist in contemporary societies have characteristics that bear the stamp of our evolutionary history and are found wherever we look. Literacy and other technologies have amplified the scope for the expression of human nature rather than transformed it. Music is a good example. Every known human society has had music (see Universals 208–217). It may have been purely vocal but many societies also had instrumental music. Modern technology, from the time of the Renaissance onwards has led to the invention of many different kinds of musical instruments which our ancestors could not have made but would surely have loved to hear and learn to play. The instruments of the symphony orchestra, which many people may now think of as old fashioned, are highly sophisticated and the end products of long chains of development. Electronics and amplification have made musical events possible on a previously unimaginable scale. The electric guitar started the rock era and its popularity suggests it taps into something fundamental about the human psyche. Systems of musical notation make it possible for music to be written down and preserved. This leads to study and further development. The huge symphonic works of the nineteenth and twentieth centuries by composers as diverse as Bruckner, Mahler, Strauss, and Shostakovich would not have been possible without written musical notation. Contemporary societies continue to place a high value on music and it is used for the purposes it has always been used for. It provides social cohesion but is also used to demonstrate power and wealth. Musical gatherings such as the Bayreuth festival, which celebrates the operas of Richard Wagner, have political and social as well as musical functions, and no doubt music has always been used in this way. The musical instinct is as old as humanity even though the ways in which it is developed and displayed have changed as new cultural forms are invented.

The point of the Darwinian orientation of the book is to use the fundamental evolutionary understanding of the nature and purposes of the human organism in its original, wild, non-literate state to gauge what effects literacy has had. Without a sound understanding of human nature we cannot be in a position to understand the impact of literacy on human life and culture. We will also find it difficult to understand how best to use the powerful leverage that literacy provides to benefit rather than disadvantage those parts of the human community whose lives are marginalised and threatened by contemporary global trends. The Darwinian orientation facilitates an investigation of the consequences of literacy but not primarily via a comparison of literate and non-literate societies, as attempted in the classic paper by Goody & Watt (1963) which has proved so controversial. The Darwinian orientation starts from the evidence that humans have universal species-specific characteristics which predispose us to think and behave in certain kinds of ways. This perspective differs markedly from the more common form of understanding in social science which supposes humans to have essentially unlimited mental and behavioural plasticity on which varied cultural practices stamp whatever specific forms we observe. Humans, it is said, construct their nature via culture. The analyses of Berger and Luckmann and of Gergen, discussed in Chapter 2, are of this kind, and so is the analysis of Goody and Watt, who said at the start of their paper that 'whereas the social organisation of animals was mainly instinctive and genetically transmitted, that of man was largely learned and transmitted verbally through the cultural heritage.' (Goody & Watt, 1963, p. 304).

There is a key theoretical point here which bears on how the study of literacy can be conducted. If human behaviour were as variable, plastic, and culturally determined as the analyses cited suggest, then the only path to an understanding of the effects of literacy would be by making comparisons between societies that are literate and those that are not. However, comparisons of this type are made difficult, perhaps impossibly so, by the fact that there is no clear line to divide those societies which are deemed literate from those which are not. It's fairly easy to say when an individual has become literate; very roughly it's when they can read and write and this can be established by observation or testing. It's essentially impossible to say when a society has become literate. Is it when more than 50% of its members can read and write, or is some other value better? Is it, perhaps, when the major institutions of the society depend on literacy, or when there's a written system of laws? There is a reasonably clear criterion for individual literacy, but not for societal literacy. This has been one aspect of the critiques of Goody and Watt's argument. One can, of course, point to societies in which there is greater or lesser literacy, but this does not provide the kind of clear cut comparison that the literate/illiterate comparison invites us to expect.

3.2 Darwinism provides a new approach to the study of literacy

The Darwinian approach, by contrast, does not require us to make potentially invidious comparisons between societies characterised by different levels of literate development. Instead, it begins with an enumeration of universal species-specific characteristics that are common to individuals in all human societies and studies how these could be affected by the acquisition of literacy. A focus on human universals as a part of the study of literacy thus takes the investigation in a completely different direction from one which starts by considering non-literate minds as 'primitive' or 'deficient' in some way. It focuses on the universal characteristics of humanity rather than on comparisons which tend to invoke judgements of superiority and inferiority. Comparisons can be made between (relatively) literate and non-literate societies to illuminate these understandings, but they are adjuncts to the study of the effects of literacy rather than its inescapable core, and may demonstrate losses from literacy as well as gains. Our memories may have become less powerful as a result of writing, which reduces the burden of remembering. It is also worth noting that many of the most prominent species-specific characteristics of humans have to do with social instincts and organisation, and thus the interaction of literacy skills with social practices becomes a fundamental aspect of the study of literacy from this new perspective.

The shifts in method and orientation that the Darwinian perspective provides are so important that, at the risk of tiresome repetition, I shall reiterate them once more in a slightly different way. Much conventional social science starts from relativistic pre-suppositions (cf. Berger & Luckmann, 1966, Chapter 2): it is assumed that there are multiple realities; 'human nature' is taken to be culturally determined and indefinitely plastic and in consequence, behaviour patterns and social practices across cultures need have nothing in common. They are constructions made by the people who use them with characteristics that reflect the details of their needs and circumstances. Given this relativistic framework, either literacy does not have constant effects across cultures, in which case its varied effects are determined by socio-cultural practices or, if it does have constant effects, it must be because they are independent of particular social and cultural arrangements, that is to say that they are autonomous. In this way, the relativistic starting point sets up a seemingly inescapable opposition between literacy understood as autonomous skills and literacy understood as sets of social practices. The Darwinian orientation rejects the relativistic starting point, and it is able, in consequence, to see that literacy has to be understood in both ways. Universal human nature has many characteristics– none, some, or all of which might be affected by literacy. Literacy consists of tools which require intellectual skills and which are used in contexts involving specific social practices. There is no conflict between skills and social practices, and thus we escape from the corrosive effects of artificial opposition between two types of understanding, both of which are essential.

Darwinism offers two routes to an understanding of human nature. One, as already mentioned, is via the study of universals. The other, in a sense deeper, route is to consider the processes of evolution which have led to the universals that we observe. The key ideas of evolutionary theory are straightforward to state, but they have had extraordinarily complex consequences which are, as yet, only very imperfectly understood. Evolutionary processes are the topic of Chapters 5 and 6. Here the focus is on the universals themselves as they are manifested in behaviour, rather than on the processes that have produced them.

3.3   Universal human nature

A universal is 'a trait or complex present in all individuals (or all individuals of a particular sex and age range), all societies, all cultures, or all languages' (Brown 1991, p. 42). Chapter 6 of Brown's book describes the characteristics of what he calls the 'Universal People', and Pinker (2002) has constructed an alphabetical list, based on Brown's work which is included, with minor additions, at the end of this chapter. Basic emotions and their associated facial expressions are examples of individual-level universals. Paul Ekman and his colleagues (Ekman & Davidson, 1994) have established that all humans express fundamental emotions such as happiness, anger, and disgust via the same facial expressions. This body of research continues a tradition started by Darwin, who published a book on the topic in 1872. The existence of statuses, roles, and a division of labour between men and women are examples of social universals. Lloyd and Gay (1981) and Staal (1988) discuss universals of human thought. In Brown's analysis, individual-level universals are seen to underlie social and cultural universals, and thus the individual level of analysis is privileged. A focus on individuals is appropriate for a Darwinian analysis too. The point is not to deny the existence of large scale processes; much Darwinian analysis, for example, is at the level of populations. However, natural selection operates on individuals and has its primary effects at the level of individuals. Larger scale effects are emergent properties of lower-level effects. Brown notes at the start of Chapter 6 of his book that his description of the universal people is tentative. He suggests that some universals will not yet have been discovered and that some current candidates will ultimately prove not to be universal. Caution is clearly wise in this regard; linguistic universals, for example, which figure prominently in Brown's list, have been called into question in recent work (Evans and Levinson, 2009) and the important characteristic of collective intentionality (Searle, 1995; Tomasello, 2008, 2009) is not on Brown's list but is probably a universal.

Inspection of the list of universals at the end of the chapter shows that there are many things which are characteristic of all human individuals and societies, regardless of whether they are literate or not. Some characteristics are what we would generally think of as positive; they are things such as empathy, a sense of fairness, hospitality, and gift giving. Others would generally be thought negative, including conflict, envy, and the use of language to mislead or misinform. The list will be familiar to everyone who reads it and it should be clear that it applies equally to literate and non-literate societies. Many of the universals can be recognised as foundations on which literate activities have been built. Advanced mathematics has been developed from the foundations of number terms, binary cognitive distinctions, and logical notions. The natural and social sciences require conjectural reasoning and classifications of the natural world, of human propensities, of kin relationships, and of mental states among others. Mass media may be derived from imagery, gossip, etiquette, and folklore as well as from language employed to manipulate others. There is also an understanding of human culture as unique and distinct from the rest of nature. The fact that human culture is unique and distinct from the rest of nature, does not mean that it is not part of nature. Many animals have distinctive characteristics which are unique to them or to a small group of related animals. We do not say that the zebra is unnatural because of its unusual pattern of black and white stripes, or that the giraffe is unnatural because of the unique length of its neck. We think of these unusual patterns as parts of biodiversity. Human culture is part of biodiversity too.

3.3.1   Types of universals

It is important to understand what is meant by the term 'universal' in the context of human nature, particularly since it is used in a different way in Chapter 8 to characterise a class of Turing machines. Brown discusses various meanings of human universals in Chapter 2 of his book, which forms the basis for the short discussion here. Useful distinctions are made, among others, between manifest and innate universals, between absolute and near universals, and between 'emic' and 'etic' universals.

A manifest universal is one which is directly observable. Most of the universals on Brown's list are of this kind. An innate universal is something deeper, and typically thought of as rooted in human neurobiology. For example, 91: ethnocentrism, 139: biases in favour of the in-group, 150: close kin distinguished from distant kin, 253: preference for own children and close kin, 278: rites of passage, and 342: territoriality, are manifest universals which may all be explained, in part at least, in terms of the underlying concept of inclusive fitness, (Hamilton, 1964a, b) which is a process affecting all sexually reproducing species. Evolutionary theory provides powerful tools for explaining manifest universals in terms of a smaller number of fundamental ideas.

Absolute universals are those which have been found wherever they have been looked for, whereas 'near' universals are those for which the record is less than perfect. As Brown says, anthropologists have generally made this distinction in order to point out how unimportant it is. Errors of reporting make it inevitable that some gaps will appear in the record. It is also suggested that the sheer complexity of human behaviour and its flexibility in the face of changing circumstances make it likely that universals will sometimes be in conflict and only one will be manifest.

The distinction between 'etic' and 'emic' universals is concerned with the way that anthropologists have defined them. An emic universal is 'a part of the conceptual system of all peoples'. (Brown, 1991, p. 49). An etic universal is one which is defined in terms of cross-culturally valid, scientific frameworks. Brown uses incest to illustrate the difference. Incest avoidance, he says, is an etic concept, whereas incest taboos have emic variants and may differ from society to society. The emic/etic distinction is related to that between manifest and innate universals. Different human groups have their own emic understandings of manifest universals, which reflect the operation of innate, etic principles and processes.

From the standpoint of the study of literacy, the distinctions among types of universals are less interesting than the fact that universals are fundamental aspects of humanity in both literate and non-literate populations. They provide indicators of the range and subtlety of human dispositions and practices which existed before literacy was invented and are able to interact with it. It is precisely because human thoughts and feelings are subtle and wide ranging that literacy can act as a powerful amplifier in many different ways.

3.4   Literacy builds on human universals

Consider, for example, the universals of classification. They include the practice itself and specific classifications of age, behaviour, body parts, colours, fauna, flora, inner states, kin, sex, space, tools, and weather conditions. If there were no human tendencies to classify then numerous literate disciplines and activities related to the specific classifications might simply not exist. Literacy, in and of itself, does not guarantee the existence of life history theory, which studies age-related phenomena; ethology, which studies behaviour; anatomy, which studies body parts; aesthetics, which studies colours among other things; zoology, which studies the animals and other fauna of the world; botany, which studies the plants; psychology, which studies inner mental states as well as their behavioural consequences; anthropology, which includes the study of kinship; geometry, which studies space; technology, which studies and produces tools and techniques; or meteorology, which studies the weather. Nor, indeed, does a classification universal plus literacy guarantee the existence or development of any particular kind of literate activity. However, it is not hard to see how literacy and a tendency to classify, in conjunction with abstraction, an interest in living things and a set of basic logical notions, could, in due course, lead to the varied activities now gathered under the general heading of biological sciences.

It will, I believe, for reasons discussed earlier in the chapter, be fruitful to use universals to analyse the contested ground between those who think of literacy in terms of skills and those who place the primary emphasis on social practices. One of the striking things about the list is that most of the universals could, given a fairly loose definition of social practice, be considered to relate to social practices and even on a tight definition, at least half of them have social content. Humans are intensely social and issues to do with status and dominance are enormously important. It is not surprising, therefore, that ample evidence exists to support the assertion that many literacy practices have social manipulation of one kind or another close to the surface. On the other hand, the existence of tools, practice to improve skills, and the universals of abstraction, logic, and classification already mentioned, provide a clear basis for thinking of literacy in terms of skills. Moreover, the universal affirmation of prestige arising from proficient language use and the universals of socialisation show how skills and social practices might interact in the complex contexts of education and schooling. In short, there need not be a conflict between viewing literacy in terms of social practices and in terms of skills. Both have their roots in the complex interlinked system of universal human endowments.

3.4.1   Abstraction

Examination of the list provides a rich source for thinking about interactions between universals and literacy. The first item, abstraction in speech and thought, is one of the most interesting. Abstraction is a complex concept which has a variety of related meanings. It can refer to a process in which something is separated from its surroundings or context; it can refer to a process of summarisation; it can indicate a representation which exists apart from material instances and it can indicate something which is primarily theoretical. Brown describes abstraction as a consequence of language rather than of thought. Boroditsky (2001) provides evidence for the effects of language in thinking about abstract domains and Boroditsky and Ramscar (2002) show that abstract knowledge can be built analogically from more experience-based knowledge. The possible impact of literacy on abstract thought is both interesting and contentious. It is particularly interesting because literacy has a concrete aspect, the written or printed trace, as well as the meanings or propositions expressed in a text. It has seemed obvious to some theorists that literacy has had a decisive impact on abstract thinking. Goody and Watt (1963) argued that writing contributed to the development of syllogistic logic and to the division of subject matter into autonomous disciplines which they claimed was 'of cardinal importance in differentiating literate and non-literate cultures' (p. 331). Goody and Watt did not argue that literacy created abstract thought but that it was extended and made more powerful by literacy. Other theorists such as Ong (1982) have taken a similar view. The formal model of Turing (1936) used in this book to characterise the powers of the literate mind in Chapter 8 tends in the same direction. It has led to new understandings of the nature of formal reasoning which are simply inaccessible to the non-literate mind because they depend on a crucial distinction between thought processes and textual representations of them. All of these examples, however, rest on the prior existence of abstraction. If we were unable to separate objects from their surroundings or contexts in thought, we would not be able to give them names. If we were not able to represent something apart from its material instances, the syntactic forms of our words would have no referents– they would not mean anything. When, for example, we use the syntactic form 'cat' to represent the animal *Felis catus*, we are drawing on our capacity for abstraction in both of these ways.

Turing's results concern only the effects of literacy on syntactic abstraction and logic, not the whole of Goody and Watt's thesis. In particular, they deal with individual minds and do not address questions about differences between literate and non-literate societies. They thus leave open questions about the social issues with which Street and others have been concerned, while giving a sharp characterisation of the impact of literacy on individual minds. Turing's results are context free; they require only the structures of an individual mind and the possibility of texts. Similar points may be made about the logical discoveries of Gödel (1931) and Chaitin (1987). There is a fascinating twist to these discoveries which is discussed in Chapter 11. Claims for the impact of literacy on abstract thought have been contentious. Halverson (1992, p. 305) has described Goody and Watt's proposal about literacy and logic as 'a thin tissue of vague suggestions, gratuitous assumptions and unsupported generalizations', while Street (1984) argued that Goody and Watt overstated the significance that can be attributed to literacy in itself. I have indicated at the start of this chapter that it may be possible to find reasons for the heated nature of the debate, shown by the tone of Halverson's comments, in the shared relativistic framework within which it is situated.

The abstraction universal indicates the possibility of de-contextualisation, but many other universals demonstrate that human life and thinking have been strongly conditioned by social contexts and practices. The Universal People use language to manipulate others, to misinform and mislead, and to manage and manipulate social relations. They favour their own children and close kin, they distinguish in-groups from out-groups, and operate biases in favour of their in-groups. They gossip and tend to overestimate the objectivity of their thinking. They are aware of and tolerate inequalities of prestige and economic resources. It is not hard to see that literacy could be used to amplify these kinds of social relations and to produce the kinds of outcomes that Street has described in the 'ideological' model.

> The model stresses the significance of the socialisation process in the construction of the meaning of literacy...It distinguishes claims for the consequences of literacy from its real significance for specific social groups. It treats sceptically claims by western liberal educators for the 'openness', 'rationality' and critical awareness of what they teach, and investigates the role of such teaching in social control and the hegemony of a ruling class. (Street, 1984, p.2)

Street's position may be summarised by saying that literacy is used strategically by powerful groups to reinforce their social positions. The analysis of universals provides support for this view, which is independently plausible on historical grounds. However, the quotation from Street's book also illustrates a negative effect of the relativistic framework discussed earlier. The passage appears to distinguish the consequences of literacy from the social practices with which it is associated, but the way the distinction is made actually casts doubt on the proposition that there are such consequences. Notice the marked difference between 'the consequences of literacy' and 'claims for the consequences of literacy'. The contrast Street makes between 'claims for consequences' and 'real significance' invites the reader to consider the claims as false or misleading. The suggestion is that the real significance of literacy is not what is claimed for it and that we should be sceptical of any proposed consequences other than social control by the ruling class. This is at best a partial view, not because ruling classes do not exert control, but because the evidence that literacy can have independent consequences is overwhelming. One obvious consequence of literacy is to make it possible for certain skills to be acquired. Because I am literate, I could learn to write Shakespearean sonnets. If I were not literate I could not do so. Because I am literate, I could learn to solve partial differential equations. If I were not literate I could not do that either. Whether it would be worthwhile for me to do these things is a completely different question. Since my case is not different, in principle, from any other, we must distinguish the consequences that literacy might have from the consequences that it has in practice. This distinction is frequently unclear in much of the literacy literature. One possible explanation is that the relativistic framework encourages a mind set which makes it hard to see that literacy skills can be identified independently of the social practices in which they are embedded. Another possible explanation is that the social practices perspective on literacy emphasizes the semantic consequences of literacy to the detriment of a focus on the syntactic skills on which it rests.

3.4.2   Unified senses

The approach taken in this book is largely programmatic and I shall not attempt to deal in detail with the possible effects of literacy on all the universals in the list. Quite apart from the scale of the task, it is essentially a matter for empirical research rather than for theoretical speculation. However, there are some further points that can be made which may help to illustrate the wide range of possible interactions between literacy and universals. Universal 304 is unified senses. Brown discusses this in the context of the fact that the Universal People have a worldview.

> In some ways their worldview is structured by features of their minds. For example, from early infancy they have the ability to identify items that they know by one sense with the same items perceived in another sense, and so they see the world as a unity, not as different worlds imposed by our different sense modalities. (Brown, 1991, p. 139)

Cross modal identification is clearly an important underpinning for literacy; it is likely to be what makes it possible for literate reporting of what we see, hear, touch, taste, and smell in a single symbol system. It must also underpin symbol systems such as Braille. One interesting way to think about how the different senses provide unified information is to treat them as perceptual systems, as was done by Gibson (1966). Senses, for Gibson, are passive, whereas perceptual systems are active and exploratory. The key point he makes is that perceptual systems have in common the active seeking and registration of experience via different sensory systems. Gibson proposed that the environment provides invariant information, that is, information which remains the same across different modes of presentation, across different sensory channels, and from different perspectives. The striking differences between textual representations such as 'cat' and the animal described by the word may be bridged by cross-modal sensory activities functioning as a perceptual system.

3.4.3   Tools used to make tools

Tool use is found in all human cultures. It is also found in other species. Some chimpanzees use sticks to fish in termite mounds; others use stones, both as hammers and anvils, to crack nuts. Some birds, particularly corvids, also show considerable ingenuity in using tools. Humans are unique, however, in using tools to make tools. It is interesting and informative to think of literacy from this point of view. Literate cultures have tools for constructing texts. Among them, very obviously, are pens, pencils, quills, styli, and other markers. Perhaps less obviously, we can also think of certain kinds of texts as tools. Cookery books and instructional manuals of other kinds are texts that serve as tools. They provide both intellectual and practical guidance for the production of a range of goods and the management of many complex processes.

The computer is the pre-eminent tool for the production of texts. It is of particular interest and importance for the study of literacy because the design of computers reflects the symbol processing capacities of humans. Chapter 9 discusses computers and the internet in greater detail.

3.4.4   Male/Female, Adult/Child Differences

It is deemed politically correct in many situations to deny that human males and females differ in any fundamental respects. One reason for this point of view is that natural difference arguments have been used, particularly in ways detrimental to women and girls, to deny them equal rights with men and boys and to discriminate against them in pay, jobs, political representation, and education to name just a few important domains. As Brown points out, though, it is a universal characteristic of human cultures to see men and women and adults and children as having different natures. Properly understood, these differences do not provide any basis for discrimination or for the assumption that males are superior to females. Indeed, it is much easier, on evolutionary biological grounds to make the case for the superiority of the female sex.

From the standpoint of literacy, I want to make just two points here. First, as a matter of fact, some popular literate genres clearly assume that male/female and adult/child differences do exist and that they are of some consequence. In a survey article describing the new literacy spaces of anime, manga, and fanfiction, Rebecca Ward Black makes the following observations:

Contemporary manga genres (these categories apply to anime as well) address markedly diverse target audiences and can be broadly categorized in the following ways: (a) *josei/redikomi* manga which are, as a rule, created by female artists and feature the daily aspects of Japanese women's lives, (b) *seinen*, created by and for men with texts ranging from horror to war stories to mild pornography. Other types include the whimsical and fantasy laden (c) *kodomo*, which is intended mostly for children, (d) *shōjo* geared toward young females with its romantic themes and strong magical girl characters, and the high-action (e) *shōnen* for young and teenage boys. (Black, 2008, pp. 586–7)

I do not wish to imply that either Rebecca Black or the authors of manga genres would endorse the idea that the recognition of sex differences and adult/child differences are human universals, but it is striking to find such a close correspondence in the forms of contemporary genres which have global, not just Japanese, readerships.

Second, in a world in which girls and women continue to suffer systematic disadvantage with respect to opportunities for education and literacy training, it is important to accept that this discrimination has deep roots. That should not mean that we accept it as inevitable. It should, instead, serve to make us aware of the need to increase efforts to achieve gender parity in education and literacy. In a world in which diversity is generally celebrated, it is curious that gender diversity is either denied or used as a basis for discrimination and prejudice. These points perhaps serve to illustrate another important element on Brown's list, Universal number 228, the universal tendency to overestimate the objectivity of our thought!

3.4.5   Cooperation

A final significant point of note is that it is not hard to think of ways in which almost any of the universals on Brown's list could be enhanced by literacy. Universal 54, cooperation, is an interesting example. The rapid growth in the use of the internet builds on the human capacity for cooperation in a number of ways. The existence of open source software, for example, has initiated new ways of enhancing the quality of programs. Wikipedia may turn out to be a highly significant example of cooperation. After a shaky start it has begun to establish a reputation for accuracy and coverage that holds out significant promise for future development (Dobson and Willinsky, 2009). It is not just our capacity for language that makes collaborative projects possible. The underlying adaptation for cooperation is also essential.

3.5   Donald Brown's list of Human Universals (from Pinker 2002)

The original list was compiled in 1989. Items marked * were added after 1989. Items marked + (44, competition, and 174, lying) have been added by the author.

1. abstraction in speech and thought
2. actions under self-control distinguished from those not under control
3. aesthetics
4. affection expressed and felt
5. age grades
6. age statuses
7. age terms
8. ambivalence
9. anthropomorphization
10. anticipation*
11. antonyms
12. attachment*
13. baby talk
14. belief in supernatural/religion
15. beliefs, false
16. beliefs about death
17. beliefs about disease
18. beliefs about fortune and misfortune
19. binary cognitive distinctions
20. biological and social mother normally the same person
21. black (colour term)
22. body adornment
23. childbirth customs
24. childcare
25. childhood fears
26. childhood fear of loud noises
27. childhood fear of strangers
28. choice making (choosing alternatives)
29. classification
30. classification of age
31. classification of behavioural propensities
32. classification of body parts
33. classification of colours
34. classification of fauna
35. classification of flora
36. classification of inner states
37. classification of kin
38. classification of sex
39. classification of space
40. classification of tools
41. classification of weather conditions
42. coalitions

43. collective identities
44. competition+
45. conflict
46. conflict, consultation to deal with
47. conflict, means of dealing with
48. conflict, mediation of
49. conjectural reasoning
50. containers
51. continua (ordering as cognitive pattern)
52. contrasting marked and nonmarked sememes (meaningful elements in language)
53. cooking
54. cooperation
55. cooperative labour
56. copulation normally conducted in privacy
57. corporate (perpetual) statuses
58. coyness display
59. critical learning periods*
60. crying
61. cultural variability
62. culture
63. culture/nature distinction
64. customary greetings
65. daily routines
66. dance
67. death rituals
68. decision making
69. decision making, collective
70. differential valuations*
71. directions, giving of
72. discrepancies between speech, thought, and action
73. dispersed groups
74. distinguishing right and wrong
75. diurnality
76. divination
77. division of labour
78. division of labour by age
79. division of labour by sex
80. dominance/submission*
81. dreams
82. dream interpretation
83. economic inequalities
84. economic inequalities, consciousness of

85. emotions
86. empathy
87. entification (treating patterns and relations as things)
88. environment, adjustments to
89. envy
90. envy, symbolic means of coping with
91. ethnocentrism
92. etiquette
93. explanation
94. face (word for)
95. facial communication
96. facial expression of anger
97. facial expression of contempt
98. facial expression of disgust
99. facial expression of fear
100. facial expression of happiness
101. facial expression of sadness
102. facial expression of surprise
103. facial expressions, masking/modifying of
104. fairness (equity), concept of*
105. family (or household)
106. father and mother, separate kin terms for
107. fear of death*
108. fears
109. fears, ability to overcome some
110. feasting
111. females do more direct childcare
112. figurative speech
113. fire
114. folklore
115. food preferences
116. food sharing
117. future, attempts to predict
118. generosity admired
119. gestures
120. gift giving
121. good and bad distinguished
122. gossip
123. government
124. grammar
125. group living
126. groups that are not based on family
127. habituation*

128. hairstyles
129. hand (word for)
130. healing the sick (or attempting to)
131. hope*
132. hospitality
133. husband older than wife on average*
134. hygienic care
135. imagery*
136. incest between mother and son unthinkable or tabooed
137. incest, prevention or avoidance
138. in-group distinguished from out-group(s)
139. in-group, biases in favour of
140. inheritance rules
141. institutions (organised co-activities)*
142. insulting
143. intention
144. interest in bio-forms (living things or things that resemble them)
145. interpolation*
146. interpreting behaviour
147. intertwining (e.g. weaving)
148. jokes
149. judging others*
150. kin, close distinguished from distant
151. kin groups
152. kin terms translatable by basic relations of procreation
153. kinship statuses
154. language
155. language employed to manipulate others
156. language employed to misinform or mislead
157. language is translatable
158. language not a simple reflection of reality
159. language, prestige from proficient use of
160. law (rights and obligations)
161. law (rules of membership)
162. leaders
163. lever
164. likes and dislikes*
165. linguistic redundancy
166. logical notions
167. logical notion of 'and'
168. logical notion of 'equivalent'
169. logical notion of 'general/particular'

170. logical notion of 'not'
171. logical notion of 'opposite'
172. logical notion of 'part/whole'
173. logical notion of 'same'
174. lying+
175. magic
176. magic to increase life
177. magic to sustain life
178. magic to win love
179. making comparisons*
180. male and female and adult and child seen as having different natures
181. males dominate public/political realm
182. males engage in more coalitional violence*
183. males more aggressive
184. males more prone to lethal violence
185. males more prone to theft
186. males, on average, travel greater distances over lifetime*
187. manipulate social relations
188. marking at phonemic, syntactic, and lexical levels
189. marriage
190. materialism
191. meal times
192. meaning, most units of are nonuniversal
193. measuring
194. medicine
195. melody
196. memory
197. mentalese*
198. mental maps*
199. metaphor
200. metonym
201. mood- or consciousness-altering techniques and/or substances
202. moral sentiments*
203. moral sentiments, limited effective range of
204. morphemes
205. mother normally has consort during child-rearing years
206. mourning
207. murder proscribed
208. music
209. music, children's
210. music related in part to dance
211. music related in part to religious activity

212. music seen as art (a creation)
213. music, vocal
214. music, vocal, includes speech forms
215. musical redundancy
216. musical repetition
217. musical variation
218. myths
219. narrative
220. nomenclature (perhaps the same as classification)
221. non-bodily decorative art
222. normal distinguished from abnormal states
223. numerals (counting)
224. Oedipus complex
225. oligarchy (de facto)
226. one (numeral)
227. onomatopoeia
228. overestimating objectivity of thought
229. pain
230. past/present/future
231. person, concept of
232. personal names
233. phonemes
234. phonemes defined by sets of minimally contrasting features
235. phonemes, merging of
236. phonemes, range from 10 to 70 in number
237. phonemic change, inevitability of
238. phonemic change, rules of
239. phonemic system
240. planning
241. planning for future
242. play
243. play to perfect skills
244. poetry/rhetoric
245. poetic line, uniform length range
246. poetic lines characterized by repetition and variation
247. poetic lines demarcated by pauses
248. polysemy (one word has several related meanings)
249. possessive, intimate
250. possessive, loose
251. practice to improve skills
252. precedence, concept of (that's how the leopard got its spots)*
253. preference for own children and close kin (nepotism)
254. prestige inequalities

255. pretend play*
256. pride*
257. private inner life
258. promise
259. pronouns
260. pronouns, minimum two numbers
261. pronouns, minimum three persons
262. proper names
263. property
264. proverbs, sayings
265. proverbs, sayings – in mutually contradictory forms
266. psychological defence mechanisms
267. rape
268. rape proscribed
269. reciprocal exchanges (of labour, goods, or services) (written contracts)
270. reciprocity, negative (revenge, retaliation)
271. reciprocity, positive
272. recognition of individuals by face
273. redress of wrongs
274. resistance to abuse of power, to dominance*
275. rhythm
276. right-handedness as a population norm
277. risk taking*
278. rites of passage
279. rituals
280. role and personality seen in dynamic inter-relationship (i.e., departures from role can be explained in terms of individual personality)
281. sanctions
282. sanctions for crimes against the collectivity
283. sanctions include removal from the social unit
284. self distinguished from other
285. self as neither wholly passive nor wholly autonomous
286. self as subject and object
287. self-control*
288. self-image, awareness of (concern for what others think)*
289. self-image, manipulation of*
290. self-image, wanted to be positive*
291. self is responsible
292. semantics
293. semantic category of affecting things and people
294. semantic category of dimension

295. semantic category of giving
296. semantic category of location
297. semantic category of motion
298. semantic category of speed
299. semantic category of other physical properties
300. semantic components
301. semantic components, generation
302. semantic components, sex
303. sememes, commonly used ones are short, infrequently used ones are longer
304. senses unified
305. sex (gender) terminology is fundamentally binary
306. sex statuses
307. sexual attraction
308. sexual attractiveness
309. sex differences in spatial cognition and behaviour*
310. sexual jealousy
311. sexual modesty
312. sexual regulation
313. sexual regulation includes incest prevention
314. sexuality as focus of interest
315. shame*
316. shelter
317. sickness and death seen as related
318. snakes, wariness around
319. social structure
320. socialization
321. socialization expected from senior kin
322. socialization includes toilet training
323. spear
324. special speech for special occasions
325. statuses and roles
326. statuses, ascribed and achieved
327. statuses distinguished from individuals
328. statuses on other than sex, age, or kinship bases
329. stinginess, disapproval of*
330. stop/nonstop contrasts (in speech sounds)
331. succession
332. sucking wounds*
333. sweets preferred
334. symbolism
335. symbolic speech
336. synaesthetic metaphors*

337. synonyms
338. taboos
339. tabooed foods
340. tabooed utterances
341. taxonomy
342. territoriality
343. thumb sucking*
344. tickling*
345. time
346. time, cyclicity of
347. tools
348. tool dependency
349. tool making
350. tools for cutting
351. tools to make tools
352. tools patterned culturally
353. tools, permanent
354. tools for pounding
355. toys, playthings
356. trade
357. triangular awareness (assessing relationships among the self and two other people)
358. true and false distinguished
359. turn-taking
360. two (numeral)
361. tying material (i.e., something like string)
362. units of time
363. verbs
364. violence, some forms of proscribed
365. visiting
366. vocalic/nonvocalic contrasts in phonemes
367. vowel contrasts
368. weaning
369. weapons
370. weather control (attempts to)
371. white (colour term)
372. world view

Chapter 4

The Literate Ecology

A dictionary definition of 'ecology' is 'the scientific study of plants, animals, or peoples and institutions, in relation to environment' (Chambers Dictionary, 1993). The Turing machine model, applied to literacy, separates minds from texts and helps us to think of the fundamental relation between a mind and a text as an ecological one. Thinking more broadly, it is obvious that the literate individual is situated in an environment with specific physical and social conditions that affect the possibilities of becoming literate, remaining literate, and profiting from being literate. Clearly there are many environmental factors that need to be taken into account if we are to understand literacy properly. Consider a child in school learning to read and write. We know from the pioneering work of Heath (1983) and from other more recent studies (e.g., Lewis, Enciso, and Moje, 2007; Alexander, 2010) that the pre-school environment has an important impact on the child's readiness to acquire literacy skills. Children who have had regular exposure to stories and prior experience of books are better able to understand what is required of them than children without such prior experience. Social and cultural factors are thus of obvious importance for a rounded understanding of literacy and its environmental supports. Barton (2007) has suggested that the 'ecological metaphor' is a good way to draw together the social, cultural, and psychological factors that are important for a broad understanding of literacy:

> Ecology seems to be a useful and appropriate way of talking about literacy at the moment, and of bringing together its different strands. Using the term changes the whole endeavour of trying to understand the nature of reading and writing. Rather than isolating literacy activities from everything else in order to understand them, an ecological approach aims to understand how literacy is embedded in other human activity, its embeddedness in social life and in thought, and its position in history, in language and in learning. (Barton 2007, p. 32)

One qualification I would make to Barton's analysis is to say that we can study reading and writing, the basic activities of literacy, in isolation via the

Turing machine model, but that we must also understand their social and cultural embedding. The formal analysis adds to the wider range of considerations that Barton has described. We can, therefore, think of the literate ecology as multi-levelled. There is the intimate micro-ecology of reader and text, there is the broader ecology of the daily circumstances of the individual, and increasing in scope, there are the societal, cultural, and possibly global contexts that may have an impact on the scope and limitations of someone's literacy activities. The discussions by Brandt and Clinton (2002) and Reder and Davila (2005) are relevant here.

4.1   The ecological approach emphasises both the environment and the organism

Texts and minds are very different kinds of things. For all its intentional complexity, a text, at one level of analysis, is just a linear sequence of symbols. Minds are altogether more difficult to describe and understand partly because they are so complicated. The approach via universals in Chapter 3 takes a functional perspective which fits well with the Darwinian perspective of Chapters 5 and 6 and the formal analysis of Turing machines discussed in detail in Chapter 7. Literacy is powerful, not because of the properties of texts or minds considered in isolation from each other, interesting though these are, but because there are interactions between them. Thus an ecological approach to literacy emphasises that the properties of the reader and the text are equally important for our understanding.

The child who asks for paper to draw on, the ornithologist who starts a new field notebook, the poet who scribbles a rhyme on the back of a beer mat, and the teenager who tags an urban wall with an aerosol paint spray all demonstrate the ecological structure of literacy which has two fundamental parts: a human agent who makes marks, and an external medium on which the marks are made. Even the computer, which has all its electronics in a single box, embodies this fundamental structural distinction by having a central processing unit which controls the computer's operations, and a memory which contains programs and data in symbolic form. Turing's theory, developed originally for numerical computation but adaptable to all forms of symbolic activity involving an external medium, was concerned with the mental processes involved in writing out a sequence of digits rather than with the details of the structural architecture of writer and medium, but it too respects the distinction between them. In Turing's theory, the mind of the reader/writer is modelled by something called a finite automaton and the external medium is modelled by something called a tape. Thus we can think of the child as a finite automaton and the drawing paper as a tape, of the ornithologist as a finite automaton and the field notebook as a tape, and so on for the other examples.

4.2   The ecological approach emphasises both ideas and external representations of them

When we separate minds and texts for analytical purposes we can see clearly the difference between ideas and external representations of them. An idea is something that happens in the mind, it is something active, something that occurs at a particular time and place in the life of the individual. Ideas are ontologically subjective. Everyone has ideas; we are all thinkers, but not everyone writes. Writing thus captures and expresses just a small part of the mental life that happens continuously. The capture and representation of mental life externally, is a key property of writing. A written sentence, comment, or remark is an external representation of an idea. It is passive and it cannot be said to happen at a particular time or place, although it is recorded at a particular time and place. The passivity of text calls into question the suggestion by Brandt and Clinton (2002, pp. 348–9) that 'things' such as texts can be treated as actors. The motivation for the idea is interesting but it is a mistake to describe texts as actors. A text without a reader is a lifeless object. Brandt and Clinton propose the concept of literacy-in-action as a replacement for the concept of the literacy event:

> The concept of the literacy event is, we suggest, anthrocentric (sic). It privileges human actors over non-human actors; it suggests that literacy is not happening unless it can be shown that local human actors at the scene are oriented toward writing or reading...we also want to consider the additional question of how literacy acts as a social agent, as an independent mediator (i.e., literacy, itself, in action). (Brandt and Clinton, 2002, p. 349)

Human actors should be privileged in literacy contexts. They are the agents who do the reading, the writing, and the meaning. I think the point that Brandt and Clinton are trying to make can be approached in two ways. First, the concept of literacy-in-action as a process can be described at the level of the individual by the engagement with text which the Turing machine model describes. Second, we can use the concept of derived intentionality to capture the apparently independent meanings that texts provide to the contexts of their use. The point was made in Chapter 2 that texts, in and of themselves, are not about anything. The capacity to mean, intrinsic intentionality in Searle's terminology, is exclusively a characteristic of human agents and is a function of their connectedness to the world. Texts have derived intentionality. They serve as vehicles for the communication of meanings from one human to another. It is thus a mistake to describe them as 'independent mediators' because the meanings that they communicate (more or less accurately) are always the meanings of the humans who wrote them in the first place and who read them. Brandt and Clinton are quite right to say that texts can 'deliver meanings from other places and transform local actions into meanings bound for or relevant to other places' (p. 349) but they always do this in a derivative way and never by or for themselves. The sharp separation between texts and minds which characterises the Turing machine model helps us to keep this basic truth in focus.

The ecological perspective on literacy, with its equal emphases on minds and texts is compatible with what has been called a 'dual-inheritance' account in which the biological system of inheritance described by evolutionary biology is supplemented by a cultural system of inheritance. Cultural systems of inheritance include, but are not restricted to, the products of literacy. When there is more than one inheritance system, questions arise about the nature of the relation between them. Many theorists have supposed that systems of biological and cultural evolution work in tandem and are mutually supportive (see for example Lumsden and Wilson, 1981; Boyd and Richerson, 1985; Durham, 1991; Tomasello, 1999; Richerson and Boyd, 2005), but others have raised the possibility that cultural artefacts have lives of their own and evolve for their own purposes (Blackmore, 1999).

Dual inheritance theorists propose that the innate resources passed on by biological means are supplemented by cultural resources passed on by whatever mechanisms are available. Immediate transmission via speech or demonstration from one member of a culture to another is the principal means that most dual inheritance theorists have had in mind. Beyond the immediate transmission required for learning to read and write, literacy offers a powerful additional or alternative means of acquisition of cultural forms. When reading a book privately, we can relate to the author on our own terms. There are no immediate social imperatives that have to be obeyed. There is no requirement for the give and take of dialogue, no need to respond within a particular time, and there is the possibility of returning as many times as needed to a particular part of a text. If we contrast the here and now, the present in which we live, with the symbolic world of texts, although there is a loss of perceptual richness, there is a compensating transcendence of boundaries of space and time. Reading a book is not like having a conversation with its author, as some have suggested, since the one-sidedness of reading is a very important part of how the process works.

4.3   Literacy requires a range of types of environmental support

Ecological thinking makes it obvious that literacy requires a range of different types of environmental support. The first, very obvious, point is that literacy is not possible if there is no reading material, nothing to write on, and nothing to write with in the immediate environment. A wide ranging introduction to the materiality of texts can be found in Eliot and Rose (2009, Part II). Duffy and Waller (1985) have discussed the processes involved in making texts usable. On a slightly larger scale, literacy and education are more easily promoted if there are schools or other buildings set apart for learning and study. Schools need teachers and teachers need training, houses, salaries, and the support of the local community. Local communities are rarely entirely autonomous in contemporary societies and need financial support and political backing from central governments. Pring et al (2009) discuss the changing educational needs of 14 to 19-year-old students in England and Wales and the impact the changes have on the design of curricula and the delivery of education. Governments which are impoverished may need outside assistance with physical infrastructure and with training. The environmental supports required for widespread literacy range from the personal to the global. Anna Robinson-Pant (2005, pp. 13–14) describes how the social benefits of literacy are enhanced when literacy programmes are accompanied by environmental and infrastructure support such as credit facilities, skills training, and health centres.

4.4   The literate ecology has two principal levels

The literate ecology is multi-levelled. It includes everything ranging from the interactions between a reader and a text, to the surrounding institutions and contexts within which literacy events and practices are situated, and beyond these essentially local contexts to the broader perspectives from which international comparisons and global issues can be considered. I propose, nevertheless, that two principal levels of analysis can be described and the theory of the literate mind proposed in this book makes a two-way analytical distinction. The individual reader/writer plus a text is the *functional core* of the system, and the *surrounding institutions* are everything outside the core that has effects on it. The functional core and surrounding institutions together can be called the *literate ecology*.

4.4.1   The functional core

There is an obvious sense in which the individual reader/writer should be thought of as the core component of the literate ecology, but the definition of the *functional core* proposed here includes not just the individual, but a text or textual materials. This may seem like a strange way to proceed since one might naturally suppose that all texts and textual materials like paper and pencils should be thought of as parts of the *surrounding institutions*. There are two reasons for making the distinction in the way proposed. The first is that the individual with a novel, a magazine, a newspaper, or a notebook is a distinct functional unit, an individual ecosystem within the larger literate ecology. With a book one can, as it were, cut oneself off from the outer world. We describe people as becoming lost in the stories they are reading and oblivious to their surroundings (Nell, 1988). Because this is so, it is extremely helpful to have a theoretical division which allows us to study the interactions between a reader and an individual textual resource, be it something to read or something to write on, without having to consider the whole of the literate ecology. We assume, therefore, that the individual has textual resources available without considering the details of the environment that provides them.

Second, there is a powerful set of analytical tools based on the Turing machine model which can be used to study the properties of the *functional core*. The model describes different types of literacy processes. Chapter 7 treats them in detail. The Turing machine model was originally invented for the study of fundamental questions in mathematical logic and now forms part of the theoretical basis for computer science. However, it is also appropriate for the study of literate minds and helps us to understand what difference it makes to individuals to be able to read and write. Within the abstract conceptual framework in which the formal tools of Turing machine theory are deployed, we can show that, in a precise sense, a fully literate mind is infinitely more powerful than a non-literate mind. That power can only be realised in the context of appropriate *surrounding institutions*, but it is definable with reference to an abstract universe of texts. The theoretical analysis is carried out in a mechanistic or syntactic way and includes no moral evaluation. It has to do with what is possible in principle, not with what it might be good or bad to do, nor with any alleged fundamental changes to the properties of the individual mind such as a transformation of consciousness. It will be seen that it is possible, to a degree, to rehabilitate the discredited concept of a literacy thesis. This is done in terms of access to resources rather than in terms of qualities of individuals, and thus directs attention to the institutions within which the literate individual is situated rather than to special properties of the literate mind, although there are also changes to neural structures as a result of becoming literate. The definition of the literacy thesis in terms of access to resources shows that there are links between what Street (1984) described as the 'autonomous' and 'ideological' models of literacy. It becomes possible to see how to preserve the intuition that literacy does make an important difference without falling prey to the criticisms levelled at classical theories of the literacy thesis and at the idea that there is a great divide between literate and non-literate societies.

4.4.2   The surrounding institutions

The *surrounding institutions* include everything that has an impact on the literate performance of the *functional core*. There is no clear boundary between those things that do have such an impact and those that do not, but it is clear that some things are more important than others. The lack of a clear boundary does not cause a theoretical problem. Understanding the impact of institutions on individual literacy attainment is more a matter for empirical research than for basic theoretical analysis, and variability from one literate environment to another is expected. The term *institution* draws attention to the fact that the primary structures requiring analysis are social structures like education policies and budgets for adult literacy training. Most of these social structures lead to or imply physical infrastructure requirements, schools and books, for example, but the decisions made about physical projects are primarily political and societal and it is thus appropriate for the analysis to be structured in terms of the political and social institutions which enable or frustrate infrastructure developments.

Thinking outwards, as it were, from the individual, one can identify numerous social practices and institutions which have impacts on literacy skills and their performance. The immediate home environment of the developing child is an important source of later differences in literate performance (Heath, 1983). The presence of books in the house is a positive indicator, as is the educational status of parents, particularly the mother. The school environment, assuming the child goes to school, is another source of important influences. Curricular issues, literacy teaching methods, and peer pressures all modulate a child's achievements. Peer pressure operates on specific individuals, but also more generally on subject choices for advanced study and career decisions which are made within a social framework of assumptions which, among other things, are gendered. Moving further outwards, local education authority policies and national government education policies including assessment regimes and strategic goals all need to be considered as potential influences on individual outcomes. Political targets for tertiary sector participation interact with individual motivation to influence choices about universities and degree subjects for those who are able to proceed beyond secondary education and wish to do so. Social and economic backgrounds continue to influence who goes where and what they study. Within the university system, the whole apparatus of academic disciplines and specialisation influences what one knows, how knowledge is deployed, what topics are favoured for research, and what kinds of outputs should be produced. Scholars in the humanities, for example, tend to produce monographs in order to build their careers, whereas a researcher in a branch of genomic science is far more likely to write journal articles, often in collaboration with a substantial number of colleagues.

Within a given society, the political system and the state of economic development influence what is preferred and sometimes what is permitted to populations in terms of education and training, both elementary and advanced. Economies which depend on advanced intellectual skills and have substantial autonomous commercial and industrial sectors, find a need to respond to the educational requirements of these sectors in order to remain competitive. This leads to debate about educational planning versus the idea of knowledge for its own sake. Clearly the range of social and political institutions which might have an impact on the *functional core* is indefinitely large. All these things are parts of the *literate ecology*.

4.5   The literate ecology rests on a set of assumptions called the Background

I am following Searle (1983, 1992, 1995) in calling the foundations on which the literate ecology rests the *Background*. It includes all the non-intentional systems that ground and sustain the literate ecology.

> The Background is a set of non-representational mental capacities that enable all representing to take place. Intentional states only have the conditions of satisfaction that they do, and thus only are the states that they are, against a Background of abilities that are not themselves Intentional states. (Searle, 1983, p. 143)

It is clear from the quotation that Searle's focus is on mental capacities because the primary target of his analysis is to explain the conditions that make intentional states possible. This is an important part of what needs to be explained by a theory of literacy, since many of the institutions which have the strongest influences on individual literacy outcomes are social institutions which have to be understood in terms of both individual and collective intentionality. However, in addition to the *Background* factors which sustain the representational capacities of individuals and social institutions, in the case of literacy there are also fundamental physical infrastructure requirements which have to be met and biological issues such as health, age, and sex to be considered. If there are no schools or books, for example, then the task of educators is made much more difficult than it otherwise would be for entirely obvious practical reasons. The concept of the *Background* is extended to include discussion of these physical and biological factors as well as the ones that Searle himself discusses. The theoretical separation of the *Background* from the literate ecology enables the account developed here to deal with a range of issues. I shall give two examples.

4.5.1   The infrastructure needs of developing countries

There are contingent, non-intentional, biological factors in large areas of the world which have an impact on individual achievement in school and in education more generally. In many countries, getting children into school is only a small part of the environmental challenges that societies and individuals have to face. Many children are often hungry, generally malnourished, and frequently infected with parasites. The 2009 Education For All

Global Monitoring Report suggests that as many as 60 million school age children suffer from iodine deficiency, some 200 million are anaemic, and more than 400 million are infected with parasitic worms which, in addition to anaemia leave them listless and often unable to concentrate (UNESCO, 2008, p. 81). Public health programmes, parts of the *surrounding institutions,* can and do have an impact on these problems but the intestinal helminths themselves such as roundworm, hookworm, and whipworm are parts of the *Background* and need to be understood as such. They are biological vectors which have a marked impact on the mental capacities of the children who suffer from them.

4.5.2   Sex and gender

The second example concerns the vexed and contested distinction between sex and gender. There is strong evidence from around the world that girls and boys perform differently throughout their school careers and that sex- or gender-based differences continue to have an impact into the tertiary sector and probably beyond. In an age when people talk about 'the two genders' (a common usage which implicitly denies a much wider range of gender categories actually in use) and refuse to classify people in terms of sex or to admit that there could be any significant mental differences between males and females as a result of the biological accidents of their birth, it is fundamentally important that we have theoretical means at our disposal for talking about both sex and gender. The term 'gender' and all the institutions, practices, and stereotypes associated with gender are parts of the *surrounding institutions* because they are, without exception, intentional phenomena. Human biological phenomena, including sexual differentiation into males, females, and intermediate or dual forms like hermaphrodites, are non-intentional and thus parts of the *Background* although they have intentional consequences. We know, for certain, that gendered institutions have an impact on educational achievement. We know that there are patterns of advantage and disadvantage that derive from gendered assumptions that are widely made about the differing capacities and aptitudes of boys and girls. We know, as Chapter 3 shows, that there are human universals concerned with sex statuses and with sex-based divisions of labour, among other things. We also know that people are sensitive to these things and that they can and do function as self-fulfilling prophecies. If you tell girls all their lives that they are second class citizens and inferior to men, some of them will come to believe it, particularly if they learn these things from their mothers and other female kin. Stereotype threat (Steele, 2010) is a constant challenge which all humans have to face in one way or another but which has particularly damaging consequences for the most marginalised groups in society. Individual, social, and societal assumptions are of huge importance for the career trajectories that are available to people as a result of accidents of birth.

We do not know and cannot know without detailed and careful research that there are not, and could not be, outcomes which depend on biological differences between males and females, rather than on our beliefs about gender and the institutions we create. The theoretical distinction between *surrounding institutions* and the *Background* enables us to explore this complex terrain without pre-commitment either way. By making the distinction, we are also helped to see more clearly when political and social influences are at work. Analysis of the non-intentional systems of the *Background* enables us to see that factors derived from sexual differentiation as well as gender roles may have impacts on educational outcomes (Halpern, 2000). Moreover we are also in a position to see that both the denial of sex-based differences and the argument for differential treatment as a result of 'natural differences' are socially and politically grounded. The physics and biology of human beings, in and of themselves, provide no grounds for differential treatment.

Let us consider just one simple example which I hope is uncontentious. Human males are, on average, taller, heavier, and more muscular than human females. That is, perhaps aptly, described as a 'brute' fact about *Homo sapiens*. Nothing of social significance follows from that difference simply because it is a difference. However, suppose that you, as supreme commander are charged with forming an army which is going to engage in hand to hand combat with the army of an opposing country. Who would you choose for your soldiers, men or women? Suppose, as a skilful strategist, you could guess at the possible formation of the enemy army by working out what the opposing supreme commander is likely to do? It does not take a strategist of genius to work out that you would have to choose the men rather than the women, however much you might value equality of opportunity. This can be seen by hypothetical consideration of what you should do conditional on the choice of the opposing supreme commander. The analysis is game theoretic and it has a structure rather like the famous Prisoners' Dilemma. Suppose you thought the opposing commander would choose men; you would have to do the same in order to match the size and weight of the enemy. Suppose you thought the opposing commander would choose women; you would still choose men because that would give you a size and weight advantage. Either way, then, you would choose men and you would assume that the rational strategy for the opposing commander would be to do likewise. Thus you end up with two armies of men.

Notice, however, that we are now in the realm of human goals and purposes; we are talking about social goals and the institutions to achieve them. We are no longer dealing simply with biology. Social institutions may, as in this hypothetical case, be structured around genuine biological differences; soldiers are selected from the male population because they are taller and heavier on average than the women. Equally, however, social institutions may be created which deliberately specify that biological differences are not relevant to the functioning of the institution. Education in Britain is made equally available to boys and girls. The biological differences between them are deemed not to be relevant to educational opportunity. Nevertheless, the educational outcomes for boys and girls do differ. This may be because the institutional stipulations of equality are being breached, because there are underlying sex differences which affect outcomes, or because of a complex interaction between institutional factors and human biology. Similarly, since 1975 in Britain, there has been a legal requirement for men and women to be paid equally for work of equal value, although in practice there are still systematic differences. The institution of equality prescribes that biological differences are again irrelevant to pay. What these cases show is that biological differences are neutral, in principle, with regard to the creation and operation of social institutions. They may, or may not be thought relevant to the structure and functioning of the institution. In practice, we do not know whether the differences in outcomes which continue to be observed are the results of institutional factors, of biological factors, or of interactions between them.

Because this is so, it is damaging to intellectual clarity to proceed in a way which simply denies the existence or possibility of biological differences in a domain in which equality regardless of biology is an institutional requirement in order to maintain the neutrality of the institution which, one fears, might otherwise be subject to arguments for differential treatment on biological grounds. If, in fact, there is sex or gender bias in a social institution which is supposedly sex or gender blind, the way to proceed must be to understand and remedy the causes of the bias rather than to deny the possibility of a difference from which the bias arises. If the bias is the result of a real biological difference, then it is better to recognise the fact and find ways to remove it if one's goal is to maintain the neutrality of the institution. Alternatively, one might decide that perhaps the institution needs to be modified to take account of the biology. Chapter 6 shows that there are real biological differences between the sexes in human populations which are important sources of social differentiation.

4.6   The analysis of the Background is Darwinian

The examples show, I hope, that the analytical distinction between the *literate ecology* and the *Background* helps to make clear some of the areas of debate which have typically been contentious in social science. It is important to note that the distinction is analytical and not ontological. It is not a distinction about what there is, but about how it should be understood. The elements of the *literate ecology* have both intentional and non-intentional parts. The intentional mental states of the literate individuals who constitute the main subject matter of this book are physical, ontologically subjective parts of the real world, but not all the mental states of literate individuals, are intentional. The non-intentional mental states of individual readers and writers are understood via the analysis of the *Background* but are, nonetheless, states of those individuals. Similarly, the non-intentional features of the *surrounding institutions* which enable them to perform their collective, intentional functions are, nonetheless, features of those institutions. The non-intentional, biological, capacities underlying the intentional capacities of humans must be understood in Darwinian terms because there is no other plausible theory to account for them. This argument has the strong corollary that social institutions must also be understood to have Darwinian underpinnings because they are created and maintained in existence by individuals, not by phantom collective or group minds. Collective intentionality is a feature of individual minds, not a characterisation of a supra-individual entity.

Although humans are evolved creatures with biases, such as a tendency to overestimate their own objectivity, I do argue for the independence and objectivity of at least some methods of literate intellectual inquiry such as mathematics and natural science. It is, therefore, incumbent on me to show how it is possible for these activities to be grounded in social institutions with the strategic characteristics typical of evolved systems and, at the same time, to be epistemically objective. The characteristics of symbol systems which allow for this are, I think, precisely those that lead some expert users and developers of those systems to believe in mathematical Platonism. The fundamental fact about mathematical and logical symbol systems is that the structures that can be built with them have characteristics which are independent of the wishes and desires of the humans who use them, despite the fact that they are human inventions. The binary system for representing numbers, for example, is a human invention, but it is true, independently of any human belief or desire, that eight binary digits can be combined in 256 different patterns. The Mandelbrot set is another, quite remarkable, example based on the complex number plane. The objectivity of such structures is perhaps fundamentally no more surprising than the objectivity of social institutions more generally, but it is of a rather different character. Formal, axiomatic systems, to take a further example, incorporate independent, autonomous rules of inference which define both their scope and their limitations. One interesting consequence of this independence is that acknowledging the Darwinian roots of social institutions need not compromise their objectivity. It may also be that among the consequences of our Darwinian heritage is an inbuilt sensitivity to some of the fundamental structure of the universe. It is said that mathematicians seldom try to prove uninteresting theorems and it is remarkable that physicists manage to home in on fundamental theoretical postulates. Perhaps they are channelled by elements of the *Background* in ways that reflect or are analogous to how the *Background* operates with respect to non-mathematical institutions.

Chapter 5

The Evolution of Cooperation and Selfishness

The functional core of the literate ecology as defined in Chapter 4 has two components, a text and a reader/writer. In order to understand the power of literacy, we need to understand what the mind of the reader/writer contributes to this core system. From an evolutionary perspective the mind is a system that has been shaped by the lengthy history of *Homo sapiens*. Complex, highly structured, language using, meaning producing, human minds pre-date the invention of literacy by tens, possibly hundreds, of thousands of years (Stringer, 2011). Human minds were evolved in environments containing numerous physical and social challenges. There has, most probably, been some evolution in our lineage since the invention of literacy (Cochran and Harpending, 2009) but there has not been enough time for major changes to the brain. The fundamental structure of human minds is, therefore, the result of evolution in largely pre-literate environments. Chapter 3 discussed this structure in terms of human universals. In this chapter, the evolutionary processes that led to human universals are introduced. Understanding these processes provides deeper insights into the nature of non-literate and literate minds.

5.1 Evolution results in the appearance of design

The concept of design provides an interesting starting point for consideration of the human mind which we can think of as the organism's control system. When considering the mind in this way we confront a system of huge complexity and flexibility and we are faced with a fundamental question: What is the human control system for? Is it the product of deliberate design, or is it to be explained in some other way? If the human control system was designed, what were the design goals? If it was not designed, how is its apparently purposeful structure to be explained?

As a child of Roman Catholic parents, I was brought up to believe that humans were created by God for specific reasons, that they were the result of 'intelligent design' to use a current slogan. Human creation was described succinctly in a short text, sometimes known as 'The Penny Catechism', much of which I knew by heart and some of which I still remember. The catechism is strikingly familiar when I read it now although I had not looked at it for many years until it occurred to me to use it in the current context. The catechism consists of a series of questions and answers covering a wide range of aspects of Roman Catholic belief and practices. The first two questions and answers set out the basic RC view of the human being as divinely created:

1. *Who made you?*

   God made me.

2. *Why did God make you?*

   God made me to know Him, love Him, and serve Him in this world, and to be happy with Him forever in the next.

The cadences of the catechism have emotional resonances for me even now and are testimony to the psychological effects of regular recitation and the process of indoctrination. Such practices, of course, continue in a wide range of religious and other contexts across the world today.

5.2   Evolution explains the appearance of design

The idea that the human mind was designed by God with the purposes that the catechism described is one that I no longer find credible. There is, nevertheless, ample evidence that the human brain is highly structured, and if it was not designed by a conscious agent it stands in need of some other form of explanation. A powerful and compelling explanation can be given in terms of evolutionary theory and it shows that Question 1 of the catechism is misleading because by using the word 'who' it assumes the existence of an agent. The question should rather be 'What made you?' and the ultimate answer is 'An evolutionary process'. It is clear from the developmental process that begins *in utero* that the information which structures the human brain is largely, although not exclusively, provided by the foetal genome and the genome itself is a product of evolution which has acted generation after generation over billions of years. One of the great insights of Charles Darwin was to understand that complex structure of the kind we see in humans and other animals can be explained without the postulation of an intelligent creator. Evolution is a blind, mechanistic process. It has no purposes. From an evolutionary point of view, answers to questions about why there are human beings cannot be given in terms of reasons but must be given in terms of mechanisms. The evolutionary process has no reason for doing anything and thus the answer to an analogue of the catechism's second question 'Why did an evolutionary process make you?' is stark. There is no reason for our existence other than past history. Evolutionary explanations are historical, not teleological. Evolution is sometimes said to produce the appearance of deliberate design but it is precisely that; an appearance. However, human psychology is so oriented towards concepts of agency and purpose that it is easy to conclude that the appearance of design in the products of evolution is evidence for the reality of a powerful designer.

5.3   The literacy literature typically does not refer to evolutionary theory

The literacy literature is almost entirely devoid of references to evolution. From one perspective this is not surprising. Much of the literacy literature is concerned with everyday practical issues and it has a focus on literacy teaching in schools and other formal institutions. It is not a literature which, for the most part, is concerned with ultimate explanation. However, a significant portion of the literature does attempt to evaluate different theoretical accounts of the effects of literacy. One of the earliest ideas to be promoted which was subsequently heavily criticised is the idea that literacy transforms the 'primitive' mind into the 'modern' mind, or the 'savage' mind into the 'civilized' mind. Different forms of literacy were said to correspond to different stages of the move from savagery to civilisation. Rousseau's eighteenth century essay on the origin of languages is a famous example of the genre.

> The depicting of objects is appropriate to a savage people; signs of words and of propositions, to a barbaric people, and the alphabet to civilized peoples. (Moran et al, 1986, p. 17)

One might think that in order to make good a transformational thesis of this kind it would be essential to have a clear idea of the starting state. What, exactly, does it mean to characterize a non-literate human mind as 'primitive' or 'savage'? Notice that the characterisation as primitive or savage must not refer simply to the lack of literacy skills. Such a characterisation would be circular. Assuming a noncircular characterisation could be given, one would then need to compare the qualities described with those of the literate mind to try to understand exactly what transformations have ensued. By and large, theories advocating a transformational effect of literacy have not given a clear characterisation of the non-literate mind and those that have been given are often contested.

5.4   Evolutionary theory explains the non-literate mind

We can make a new departure in the study of literacy by characterising the non-literate mind in terms of universals, as discussed in Chapter 3, and by understanding universals via the theory of evolution. At present the characterisation is patchy but it will become increasingly detailed as knowledge of evolution and its effects on our lineage improves. Moreover, the evolutionary perspective is the only way to provide a satisfactory view of the range of phenomena that needs to be taken into account. Contemporary humans engage in an apparently limitless range of jobs, sports, entertainments, social interactions, intellectual pursuits, and so forth, but underlying all of them are the fundamental activities of our lives as a particular kind of animal. We require food, water, and shelter, we need the company of other humans, we seek sexual relationships and children, we care for those close to us, and we mourn our dead. The states of mind involved in these activities, and in the plethora of other activities in which humans engage, need to be understood. Familiar human activities predate agriculture and the invention of writing by many millennia. Thus the foundations on which literate lives are built are clearly rooted in the evolutionary history of our species. From this standpoint it is unlikely that literacy has effected fundamental transformations of human mentality. There hasn't been enough time. It is more plausible to suppose that literacy amplifies pre-literate universals and adds some new capabilities. Humans did not become interested in food and drink when they became literate but they have written voluminously about them and furthered the knowledge and pleasure to be gained from them. Humans did not become interested in sex when they became literate, but they have used literacy in many ways relating to sex including religious ordinances and pornography. Humans did not become interested in competition and status as a result of literacy, but they have found numerous ways of competing and building hierarchies based on literacy and its products. Humans have not become interested in power as a result of literacy, but they have constructed social institutions such as legal systems in which the uses and abuses of power are codified and debated. The better we understand ourselves in the round as evolved creatures the more able we will be to understand what is distinctive about literate life as compared with non-literate life.

5.5   Evolutionary time scales are hard to grasp intuitively

An essential starting point for a proper appreciation of Darwinian analysis is the recognition of the vast time scales involved in evolutionary processes. (It is a particular feature of the literate mind that it is capable of expressing in a comprehensible fashion ideas about time scales that are far too short or far too long to be grasped by unaided human perceptual equipment.) The universe is about 13.7 billion years old, the earth is about 4.5 billion years old, and life has existed on the earth for more than 3 billion years (Dawkins, 2005). One of the difficulties that most of us have is to get an adequate intuitive grasp of just how long the time spans involved really are. The Universal People have units of time and understand that human lives are governed by temporal cycles at various scales but they do not have an intuitive feel for the time scale of evolutionary processes. Consider the time scales that we can grasp intuitively. At the shorter end of the spectrum we can grasp durations of tenths of a second, approximately, but struggle with much shorter intervals. At the longer end of the spectrum our intuitions are tuned to the lengths of human lifetimes. If we think of a human generation as approximately 25 years, then four generations, or a century, is a span for which, as adults, we have a ready feel. Increasing familiarity with written records which now stretch back over approximately 5,000 years provides the means to think cogently about longer time spans but even a span of a thousand years is hard to grasp intuitively. If humans lived for a thousand years we would have a better feel for spans as long as that, but because our lives are limited, so too is our intuitive grasp of very long time periods.

Literacy is the principal means by which we transcend or work around such natural limitations. The point is simply made but it merits further discussion. Educated, literate people nowadays talk readily about nano-seconds and micro-seconds because the computer technology which pervades our lives operates on these time scales and we have created a vocabulary for talking about them. Similarly we talk readily about the immense time scales involved in the movements of continents because geologists have familiarised us with the concept of tectonic plates and the theory of their movements. Our native perception, however, is simply incapable of grasping these very short and very long time scales intuitively. Our ancestors had no need for such capacities and would not have benefited from them. Their, and consequently our, perceptual systems were fashioned over evolutionary time by the regularities of the natural world that were relevant to their daily lives, not by scientific research and discovery. The results of scientific enquiry enable us to know about very long and very short time scales but we cannot readily develop a feel for that knowledge to parallel our feel for mundane time scales. As a result literate minds are curious mixtures of the intuitively known and the theoretically known, and these sources of understanding can come into conflict. The extension of our understanding of time scales is an instance of the fundamental point that literacy amplifies existing capacities rather than transforming them.

The immense time period over which life has evolved on our planet is significant for a number of reasons. Among them is the fact that there has been sufficient time for an extraordinary range of life forms to be tested by evolutionary competition and for some extremely complex creatures to have been produced, including ourselves. As a result of the work of numerous theorists, among whom Charles Darwin and Alfred Russel Wallace are pre-eminent, we understand that the basic principles of the evolutionary process which produces these complex outcomes are, in essence, quite simple. It may be that it is the rather deceptive simplicity of the process, coupled with the complexity of its outcomes and the intuitively hard to grasp time scales, which is one of the factors that creates resistance to evolutionary explanations of humanity.

5.6   The evolutionary process has three fundamental drivers

The process of evolution by natural selection has three fundamental drivers: competition for scarce resources; heritable variation in characteristics; and differential reproductive success. Darwin's own summary description of the process is an excellent place to begin.

> If during the long course of ages and under varying conditions of life, organic beings vary at all in the several parts of their organisation, and I think this cannot be disputed; if there be, owing to the high geometrical powers of increase of each species, at some age, season, or year, a severe struggle for life, and this certainly cannot be disputed; then, considering the infinite complexity of the relations of all organic beings to each other and to their conditions of existence, causing an infinite diversity in structure, constitution, and habits, to be advantageous to them, I think it would be a most extraordinary fact if no variation ever had occurred useful to each being's own welfare, in the same way as so many variations have occurred useful to man. But if variations useful to any organic being do occur, assuredly individuals thus characterised will have the best chance of being preserved in the struggle for life; and from the strong principle of inheritance they will tend to produce offspring similarly characterised. This principle of preservation, I have called, for the sake of brevity, Natural Selection.
>
> (Darwin, 1859, pp. 126–7)

5.6.1   Competition for scarce resources

With respect to competition in the struggle for life, Darwin mentions the 'geometrical powers of increase of each species'. He would have thought of this geometrical increase in comparison with the constant or, at best, linearly increasing food supply which seemed possible with the agricultural technology of the time. Darwin had been influenced by the work of Thomas Malthus who proposed that increases in the human population would be kept in check by the food supply, which could not grow as fast as demand for it. In the short term Malthus's predictions have not been vindicated, in the sense that human food production is currently sufficient, in principle, to meet the needs of the global population, although death by starvation is a regular occurrence because of inequitable distribution. However, the general principle is obviously correct and some notable evolutionary theorists

have argued that a 'Malthusian crunch' involving mass starvation is simply a matter of time unless population growth is brought under control.
Diamond (2005) discusses overpopulation and other pressing challenges for
contemporary humanity. For most species, undoubtedly including humans
prior to the development of systematic agriculture, more individuals are
born than can survive to maturity because of competition for resources,
especially food and clean water. The resulting competition causes 'at some
age, season or year, a severe struggle for life'. It is easy for those of us living in affluent societies to forget the severity of the struggle but it is there,
right under our noses, if we care to look at less fortunate contemporary
human populations. Avoidable deaths from malnutrition, from waterborne
diseases, and from lack of medical care are commonplace in many human
societies and structural inequity in provision of vital resources is characteristic of all of them. Darwin's phrase 'at some age, season or year' serves
as a reminder that the struggle may be cyclical or may be more intense at
particular times of life. Infancy, late adolescence, and early adulthood are
particularly difficult times for humans whose psychological states respond
in systematic ways to deprivations and challenges at these different life
stages.

5.6.2   Heritable variation of characteristics

Variation, Darwin says, indisputably occurs both in environmental conditions and in the organisation of 'the several parts' of organic beings.
The first two chapters of *On the Origin of Species* document variability
in both domesticated and wild flora and fauna and Darwin was assiduous in studying variation himself and in finding out about it from others.
His network of correspondents was global and he engaged in painstaking
research and involved his family and friends in it. His research and that
of subsequent generations has established that ample variation exists in
natural species, although significant questions remain about how and why
it is maintained.

Given the existence of struggle and variation as premises, Darwin then
argued from the 'infinite diversity' of structure, constitution, and habits
of organisms caused by the 'infinite complexity' of their ecological inter-
relations to the intermediate conclusion that some of this diverse variation
must be useful to its possessors. Contemporary Darwinians tend automatically to look for use or function when variation is apparent but it was by no
means obvious in the mid-nineteenth century that variation was anything
other than adventitious or perhaps put in place by a benevolent creator
for his own reasons, possibly including the entertainment of his human
creatures. It was certainly one of the most important of Darwin's insights
to see variation as a driver of the evolutionary process. The argument continues from the existence not just of variation but of *useful* variation to a

further pair of conclusions: individuals with useful variations will (a) have improved chances in the struggle for life and (b) will tend to produce off-spring with similar characteristics.

5.6.3   Differential reproductive success

In terms of contemporary evolutionary understanding, the conclusions of Darwin's argument appear somewhat tentative, and a rather more targeted account of the advantages of useful variation is usually given. The simple point is that being preserved in the struggle for life, i.e., living longer than one's competitors, is of no benefit whatsoever inde-pendently of the production of offspring. Reproductive success is the currency of the evolutionary process. Organisms which die young hav-ing produced many offspring are genetically better represented in the next generation than those which live into old age but produce fewer offspring. If it is the case that increased reproduction leads to a shorter life then there is a trade-off between reproduction and survival. Since Darwin's day, significant mathematical analysis has been developed to explore the many trade-off relationships that lead to subtle nuances of selective action (Roff, 1992; Hawkes and Paine, 2006; Lawson, 2011). In general, the modern understanding places less emphasis on survival and more on numbers of offspring, but we should note that the idea of improved chances in the struggle for life had more immediate connota-tions in Darwin's day than it does now for those of us who live in afflu-ent societies with very low infant and child mortality. The early death of children was common and Victorian parents, including the Darwins, were far more aware of its threat than are members of contemporary, developed societies who have ready access to advanced medical care and rapid treatment for their children. Charles and his wife Emma suf-fered the early loss of children. Their great-great-grand-daughter, the poet Ruth Padel, has written movingly about the death of their much loved daughter, Annie, in her recent collection, *Darwin A Life in Poems* (2009).

To summarise Darwin's summary of the evolutionary process, it has three principal drivers. First, there is a struggle for resources, the most important of which are directly connected to survival and mating. Second, there is functional heritable variation in characteristics within species, *use-ful* variation, in Darwin's terms. Individuals whose characteristics predis-pose them to success in the battle for resources tend, as a result, to produce greater numbers of offspring. This differential reproductive success changes the frequency of characteristics in the population and sets the terms for the struggles of the next generation. Over geological time, species become adapted to particular ecological niches but may decline to extinction if competition for a niche is lost or if an ecological catastrophe occurs. The process is blind, stark, and often brutal. The genius of Darwin and Wallace lay in seeing that it was not necessary to postulate a designer or any conscious agent of change at all to explain the variability of forms of life and the processes of birth, living, and death.

Darwin described and documented much of the 'infinite complexity of the relations of all organic beings to each other and to their conditions of existence' and the 'infinite diversity in structure, constitution, and habits' which resulted from this diversity. Since the publication of *On the Origin of Species* 150 years ago, a great deal more has been learned but Darwin's writings are still an important resource. Everything he wrote about evolution can be found online at http://darwin-online.org.uk/

5.7   Competition leads to the evolution of selfishness

The fundamental driver of competitive struggle is scarcity of resources and the fundamental evolved human response to chronic scarcity has to be 'me first'. Why should selfishness be the fundamental response? Why could it not be 'you first' or 'share and share alike'? Let us consider scarcity of food as an example. Scarcity is a simple concept: it means that there is not enough for everyone. In the starkest cases it implies that those who eat survive and that those who do not eat die. 'Share and share alike' is a precarious strategy in extreme circumstances; it carries the risk that both or all parties to the sharing will die, albeit more slowly than otherwise. 'You first' is tantamount to suicide. A strategy where you eat and I don't is noble, but evolutionarily not sustainable because the genes for the strategy will be lost from the population. 'Me first' means that I eat and you don't. It is an ignoble strategy perhaps, but effective with respect to the propagation of the genes that underlie it. If we consider a population in conditions of chronic scarcity and suppose that each individual can act according to 'me first', 'you first', or 'share and share alike', who will prosper? Clearly those who adopt 'me first'. This is the harsh logic of natural selection. There are circumstances in which the stark brutality of these choices is avoided or softened by considerations of genetic relatedness and reciprocity, but it is important to appreciate that moral sentiment, divorced from the consideration of outcomes, has no part to play in the evolutionary analysis of difficult choices. What we might prefer to think of ourselves and others and what we would actually do in conditions of extreme need are likely to be different. There would certainly have been those in ancestral populations who, for whatever reason, adopted 'you first' or 'share and share alike', but it is highly unlikely that they would have had descendants if there were significant numbers of 'me first' players in the population. If there were, they would be overwhelmingly more likely to have been ancestors, and, if the trait were heritable, then their descendants would also be 'me first' players.

5.7.1 War and conflict are signals of human competitiveness

One might, perhaps, question the Malthusian assumption on which the struggle argument depends and suggest that scarcity has not been a regular feature of human environments, and hence that strategies like 'me first' are not fundamental characteristics of the human psychological endowment. However, although it may be impossible to prove that shortages of food and other resources have been endemic in human evolutionary history, recent genetic evidence suggesting bottlenecks in the size of the human population at various times (Hunley, Healey, and Long, 2009) is clearly compatible with acute shortages of resources, and the existence of war and conflict in all known human societies points clearly to a readiness to compete. The Italian chemist Primo Levi, writing about his experiences in a Nazi concentration camp during the Second World War in his remarkable book *If This is a Man*, described the camp as 'a gigantic biological and social experiment':

> Thousands of individuals, differing in age, condition, origin, language, culture and customs, are enclosed within barbed wire: there they live a regular, controlled life which is identical for all and inadequate to all needs, and which is more rigorous than any experimenter could have set up to establish what is essential and what adventitious to the conduct of the human animal in the struggle for life. (p. 93)

Levi said that under those conditions two 'particularly well differentiated categories' of people emerged, those who perished and those who survived, 'the drowned' and 'the saved', as he described them. An important characteristic of the saved was an attitude in which 'me first' was predominant, although Levi's analysis is more subtle than this simple description might suggest. He did not believe that 'man is fundamentally brutal, egoistic and stupid in his conduct once every civilized institution is taken away'. His central point was this: if the normal social customs and institutions are removed and 'everyone is desperately and ferociously alone' then 'the struggle to survive is without respite'. Under such circumstances 'me first' has to be in operation if one is to survive rather than to drown.

> One has to fight against the current; to battle every day and every hour against exhaustion, hunger, cold and the resulting inertia; to resist enemies and have no pity for rivals...to throttle all dignity and kill all conscience, to climb down into the arena as a beast against other beasts, to let oneself be guided by those unsuspected subterranean forces which sustain families and individuals in cruel times...Survival without

renunciation of any part of one's own moral world...was conceded only to a very few superior individuals, made of the stuff of martyrs and saints. (p. 98)

Given recurrent shortage of resources, 'me first' behaviour has clearly undergone positive selection and, as a result, exists as a fundamental tendency in the behavioural and psychological repertoire of *Homo sapiens*. In genetic terms, with the exception of identical twins, humans are unique and thus it is to be expected that when scarcity prevails, a tendency to self-interest will come to the surface, although it will be moderated in some circumstances, particularly in the presence of close genetic kin.

5.8   Selfishness is relevant to the study of literacy

The fundamental tendency to self-interest is relevant to the study of literacy in a variety of ways. I shall consider just one example here. The understanding that self-interest is built into the human psyche helps to explain the kinds of phenomena that led Street (1984) to postulate the ideological model of literacy. Street did not include self-serving biases as an explicit element of the model in his list of its six fundamental characteristics (1984, p. 8), but such biases are indirectly indicated in the references made to social stratification and the political and ideological significance of literacy. Moreover, in the prolegomenon to the book, Street suggested that the qualities of literacy were frequently used 'to legitimise assertions that might otherwise appear self-interested and ethnocentric' (p. x). This is both intuitively plausible and supported by a considerable body of recent evidence, some of which is summarised in Larson (2007). It is also possible to see evidence of the political uses of literacy in some of the earliest known texts. Damerow (1996), writing about food production and social status as documented in Proto-Cuneiform texts from southern Mesopotamia, suggests that the archaic writing system was 'essentially an instrument used by elites controlling major parts or even the entire production of the society' (p. 151). A point worth making is that if writing had not been a powerful force for self-interest, elites would not have bothered with it. We can thus recognise both the 'autonomous' qualities of literacy and the fact that self-interest has deep roots and will tend to surface when individual interests are at stake.

The example shows that individual self-interest is a strong driving force in contemporary human affairs and has left its mark on the practices associated with literacy. Literacy is an intellectual tool and we should expect it to be used strategically to promote self-interest, as are other tools. However, individual self-interest is not the only outcome of the evolutionary process that has shaped human minds. Competition and conflict are powerful driving forces, but so are co-operation and mutualism.

5.9   Altruism and co-operation are also products of evolution

Humans are profoundly social beings, as the list of universals in Chapter 3 shows, and circumstances are often such that sharing is beneficial and would have been beneficial in the environments which shaped the traits and dispositions we have inherited from our ancestors. As a result, alongside deep rooted capacities for self-interested behaviour and conflict, evolution has also selected various forms of co-operative behaviour as important aspects of human sociality. Many of the world's great religious scriptures are largely concerned with the warring impulses towards conflict and co-operation which are often characterised in terms of the struggle between good and evil, between right and wrong. From an evolutionary standpoint, although the descriptive work is often compelling, the correct account of the origins of these dispositions is missing.

Co-operation and mutualism can be understood without difficulty from an evolutionary perspective when they are beneficial to both or all parties. Sexual relations between men and women, for example, are mutually beneficial because they lead to the propagation of both male and female genes. Alliances between members of a tribe tend to be beneficial because they enable concerted action to be taken to prevent aggression from, or to promote aggression against, neighbouring groups. However, there are forms of co-operation which are hard to understand.

5.9.1   Altruism is an evolutionary puzzle

Altruistic behaviour is particularly challenging when an altruistic act is defined as one which reduces the reproductive success of the actor and benefits the reproductive success of the recipient. Such acts appear to be examples of what have been described as 'you first' behaviours, and the analysis suggested that they should lead to extinction of the genes supporting them. If you act altruistically for my benefit then, by definition, the next generation will contain more of my descendants and fewer of yours. If you have any descendants and they have inherited your altruistic genes then they will be at even greater risk, because the proportion of non-altruists, people like me, will have increased. After relatively few generations we should expect the genes promoting altruism to have been lost from the population.

In the passage from the *Origin of Species* quoted earlier, Darwin talks about the 'strong principle of inheritance' by means of which characteristics are passed from one generation to another such that offspring tend to resemble their parents more closely than they resemble other members of the parental generation. Darwin did not understand the mechanisms of inheritance, although Gregor Mendel, the Augustinian monk after whom Mendelian genetics is named, had published his work during Darwin's lifetime. The first systematic synthesis of Darwin's work on evolution and Mendel's on genetics was not made until 1930 when Ronald Fisher's seminal book *The Genetical Theory of Natural Selection* was published. Fisher's mathematical work established the foundations for the contemporary understanding that natural selection works by changing population gene frequencies and hence that the genetic level rather than the individual level of analysis is fundamental to evolutionary biology even though selection acts on organisms.

5.9.2   Kin selection theory solves the puzzle of altruism

Fisher's work paved the way for that of William Hamilton, the pre-eminent twentieth century biologist of social evolution, who solved the problem of altruism. At the start of a now famous paper, Hamilton summarised the argument for thinking that natural selection operates largely to produce selfish individuals:

> With very few exceptions, the only parts of the theory of natural selection which have been supported by mathematical models admit no possibility of the evolution of any characters which are on average to the disadvantage of the individuals possessing them. If natural selection followed the classical models exclusively, species would not show any behaviour more positively social than the coming together of the sexes and parental care. (Hamilton, 1964a, p. 31)

The challenge in the human case is obvious. Some humans do, as a matter of fact, exhibit more social behaviour than is involved in sexual partnerships and parental care, and thus the 'classical models' to which Hamilton referred must either be wrong or incomplete. Hamilton's theory showed that they were incomplete. He demonstrated that it was possible for a behaviour which diminished its possessor's direct reproduction to be positively selected, provided that the genes underlying the behaviour increased in frequency as a result of it. That could happen if the beneficiary of an altruistic act was sufficiently closely related to the actor. In a short paper published before the one quoted above, Hamilton gave a succinct description of the circumstances which would be needed for this to occur.

> As a simple but admittedly crude model we may imagine a pair of genes *g* and *G* such that *G* tends to cause some kind of altruistic behaviour while *g* is null. Despite the principle of 'survival of the fittest' the ultimate criterion which determines whether *G* will spread is not whether the behaviour is to the benefit of the behaver but whether it is to the benefit of the gene *G*; and this will be the case if the average net result of the behaviour is to add to the gene pool a handful of genes containing

G in higher concentration than does the gene pool itself. With altruism this will happen only if the affected individual is a relative of the altruist, therefore having an increased chance of carrying the gene, and if the advantage conferred is large enough compared to the personal disadvantage to offset the regression, or 'dilution', of the altruist's genotype in the relative in question...Thus a gene causing altruistic behaviour towards brothers and sisters will be selected only if the behaviour and circumstances are generally such that the gain is more than twice the loss; for half-brothers it must be more than four times the loss; and so on. To put the matter more vividly, an animal acting on this principle would sacrifice its life if it could thereby save more than two brothers, but not for less. (Hamilton, 1963, p. 7)

Hamilton's 'kin selection' theory, as it is now known, explains the commonly observed tendency of humans to behave altruistically to close relatives much more often than to genetic strangers. It also explains why conflicts between relatives tend to be more restrained than those between strangers. By parity of reasoning, Hamilton's theory also implies that selfish and aggressive behaviour will be observed much more frequently with respect to strangers than with respect to genetic relatives.

5.10   Group selection is a weaker force than individual selection

It is important, both in general and in the context of literacy, to understand group level social processes as well as individual processes. In view of the tendency for selection at the level of individuals to produce 'me first' behaviour except towards close genetic kin, an important question is whether selection for co-operative behaviour can occur at the level of groups despite the selfish tendencies of individuals. One might think that groups would be able to generate altruistic behaviour and to suppress selfish behaviour by virtue of the policing which is possible when members' activities are open to group inspection. One might also expect greater homogeneity of behaviour in groups as a result of the possibility of enforcing conformity to group norms. Darwin in *The Descent of Man* suggested something of the kind:

[A]fter the power of language had been acquired and the wishes of the members of the same community could be distinctly expressed, the common opinion how each member ought to act for the public good, would naturally become to a large extent the guide to action. (Darwin, 1871, p. 72)

He also made explicit the possibility of natural selection acting at the level of groups to improve 'the standard of morality':

> It must not be forgotten that although a high standard of morality gives but a slight or no advantage to each individual man and his children over the other men of the same tribe, yet that an advancement in the standard of morality and an increase in the number of well-endowed men will certainly give an immense advantage to one tribe over another. There can be no doubt that a tribe including many members who, from possessing in a high degree the spirit of patriotism, fidelity, obedience, courage, and sympathy, were always ready to give aid to each other and to sacrifice themselves for the common good, would be victorious over most other tribes; and this would be natural selection. At all times throughout the world tribes have supplanted other tribes; and as morality is one element in their success, the standard of morality and the number of well-endowed men will thus everywhere tend to rise and increase. (Darwin, 1871, p. 166)

This passage has frequently been cited by contemporary theorists exploring the possibility that altruism can evolve via selection at the level of groups (Sober and Wilson, 1998; Traulsen and Nowak, 2006; Wilson and Wilson, 2007). It is sometimes treated as a group-level solution to the problem of altruism:

> The solution, according to Darwin, is that groups containing mostly altruists have a decisive advantage over groups containing mostly selfish individuals, even if selfish individuals have the advantage over altruists within each group. (Wilson and Wilson, 2007, p. 43)

Hamilton also referred to this passage but in a more cautious way. In a paper published in 1975, the year in which E.O. Wilson's *Sociobiology* appeared and sparked a storm of controversy, Hamilton discussed human social behaviour using a mathematical model of natural selection, based on the work of Price (1970, 1972). With respect to Darwin's infrequent endorsements of groups as units of selection he said

> I believe even these limited concessions were incautious, and value his judgement more where, discussing the evolution of courage and self-sacrifice in man, he left a difficulty apparent and unresolved. He saw that such traits would naturally be counterselected *within* a social group whereas in competition *between* groups the groups with the most of such qualities would be the ones best fitted to survive and increase. (Hamilton, 1975, pp. 330–1)

5.10.1   Group selection is controversial

The 'group selection' question has been a controversial issue in evolutionary biology for more than 40 years. Prior to the 1960s, the balance of opinion suggested that explanations of social behaviour in terms of 'the good of the species' were plausible both in theory and in practice. Such explanations proposed that selection at the level of groups could produce social adaptations. If a group such as a species required self-sacrifice on the part of some of its members to prevent resource depletion or to warn of the proximity of predators, for example, such altruistic behaviour could be evolved. One of the most well known texts proposing a view of this kind was *Animal Dispersion in Relation to Social Behaviour* by V.C. Wynne-Edwards (1962). The group selection argument was strongly criticised by G.C. Williams in *Adaptation and Natural Selection* (1966), which proposed that every apparent example of group selection could be explained in terms of individual selection. Williams' book became the basis of the orthodoxy which still largely prevails. Richard Dawkins' *The Selfish Gene* (1976), for example, was strongly influenced by Williams' work.

One of the key arguments against group selection was the inevitability of free-riding. Suppose there were a species in which altruistic self-sacrifice had been evolved for the good of the group. A non-altruistic mutant member would do better, on average, than the altruistic members and would, therefore, have more offspring. If the non-altruistic trait were heritable it would, in time, come to dominate the population. Since there is no reason in principle why such a mutation should not arise, the possibility of a group-related adaptation is fatally weakened. Williams argued that 'group-related adaptations do not, in fact, exist' (1966, p. 93). Despite this very strong argument, there is continued support for group selection. Traulsen and Nowak (2006, p. 10952), for example, claim that 'group selection is an important organizing principle that permeates evolutionary processes from the emergence of the first cells to eusociality and the economics of nations.'

The theoretical underpinning for much of the current work on group selection is found in the work of George Price. Price developed a new equation which describes evolutionary change (see Price 1995 for a relatively nontechnical introduction). Price's equation is based on the covariance between reproductive fitness and a specific characteristic such as altruism. Frank (1995, p. 374) says that 'The equation itself cannot reduce the inherent complexity of models, but the simple covariance relationship between a character and fitness provides a compact way to see the essential features of social evolution.' The significance of Price's equation for the group selection controversy is that it has two components. One component represents selection between groups, and the other selection within groups. Price's formulation thus shows that group selection is real but, as Hamilton made clear, 'being able to point to a relevant and generally non-zero part of

selective change is far from showing that group selection can override individual selection when the two are in conflict' (1975, p. 333). When a population is randomly divided into groups the inter-group selection component
is characteristically much weaker than the intra-group component because
the between-groups variance is much smaller than the within-groups variance. For group selection to succeed, the between-groups variance has to be
increased relative to the within-groups variance. This is typically achieved
by making the characteristic of interest assort positively with its own type.
In the case of altruism, for example, it means that altruists must be grouped
to some degree with other altruists rather than with the selfish. This makes
intuitive sense because it means that the benefits of altruism are then select-
ively targeted on other altruists. Hamilton was able to specify the degree
to which grouping was required in a relatively simple model which, with
suitable redefinition, can be applied to human groups. He also showed
that the level of migration between groups is an important determining
factor with regard to the level of altruism which can be reached within a
group. Although within-group relatedness is important, it is also essential
that a certain amount of migration should occur, otherwise groups become
inbred. There is, therefore, a delicate balance to be struck between protect-
ing the group from outsiders and reinforcing the group with outsiders.

5.10.2   Group selection implies hostility towards outgroups

One important feature of group selection is that the success of one group
comes at a cost to others. The conditions that are conducive to group selection mean that relatedness builds up within groups and declines between
groups. That, in its turn, implies that amicable behaviour increases towards
members of one's own group and, at the same time, hostile behaviour
increases towards members of other groups. Hamilton explored the possibility that violent conflict between groups with low relatedness could be
adaptive.

> Close frontiers to migrants a little more, or slightly increase group mobil-
> ity, and it is possible to imagine the sudden success of a policy which
> makes any frontier incident an occasion for an attempt at violent incur-
> sion by the more populous group with losers killed, enslaved, or driven
> off. (Hamilton, 1975, p. 342)

The rewards of conflict are potentially increased once technology and agriculture are in place because there is more to fight over.

> The rewards of the victors in warfare obviously increase for peoples past
> the neolithic revolution. There are tools, livestock, stores of food, lux-
> ury goods to be seized, and even a possibility for the victors to impose

themselves for a long period as a parasitical upper class ... The occurrence of quasi-warlike group interactions in various higher primates ... strongly suggests that something like warfare may have become adaptive far down in the hominid stock. (Hamilton, 1975, p. 344)

It is clear from a survey of the current global situation that warfare remains a potent part of the human behavioural repertoire. In 2007, the United Nations High Commission for Refugees estimated that there were some 25 million people displaced within their own countries as a result of armed conflict (UNHCR Global Report 2007, p. 47). Group selection of altruistic behaviour is, therefore, a mixed blessing because it does not replace selfish behaviour and it does not readily extend beyond the boundaries of local groups. Indeed it is possible that inter-group conflicts are made more bitter and violent by the polarisation resulting from group selection.

5.11   Evolution and education for all

The evolutionary analysis of social behaviour is far more complex than the simple sketch given above suggests, but there is, I hope, sufficient in what has been said to indicate why evolutionary thinking is relevant to the study of literacy. Perhaps the single most important summary point to make is that cultural factors, including the products of literacy, interact with genetic factors but have not replaced them. Group level processes are often more public and more obvious than the lower level individual processes on which they rest, but they are not more powerful. Consider, as an example, the Education for All initiative which is managed by UNESCO. The initiative was started in 2000 with the modest goal of achieving universal primary education (UPE) by 2015. The initiative is a group-level process to which the majority of the world's governments have committed themselves. Global monitoring reports are produced annually. The 2006 report (UNESCO, 2006) dealt specifically with literacy. The costs involved are considerable but pale into insignificance by comparison with the sums that have been spent to shore up the global financial system. Progress towards UPE has been patchy and interim goals have already been missed, in part because donors have not lived up to their commitments.

A simple explanation for why donors have behaved in this way is that they do not actually see universal primary education as a sufficiently important priority. Group-level processes that lead to agreement in principle to fund worthwhile objectives are simply not strong enough to compete with the demands of local agendas and, by and large, the populations on whose behalf funding decisions are made by governments are rarely sufficiently exercised by inequality to take significant action to reduce it. The reasons why developing countries are not spending enough themselves are complex, but it may also be explained in part by group differentiation within those countries. The 2009 Global Monitoring Report includes statistics comparing the richest and poorest 20% of national populations with respect to a range of key indicators. The report makes it clear that

> rich and poor live in different worlds...In many of the world's poorest countries the richest households already enjoy UPE while the poor lag far behind. (UNESCO, 2009, p. 73)

It is plausible to suppose that in these poor countries the richest people are more likely than the poorest to be able to exercise political influence with respect to providing funding for education for the disadvantaged. The data suggest that for them, as for rich donor countries, this is often not a high priority. To make these points is not to deny the progress which has been made. Globally agreed cultural imperatives do make a difference and in some cases the advances have been spectacular. However, it has to be recognised that evolution, acting on human groups, has produced a human nature which not only tolerates but can actively encourage inequality. Consider the following. It deals specifically with the Arab world but there is no reason to suggest that the rest of the world is much different.

> It would not be unreasonable to suggest that insofar as education is concerned, there a class apartheid in place in most of the Arab world. Those with means bypass the perils of the public educational systems and send their children to private schools, where they almost always master a former colonial language and go on to seek their place in the global economy. And the majority, who cannot afford this road to the future, go around in circles created by those who will not change the situation because the children of the poor are not threatening their grip on power. (Haeri, 2009, p. 429)

The global financial crisis, arguably caused by greed and selfishness on a massive scale, has made things worse. The 2010 EFA Global Monitoring Report is entitled 'Reaching the marginalized' and it warns that progress towards the EFA goals could be stalled or go into reverse as a result of the crisis.

> The international community has not responded effectively to the challenges facing the poorest countries. Rich-country governments and successive summits of the Group of 20 and Group of 8 have moved financial mountains to stabilize financial systems, but have provided an aid molehill for the world's most vulnerable people. (UNESCO, 2010, pp. 3–4)

The Education For All program is discussed further in Chapter 12. A sense of fairness, co-operation, empathy, and admiration for generosity are all parts of the universal human endowment but so are the capacity for conflict, biases in favour of in-groups, and preferences for kin over strangers. Recognition of the divided, Manichean nature of human nature will not, by itself solve the problems it creates but it may help us to construct social institutions which will mitigate the worst excesses and provide stronger foundations for our pro-social impulses. A recent book by Wilkinson and Pickett (2009) presents a wide range of evidence making the case that equality is better for everyone and this gives us positive reasons to try to curb our natural tendency to want more for ourselves than for others.

Chapter 6

Sexual Selection, Sex Differences, and Social Evolution

Chapter 5 discussed some of the principles of evolution by natural selection with a focus on cooperation and conflict as fundamental aspects of universal human nature. Natural selection is often understood in terms of 'survival of the fittest', which brings to mind qualities of organisms which enable some to survive and prosper at the expense of others. A fast, agile, gazelle, for example, is more likely to be able to escape from a cheetah than a slower or less agile one. Similarly, a cheetah with great speed and endurance is likely to be more successful as a hunter than a slower one or one which quickly becomes exhausted. More acute vision, hearing, and sense of smell all contribute to the likelihood that a particular animal will be able to find food, shelter, or a mate and defend them against potential robbers.

6.1 Sexual selection

There are, however, some evolved characteristics which resist explanation in terms of survival advantage. Many birds, for example, are brightly coloured, which makes them more visible to predators, and some have elaborate ornaments which can be detrimental to survival. The tail of the peacock is a famous example (Cronin, 1991). A peacock's tail may be so large that it hinders his ability to become airborne and thus makes him much more vulnerable to predation than he would otherwise be. Darwin was well aware of characteristics such as the peacock's tail and thought hard about how to fit them into his theory which suggested that characteristics promoting survival would be conserved while those that imperilled survival would gradually disappear. In due course he came to understand that characteristics like ornaments could be explained in terms of reproductive advantage rather than survival advantage, and he developed this understanding in the theory of sexual selection, building on evidence from a wide range of species (Darwin, 1871). Reproductive success is the currency of the evolutionary process. A moment's reflection on our own histories helps to make this clear. Every human owes his or her existence to successful parental reproductive activity. Each parent similarly depended on the successful reproduction of the previous generation, and so on back to the beginnings of life. From an evolutionary standpoint, survival is important only to the extent that it keeps alive the possibility of reproduction. A long life with no offspring makes no direct contribution to the population gene pool. A short life with lots of offspring makes a substantial contribution. Darwin's thinking led him to the conclusion that characteristics such as the peacock's tail could undergo positive selection if their reproductive advantages outweighed their survival disadvantages.

6.1.1 Competition and choice differ between the sexes

One of the principal drivers of natural selection is competition for resources. In the case of sexual selection the resources in question are mates and opportunities for mating. Males and females both need mates, of course, but Darwin observed that competition for mates appeared to be stronger among males than among females.

> It is certain that with almost all animals there is a struggle between the males for the possession of the female. This fact is so notorious that it would be superfluous to give instances. Hence the females, supposing that their mental capacity sufficed for the exertion of a choice, could select one out of several males. But in numerous cases it appears as if it had been specially arranged that there should be a struggle between many males... On the whole there can be no doubt that with almost all animals, in which the sexes are separate, there is a constantly recurrent struggle between the males for the possession of the females. (Darwin, 1871, Part II, Ch. VIII, pp. 259–60)

Conversely, females generally appeared to be more particular than males about their choice of mates. Darwin was unable to explain this asymmetrical pattern of males generally competing more fiercely than females and females generally exercising more careful choice than males. The theories on which our current understanding rest are relatively recent achievements. Trivers (1972) developed parental investment theory, which proposes that the relative investment of the sexes in offspring is the key variable controlling how sexual selection works. Andersson (1994) gives a detailed theoretical account of sexual selection theory across a wide range of species and Kokko and Jennions (2008) fill in some gaps in Trivers' theory. Sear (2011) provides an introduction to the evolutionary literature on human parenting and families. It took time for the importance of sexual selection to be understood properly because it fell out of fashion after Darwin's death and its significance was not clearly understood until Fisher discussed it in the 1930s. Even then, it was not readily adopted. One reason for its shaky start was that many theorists found the important role it gave to female choice an unpalatable idea.

6.1.2   A model of parental investment

As an introduction to some of the key ideas, consider an investment scenario which requires pairs of investors in partnership. Investors are drawn from two groups, A and B, of equal numbers. An investment pair consists of a group A member and a group B member. The group A partner contributes £10 and the group B partner £1,000. The return to each is the same, a half-share in an indivisible asset which benefits both partners equally. The value of this asset varies from pair to pair. Each partner has £10,000 in total to invest, they have free choices about who to invest with from the other group, investment decisions are mutual, and the qualities of the partners have effects on the value of the return that they get. We assume that all players of the game are motivated to invest.

Two questions naturally arise: (1) Which group would you prefer to be in? (2) Would you expect the group A and group B members to have the same or different strategies with regard to choosing partners? Informal investigations show that the initial reaction of many people is to choose to be in group A because they get the same payoff as group B members for a lower investment; answers to the question about strategies are less clear cut.

Let us consider the second question first. It seems reasonable to suppose that group B investors would inevitably be more cautious about choosing partners because they have only ten investment chances, but much might depend on the conditions under which choices are made and the kinds of information that are available about group A members and how their qualities affect the investment outcome.

Turning now to the first question, group A membership might well seem preferable, since group A members have many more investment chances than group B members and have half-shares in assets to which they contribute one per cent of the group B members' contributions. However, this preference seems less obvious once the implications of the other conditions for the investment are considered, namely that the A and B groups are of equal size, that decisions require the consent of both partners, and that resources are finite. The most salient fact, when the A and B groups are of equal size and the total resources of each group are equal, is that most of the A group potential choices cannot be actualised. Suppose there were 100 members in each group. An A group member can make 1,000 investment choices at £10 each. Thus the A pool has 100,000 possible choices in all. Each B group member, by contrast, can make only 10 choices at £1000 each. Thus there are 1,000 possible choices in the B pool. Since each A group choice must be matched by a mutual B group choice, 99,000 of the potential choices in the A pool must be unrealised even when all the B group choices are realised. It is also relevant to note that because there are only 1,000 choices in the B group, if one member of the A group were clearly preferable as an investment partner, that member could be chosen by all the group B investors for all their investments, leaving the remaining 99 A group investors without any partners at all. Even if all the A group members were equally attractive as investment partners and the B group members were essentially choosing at random, most A group members would still inevitably fall a long way short of their maximum investment potential and some might have no opportunities at all. Under these circumstances it might appear that being a member of the B group is a better option; it is highly likely that all one's investment opportunities will be actualised should one so wish, since there will always be A group members with unused investment capacity.

6.1.3 Differential parental investment in humans

The investment scenario makes some points which are relevant to thinking about sexual selection and the observed asymmetry between competitive males and choosy females. Consider the initial investment that humans make in the production of children. To begin with, men provide sperm and women provide eggs. There is an immediate investment asymmetry because male and female gametes are of unequal size. The technical term for this is 'anisogamy' and the sexes are defined in terms of it. The female sex is the one with the larger gametes. Eggs are much bigger than sperm. Females thus provide more in terms of the basic cellular material needed to produce an offspring. Pursuing the idea a little further, a useful concept is minimal obligatory investment. This is the bare minimum required from the two sexes to produce a child. For men, the obligatory investment really is minimal. Since conception is possible, if unlikely, from a single coupling, the minimal obligatory investment for a man is an ejaculate of sperm plus the time it takes to copulate. For a woman, by contrast, an egg plus the time taken to copulate is a tiny fraction of her obligatory investment. The nine-month gestation period, the metabolic costs, and the physical challenges of pregnancy vastly outweigh the man's contribution. Moreover, in ancestral populations, a child successfully brought to term would also have needed suckling for a lengthy period until weaning was complete. Female obligatory investment in children thus dwarfs the male contribution. Thinking in terms of the investment game described, women are represented by group B, men by group A, but a woman's minimal obligatory investment in a child is much more than 100 times greater than a man's.

It is true, of course, that men in general invest much more than the obligatory minimum in their children and human males are highly unusual among primates for their general level of investment. This tends to mask the difference in minimal obligatory investment, but it is essential that we remain aware of it because it is a real difference and it has contributed to the evolution of psychological differences between men and women. Human beings are the result of a lengthy evolutionary process whose basic operation is to shape its products for more successful reproduction. Human anatomy, physiology, psychology, and metabolism are the way they are because they better promote the production of more humans than previous variants. Contemporary life in literate cultures offers so many possibilities apart from survival and the rearing of children that it is easy to forget or ignore this fundamental truth.

6.1.4   Interactions between the sexes

Thinking about the investment game again can take us further in the investigation of the shaping of human psychology by the demands of reproduction. The scenario is simplified and thus inaccurate in some respects, but it serves to sharpen appreciation of some of the underlying dynamics of interactions both within and between the sexes. In particular, the marked asymmetry of investment between the two groups has further consequences. In the investment game it was stipulated that both A and B group members had the freedom to choose their investment partners. It was also clear that most A group choices could not be realised. The asymmetry creates what is known as a selection pressure. The scenario clearly demonstrates that As have to be more assiduous in seeking investment opportunities than Bs. An A must try to persuade all the Bs to choose him because his investment potential can only be fully realised if all the Bs make all their choices in his favour. He should, therefore, feel equal, and ardent, enthusiasm for all of them unless he is so confident of his qualities that he can rely on being chosen by them without much effort. Bs, by contrast, can realise their full investment potential by making all their choices in favour of a single A. At most they can choose ten different As. Since the outcomes depend on the qualities of the As and there is no shortage of As to choose from they can afford to be selective, and they should be.

The model states that the qualities of the As and Bs contribute to the value of the indivisible shared asset, which is the outcome of their mutual investment, but nothing has been said about what those qualities are. This is a weakness of the model but, given the particular conditions of the scenario, it is clear that the qualities of the Bs are unimportant for the As because they should try to invest with all of them. The qualities of the As are important to the Bs and we can say some general things about them without knowing specific details. If there is a clear ranking of the As in terms of their qualities, and no two are of equal value, then, assuming the Bs can accurately assess the As, their choices should converge on the top ranked A and all their investments should be made with him. If there is a tie at the top of the rankings then the Bs should be indifferent with respect to the top ranked As and their investments should be distributed at random among them. If the As are all of equal value then the Bs choices among them will be random. The net result of all this is that there will be greater variance in investment outcomes among the As than among the Bs.

The selection pressure on As can be explored in terms of a question. What could As do to improve their chances of being chosen as investment partners? They could vigorously court Bs, advertising qualities relevant to the likely success of the investment outcome; they could try to dispose of rivals; they could try to coerce the Bs. These options are not necessarily exclusive and there is evidence that each of them, with numerous variants, has succeeded in real contexts. Let us consider courting behaviour first. As are likely to persuade, cajole, charm, or flatter the Bs. They must present themselves in the best possible light by fair means or foul. Those with good qualities should emphasize them and those with poor qualities should pretend that they are better than they are.

With regard to disposing of rivals, one sure way for an A to improve the odds of being chosen would be to find ways to get rid of his competitors. This might be done by fighting, by threats, by derogation, by the formation of alliances, or by some combination of these. A fight to the death between two As is a possibility, but it carries high risks: it guarantees the permanent removal of one of them but requires confidence of victory and leaves open the possibility of injury which might make the victor vulnerable to attack from another uninjured A. A threat to fight might be better but it would depend on being able to convince one's rival about the outcome if the fight actually occurred. An alliance with another A might also work and it could improve the chances of making a successful threat or of winning in a fight, but would then require some form of sharing or a further dispute.

In each case, if the outcome were dependent on physical resources then being bigger seems better. All else being equal, if a small creature fights a big creature the big one is likely to win. There are stories such as the biblical tale of David and Goliath where brain triumphs over brawn, but if the rivals are roughly equal in brain power then brawn is likely to be decisive. The same is true of threats: threats of violence from big creatures are more likely to be taken seriously than threats from smaller ones. Moreover, being large may help, not just in ousting rivals but in advertising quality and in coercion. If competition with other A group members is something which B group members take into account when making their choices then being big is a quality that B group members may view positively. Furthermore, if being big helps in ousting competitors, it is also likely to help if coercion of B group members is a possibility.

How might B group members' choices be conditioned by selection pressures? Given the limited number of investment choices that B group members can make, the large number of As available to choose from and the possibility that many or all Bs might choose to invest with the same A, it may serve Bs to be inclined to share information about As' qualities among themselves. There would be no need for competition among Bs because a single A could meet all their needs for investment partners. Given the need to choose wisely and the lack of competition with other Bs, it might also be advantageous for the Bs to have the As advertise their qualities in a public forum where easy comparisons could be made among them. This would save time and promote efficient choosing.

The investment scenario models the primary physiological differences between men and women with respect to the production of offspring, and highlights some possible psychological consequences. The principal drivers of the model are the asymmetry of male and female investments, the equal size of the male and female populations, the requirement for paired action, and the assumption that investors are keen to invest. Given the specific conditions of the scenario, choice is important for women but not for men, and competition to be chosen is important for men but not for women. If the conditions are realistic and the scenario, or something like it, has happened over many generations with the characteristics of the successful being inherited by their offspring, then we can see how greater competitiveness may have evolved in males and greater choosiness in females, thus explaining the pattern that Darwin observed. Are the conditions realistic when thinking about human populations?

There is no doubt about the investment asymmetry from a physiological point of view; women contribute far more in terms of bodily resources to the production of children than men do, and human nature has been shaped by this fundamental fact. However men can and do invest in other ways by providing care and other resources for their women and their children. The extent of this provisioning is a matter for debate; it may have lessened direct male competitiveness for mates by offering males alternative strategies, but it has not abolished it. Resource acquisition and holding offer males an alternative method of competition, but they are also independently important for the development of sex differences in social groups. If, for example, resource acquisition is physically demanding, as in the case of hunting, males will be seen as more valuable.

6.2   Competition and choice

The distinction between male competition and female choice is much more subtle in reality than in the model. Male choice and female competition also exist for reasons which are not captured by the model. For example, the model makes no distinctions in terms of age but age is an important parameter in human reproduction and more so for women than for men. Women are potentially fertile from menarche, at around 12 or 13, to the menopause, which occurs at about the age of 50. Their reproductive careers are therefore time limited, and the concept of reproductive value has been developed to provide a quantitative estimate (Fisher, 1999, Chapter 2). Reproductive value peaks in the teens, just before women become physiologically capable of reproducing (or just before they start reproducing, in societies where age at first birth is delayed), since reproductive value equals expected total future reproduction. Women's age-specific fertility rates peak in their twenties (usually their early twenties), and decline quite quickly thereafter. Men become fertile when they begin to produce viable sperm and remain fertile, in principle, for the rest of their lives, although sperm quality declines significantly with age. There is, therefore, a selection pressure on men to choose younger women if they are to maximise their own success, because the future reproductive potential of younger women is greater. In consequence, there is also a pressure for competition among females to emphasize their future reproductive value.

6.3   Sex ratios

The sexes are roughly numerically equal in human populations. The sex ratio, expressed as the number of males to females in the population, differs slightly at different points in the life cycle, but is self-stabilizing at approximately 1:1. Thus the assumption of equal numbers of As and Bs in the model is a reasonable approximation to the reality of human life in many parts of the world. However, in some countries, certainly in China and India, sex ratios have become male biased as a result of societal practices that have led to selective offspring selection (Hudson and den Boer, 2004). *Homo sapiens* is modestly dimorphic in body size and strength. Males, on average, are bigger and more muscular than females. The dimorphism is the result of male-male competition for access to females and it results in the ability of men to dominate women physically if it pays them to do so. This size difference can have paradoxical results when resource holding and protection are at issue. Even though women and access to them are resources that males struggle to acquire and protect, they can sometimes be sacrificed in order to produce males who can safeguard existing resources.

6.4   Fertility rates

The assumption that investors are keen to invest and to maximise their investment opportunities is much more questionable. Most people wish to have at least one child but some choose not to reproduce at all. In contemporary developed societies fertility is dropping and in some countries it is below replacement level. In other societies, typically less developed ones, fertility rates remain high. There is a negative correlation between literacy and fertility, but it is not fully understood and requires further study. Early confident assertions of a causal relation between increased literacy and decreased fertility have been questioned and evidence has accumulated that shows a range of relations within the overall picture. Graff (1995, Chapter 6) presents a review of some of the evidence from an historical standpoint.

6.5   Sexual selection and human universals

In summary it is clear that evolution has produced differences between the sexes which are reflected in the universals discussed in Chapter 3. The Universal People expect that the biological and social mother will normally be the same person; females do more direct childcare and there is, more generally, a division of labour by sex. Husbands are older than their wives on average; males and females and adults and children are seen as having different natures; males dominate in the public and political realms; they are more aggressive; they engage in more group-based violence; they steal more and they travel greater distances on average during their lifetimes. Sex and gender terminology is fundamentally binary; there are sex differences in cognition and behaviour, and sexual behaviour is regulated.

The investment asymmetry suggests that Bs are, in some sense, more fundamental to the population than As, since many or most of the As are redundant. Bs also have the opportunity to exert much more control over the investment process (Waage, 1997). Access to the Bs is the limiting factor on the success of the As. One might wonder, therefore, given their greater contribution to reproduction, why women and girls are frequently treated as second-class citizens both in general and in particular in the context of access to education and literacy training. One obvious answer to the question is societal and cultural traditions, but this answer simply invites a further question as to why the social and cultural traditions are as they are. One possible answer is that it is in the interests of men to construct and maintain social institutions which improve their access to, and control over, reproduction. This simple explanation offers a partial truth but societal group structures and access to resources are also important. Literacy could make a substantial contribution to these institutions and thus control over access to literacy could contribute to male domination.

6.6   Sex differences and literacy

Sex differences are relevant to the study of literacy because they are fundamental to human relations generally and also because of the persistent sex-based global inequality of access to literacy training and education. The Education for All (EFA) Global Monitoring Report for 2011 estimates that some 795 million adults, about 16% of the global adult population, lack basic literacy skills. Approximately two-thirds of them (64%) are women. From an evolutionary perspective, the existence of a marked sex difference such as this, is an indicator that the reproductive interests of men and women may diverge with respect to the issue in question. Why are the skills of literacy involved in matters to do with reproduction? This is a complex question but one possible answer is simply stated. If it appears to people that their reproductive (and other) interests are better served by educating sons and denying education to daughters this will tend to happen if it is not prevented by legislation. If, for example, men on average wish to have more children than they currently do and women wish to have fewer, and if, as seems to be the case, access to literacy empowers women to take greater control over their reproductive futures, then men may see literate wives as challenging their reproductive goals. Thus they could think of restrict-ing their wives' access to literacy as a way of furthering their reproductive interests. Data presented by Zlidar et al (2003) and Salem (2004) are con-sistent with this possibility.

6.7   The social functions of the intellect

Sexual selection and parental investment highlight the fundamental impor-tance of social variables in evolution and there is a substantial body of research, much of it stemming from a classic paper by Nicholas Humphrey (1976), which explores the thesis that humans are highly intelligent because they have to cope with the challenges of living in complex social environ-ments. This idea is significant for students of literacy because it helps us to understand the strategic and ideological practices which some theorists take to constitute the core meanings of literacy (Street, 1984; Barton, 2007; Gee, 2008). In later chapters I propose that the stability of autonomous literate representations provides an intellectual space in which reflection is possible, separated from the constantly changing flux of the social environ-ment. The point is not that the practices of literacy are independent of the social environment, but that texts are or can be independent, at least to a degree.

Humphrey starts from two assumptions: first that evolution is an eco-nomical process and does not make creatures with capabilities which exceed the requirements of their way of living; second that human creative intelligence is a much more developed capability than is required solely by the practical demands of living, for instance, in activities such as hunt-ing, searching, and navigating. Humans have brains which are larger than expected for creatures of similar size and brain tissue is metabolically expensive (Aiello and Wheeler, 1995). It appears, then, that human intel-lect must be devoted to something other than the demands of subsistence living. Humphrey argues that 'the chief role of creative intellect is to hold society together' (p. 307) Society, he says, is the repository of the informa-tion that humans need to manage their daily lives and it also provides the environment in which learning can occur. It is management of that social environment which provides the principal challenge to humans.

[T]he life of social animals is highly problematical. In a complex society, such as those we know exist in higher primates, there are benefits to be gained for each individual member both from preserving the overall structure of the group and at the same time from exploiting and out-ma-noeuvring others within it. Thus social primates are required by the very nature of the system they create and maintain to be calculating beings; they must be able to calculate the consequences of their own behaviour, to calculate the likely behaviour of others, to calculate the balance of advantage and loss – and all this in a context where the evidence on which their calculations are based is ephemeral, ambiguous and liable to change, not least as a consequence of their own actions. (Humphrey, 1976, p. 309)

He goes on to suggest that the intellectual skills required to manage these challenges are of the highest order and require constant attention and responsiveness to what is happening in the immediate environment. Accumulated knowledge is not sufficient for the 'game of social plot and counter-plot' (p. 309). Social skills require flexible forward planning as well as acute perception.

Humphrey proposes that the outcome of evolution 'has been the gift-ing of members of the human species with remarkable powers of social foresight and understanding' (p. 312). This outcome prompts a question of great significance. If human intellect has evolved primarily for thinking about and managing people and social institutions, how does it fare with non-social issues? Humphrey suggests that social evolution will have led to intelligence which is focused on transactions with other agents as its 'customary mode' (p. 313). This transactional mode may lead people to treat inanimate entities as agents, a tendency which Chapter 3 suggests is a human universal.

There are many examples of fallacious reasoning which would fit such an interpretation. The most obvious cases are those where men do in fact openly resort to animistic thinking about natural phenomena. Thus primitive – and not so primitive – peoples commonly attempt to *bargain* with nature, through prayer, through sacrifice or through ritual persua-sion. In doing so they are explicitly adopting a social model, expecting nature to participate in a transaction. But nature will not transact with men; she goes her own way regardless – while her would-be interlocutors feel grateful or feel slighted as the case befits. (Humphrey, 1976, p. 313)

Towards the end of the paper Humphrey says that the rise of scientific thinking has depended on humans finding ways to escape from the trans-actional, anthropomorphizing style of reasoning which comes naturally as a result of social evolution but he warns that 'there are everywhere signs of a return to more magical systems of interpretation' (p. 315). Part of the power of literacy, I believe, lies in the help it gives us to escape the transactional style of reasoning, although there are no guarantees, and that is not its only function. Objectivity and detachment are achieved slowly and occasionally, if at all. It is certainly not the case that simply becoming literate turns us into cool, logical thinkers capable of viewing ourselves and others with a clear and unbiased eye.

The study of social intelligence has blossomed since the publication of Humphrey's paper which has been widely cited (Emery, Clayton, and Frith, 2007). The concept of 'Machiavellian Intelligence' has been the subject of intensive exploration (Byrne and Whiten, 1988; Whiten and Byrne, 1997), and other related proposals, such as the suggestion that humans have large brains to promote social cohesion through gossip (Dunbar, 1996) have been explored. Frank (1998) has studied the evolutionary processes that can occur when there is tension between conflict and co-operation. Sozou (2009) has modelled the complex phenomenon of social discounting. All of these developments are potentially of interest to students of literacy but I focus on just two lines of enquiry here. The first is interesting for the unusual light it sheds on the scope of the evolutionary process; the second focuses on the co-operative rather than the competitive aspects of social evolution.

6.7.1 Selection for unpredictability

One of the principal challenges for social creatures is the need for forward planning. That need may take the form of having to predict what an opponent in a competitive exchange is likely to do, or in trying to assess the future reliability of a current ally, or in trying to gauge the sexual receptivity of a potential mate. Forward planning is made easier if the behaviour of other social actors is predictable, and more difficult if their behaviour is unpredictable. Maximum advantage would accrue to an actor who was able to remain unpredictable while predicting the behaviour of others. Building on work by Driver and Humphries (1988), Geoffrey Miller has proposed that evolution has selected for unpredictable behaviour in a variety of contexts (Miller, 1997, 2000, Chapter 11). This suggestion makes a very interesting counterpoint to the argument, sometimes heard from critics of evolutionary thinking, that genes cannot play much, if any, part in human behaviour because if it were so, our behaviour would be 'genetically determined' and thus it would be unable to vary flexibly to meet changing circumstances. The simple answer is that this challenge mistakes the level at which genes operate.

> Genes rarely determine specific behaviours, but they often determine the ways in which environmental cues activate behaviours. Many behaviours are fairly predictable if you know what an organism is perceiving

at the moment. This predictability comes from the demands of optimality: for any given environmental situation, there is often one best thing to do...However, there are situations in which it is a very bad idea to be predictable. If another organism is trying to predict what you will do in order to catch you and eat you, you had better behave a bit more randomly. Selection may favour brain circuits that randomize responses, to produce adaptively unpredictable behaviour. (Miller, 2000, pp. 393–4)

Miller builds on this idea to create a theory of the human mind as a device in which creative, unpredictable behaviour is valuable not just for its survival advantages but also in the service of courtship and the search for mates. He proposes that creativity in all its many forms can be explained as a positive outcome of sexual selection in favour of the unusual and the novel. The idea is easily put to an informal test. Who would you prefer to have as a long-term sexual partner? Someone who is boring, predictable, and with nothing to say, or someone who has novel ideas, is curious about the world, and wants to engage your interest? If Miller is right, his ideas will help us to understand literate as well as other forms of creativity.

6.7.2   Collective intentionality

Unpredictable, protean behaviour is clearly of advantage in competitive social contexts and much of the literature about social evolution has stressed its competitive aspects. However, there has also been a line of development which has examined the evolution of cooperative social behaviour. Humphrey described this in terms of sympathy.

> By sympathy I mean a tendency on the part of one social partner to identify himself with the other and so to make the other's goals to some extent his own. (Humphrey, 1976, p. 313)

Michael Tomasello and his colleagues have developed a theory of 'shared' or 'collective' intentionality, a uniquely human attribute which makes possible the activities underpinning and constituting human culture, including the creation and use of mathematical and linguistic symbols. The theory has been refined over a period of more than a decade to take account of new findings derived from research with humans and other primates. An early version of the theory (Tomasello, Kruger, and Ratner, 1993) proposed that humans were able to accumulate cultural artefacts and practices because they could learn from each other in ways that nonhuman animals could not. Human beings, they said,

> understand and take the perspective of others in a manner and to a degree that allows them to participate more intimately than nonhuman

animals in the knowledge and skills of conspecifics. (Tomasello, Kruger, and Ratner, 1993, p. 495)

The emphasis was on individual cognition and the extent to which one individual understands another. Understanding what someone intends to do with a tool, for example, is important because it enables systematic modifications to be made. If I understand why you have invented a fishhook but I observe that it readily slips out of the mouth and allows the fish to escape, I may see how to improve it by adding a barb. The intellectual challenge is shared. I can build on your insight because I know what you were trying to do but I have not had to invent both the hooked shape and the barb. A later fisherman using the barbed hook may observe that the fish no longer escapes but that the line works loose as the fish struggles. This observation may lead to a new, more secure way of tying the hook to the line and so on. The cumulative effects are powerful not just because the cognitive effort involved in innovation is shared, but also because the opportunities for the crucial observations to occur are increased when every member of a group understands what is going on. The cumulative process has been called the 'ratchet-effect' because 'each modification stays firmly in place in the group until further modifications are made' (p. 495). Literate works are eminently suitable means for storing cultural ratchets.

The failure of chimpanzees and other animals to achieve lasting cultural modifications was put down to their having insufficient understanding of the intentions of their fellows. Further research showed, however, that some nonhuman primates understood more about the intentions of their fellows than had previously been thought, without thereby acquiring a human-like capacity for culture. Tomasello, Carpenter, Call, Behne, and Moll (2005) proposed that the crucial difference which enabled human culture was a unique adaptation for shared understanding.

> We propose that human beings, and only human beings, are biologically adapted for participating in collaborative activities involving shared goals and socially co-ordinated action plans (joint intentions). Interactions of this type require not only an understanding of the goals, intentions, and perceptions of other persons, but also, in addition, a motivation to share these things in interaction with others – and perhaps special forms of dialogic cognitive representation for doing so. The motivations and skills for participating in this kind of "we" intentionality are woven into the earliest stages of human ontogeny and underlie young children's developing ability to participate in the collectivity that is human cognition. (Tomasello et al, 2005, p. 676)

Moll and Tomasello (2007) have taken the argument a step further. In what they have called the Vygotskian intelligence hypothesis, they propose

that 'participation in interactions involving shared intentionality transforms human cognition in fundamental ways' (Moll and Tomasello, 2007,
p. 645). Participation, they say, creates the concept of perspective, the
appreciation that someone else can see the same thing as I can, but from a
different point of view.

> The ability to take the perspective of others – which spawns the under-
> standing of false beliefs, perspectival cognitive representations and col-
> lective/institutional reality – is only possible for organisms that can
> participate in social interactions involving shared intentionality, espe-
> cially interactions involving joint attention. Let us be very clear on this
> point. Participation in these interactions is critical. A child raised on a
> desert island would have all of the biological preparations for participa-
> tion in interactions involving shared intentionality, but because she did
> not actually participate in such interactions, she would have nothing to
> internalize into perspectival cognitive representations. Ontogeny in this
> case is critical. (Moll and Tomasello, 2007, p. 646)

Mention of the desert island brings us back to Humphrey's prescient paper
in which the world of Robinson Crusoe was discussed. But there is a contrast of approach. Whereas Moll and Tomasello argue that social interaction and cooperation are crucial for development, Humphrey emphasizes
the challenges they pose.

> My view – and Defoe's, as I understand him – is that it was the arrival of
> Man Friday on the scene which really made things difficult for Crusoe.
> If Monday and Tuesday, Wednesday and Thursday had turned up as
> well then Crusoe would have had every need to keep his wits about him.
> (Humphrey, 1976, p. 305)

The contrast between social co-operation and social competition does
not involve a contradiction but emphasizes further, if further emphasis is
needed, that evolution has led to a situation in which both co-operative
and selfish impulses have deep roots. These warring impulses are equally
fundamental parts of human nature, both of which have to be taken into
account if we are to understand the powerful impacts of literacy, for good
and for ill.

Chapter 7

Turing Machines: Syntactic Foundations for the Study of Literacy

In the normal course of events we read texts in order to understand them, and authors write in the hope that their texts will be meaningful to their readers. At this point in the book, although my goal is ultimately to illuminate some keys issues about meaning, I am going to explore literacy from a purely syntactic point of view. The syntactic point of view considers the forms or structures of texts independently of what they mean. This is quite a challenging thing to do, but even more challenging is to consider minds from a purely syntactic point of view. The main reason for doing this is that the syntactic point of view puts the powerful resources of computer theory at our disposal. We are concerned here with what is called the 'micro-ecology' of literacy in Chapter 1 and the 'functional core' in Chapter 4. The focus is on the individual mind engaged in reading or writing a text. The chapter starts by exploring texts in purely syntactic terms. It then tackles the problem of thinking of minds in syntactic terms. Finally the two are put together and the marriage produces the class of abstract structures called Turing machines, which can be used to describe literate processes. The point of the exercise is to consider the properties of the systems of symbols that carry the meanings with which literacy is mainly concerned. Chapter 2.8 introduced the syntactic study of texts; here we take things further and work from the most basic considerations possible.

7.1   A syntactic perspective on texts

Human societies have produced many different writing systems (Coulmas, 1996). The differences among them have implications for how easy or difficult they are to learn (Joshi and Aaron, 2005). Some languages, Finnish for example, have regular correspondences between sounds and how they are written down. This makes literacy acquisition relatively easy. Other languages, English for example, have irregular correspondences between written and spoken forms and this makes literacy acquisition much harder.

In this chapter we are concerned with properties of writing systems which are even more basic than that. In fact they are so basic that they can be explored in terms of the binary alphabet, which can be regarded as the fundamental writing system in which all others can be represented. Consider the following.

> Every English sentence can be represented as a sequence of ASCII codes.

This is a perfectly good English sentence. It has both a syntactic form and an obvious meaning. It also has the advantage of being true. Several aspects of its syntax are readily discernible. It has 12 words, if we count 'ASCII' as a word, and it has a grammatical structure which can be described in terms of nouns, verbs, etc. The website http://www.convertbinary.com/ translates alphabetic texts into binary. When given 'Every English sentence ...' it produces the binary representations of the underlying ASCII characters.

```
01000101011101100110010101110010011110010010000001000101
01101110011001110110110001101001011100110110100000100000
01110011011001010110111001110100011001010110111001100011
01100101001000000110001101100001011011100010000001100010
01100101001000000111001001100101011100000111001001100101
01110011011001010110111001110100011001010110010000100000
01100001011100110010000001100001001000000111001101100101
01110001011101011001010110111001100011011100101001000000
01101111011001100010000001000001010100110100001101001001
01001001001000000110001101101111011101100110010101110011
00101110
```

This is the kind of stuff with which we are going to work. One great advantage of doing syntactic exploration using binary representations of texts is that there are no meanings to interfere with our concentration on the syntax, but we know, in a sense, that binary sequences are able to convey the same information as English sentences so that we are losing nothing essential. Doueihi (2011, p. 28) cites a legal decision from the United States which supports the point! There's a sort of pleasing simplicity about this basic level of textual syntax even though, at first sight, there's not much we can do with it. What we can do, for a start, is to think about the layout of texts in whatever medium we choose. It's normal practice, adhered to in this book as you see, to arrange symbols in a two-dimensional array called a page. It's convenient because lots of symbols can be displayed on a single page and pages are bound together in books but it's not the only way. Some literate societies have used clay tablets, others have used papyrus scrolls. A way which is conceptually even simpler is to write symbols in a one-dimensional array or string. Any page of text can, in principle at least, be re-arranged as a string by cutting it into lines and gluing them together in the appropriate order. Please don't do that to this book! For us it would be inconvenient to read texts arranged in that way and the 2D format is much more practical, but for the sake of simplicity and because that is what Turing machines read and write, we will consider texts, in the most basic sense, as one-dimensional strings of binary symbols.

We now turn to the question of how many binary texts there could be. This parallels the discussion of the number of four-letter English word forms discussed in Chapter 2. Because we want to be as basic as possible we will start from the consideration of what can be called the 'null text'. This is a text with no symbols at all. You might find it a bit odd even to think of the null text as a text since it has no symbols, but it's a kind of way of thinking that mathematicians and logicians like. It provides a firm foundation, akin to counting from 0 rather than from 1. The null text is of zero length. There are two binary texts of length one, i.e. the symbols 0 and 1. From these simple beginnings the full splendour of the world of binary texts starts to blossom. There are four texts of length two, because each text of length one can have either of the symbols in the second position. Thus we get 00, 01, 10, and 11 as the set of possible binary texts of length two. Exactly the same principle applies to each successive lengthening. There are eight texts of length three, sixteen of length four, and so on. We get double the number of possible texts each time we increase the length by one symbol. This is an important property because symbols can be written at almost no cost. Notice how different this is from most of the physical things we want and need. If we wish to double the food supply, someone has to put in the work of growing the plants, rearing the animals, and so forth. But we can double the number of texts simply by inscribing more symbols. From a purely syntactic point of view, then, texts are cheap and abundant. There are 2^n binary texts of length n, that is 2 multiplied by itself n times. We can also easily calculate the total number of texts up to and including a given length. Suppose we take $n = 4$. Then we have 16 + 8 + 4 + 2 = 30 texts of length less than or equal to four which is $2^{n+1} - 2$ altogether.

The doubling of syntactic forms for each unit increase in the length of binary texts means that the numbers of possible forms quickly become enormously large and it is this that enables a simple syntactic system to provide vehicles for immense numbers of meanings. Consider the 'tweet', generally thought of as a short text. Tweets have a maximum of 140 characters, so we can calculate that there are 2^{140} binary tweets of maximum length and $2^{141} - 2$ tweets in total. $2^{140} =$

1,393,796,574,908,163,946,345,982,392,040,522,594,123,776

That, in words, is more than one million, trillion, trillion, trillion binary tweets. Although it's a huge number it is dwarfed by a more realistic estimate when we take into account the fact that tweets are not normally written in binary. If we use the 26 symbols of the familiar roman lower case alphabet with the space and the full stop added for punctuation there are $28^{140} =$

40,005,931,584,209,889,636,110,772,996,008,684,488,977,269,31
5,747,493,504,140,826,783,189,592,734,348,541,947,162,410,840,
032,188,476,940,609,170,458,859,923,108,791,960,626,933,770,
898,132,701,516,052,183,742,155,037,471,746,659,320,060,880,
513,376,479,265,922,482,176

possible tweets. In general, the number of possible texts is a function of their length and the number of symbols in the alphabet. For an alphabet of m symbols and texts of length n, there are m^n possible texts. The calculations here are courtesy of WolframAlpha from http://www.wolframalpha.com/. Clearly, most of the possible tweets would not make sense in English or any other language because they are random strings of letters, but even so, the number which could be read as meaningful messages is enormous. It's partly for that reason that no one worries about being unable to formulate a message to say what they want to say. Part of the art, of course, is finding striking and witty ways to express a message in only 140 characters, but even for the artless, the form provides vehicles for vastly many different meanings.

The texts considered so far have been finite in length but there are circumstances in which it makes sense to think of texts that are infinitely long. Infinity is a tricky concept and the idea of an infinitely long text is one that makes many people feel uncomfortable. Rucker (1995) provides an introduction to the science and philosophy of infinity, and Dauben (1979) explores the seminal work of the mathematician Georg Cantor who first studied the domain of transfinite numbers systematically. Rather than trying to imagine a completed text which is infinitely long, it's generally easier to think of a text which could always be added to. If there were an infinite amount of time and space available then a text which was constantly added to would, after an infinite amount of time, be infinitely long, although after any finite amount of time it would be of only finite length. For most practical literacy purposes, there is no reason to consider infinite texts, but in certain quite familiar contexts we need to allow for texts that grow endlessly. Most people are familiar with pi (π), the number representing the ratio of the circumference of a circle to its diameter, and many will be familiar with the first few digits of its decimal representation, 3.14159. It may be a less familiar fact that to express pi with full precision requires an infinite number of digits– i.e., an infinitely long text. Pi is an example of a 'transcendental number' and mathematicians know of many other numbers which are of the same kind. These numbers can be expressed in the binary system. If, then, we wish our account of literacy to cope with the representations of numbers as well as with alphabetical texts, we need to acknowledge the possibility of infinitely long texts.

We thus arrive at the most general possible representation of a text. It is a sequence of binary symbols which can be of any length. Assuming that it takes at least some time to write down each symbol then a text will be of finite length after any finite amount of time, but it could become infinitely long after an infinite amount of time. The set of all binary texts of all lengths is an infinite set which I shall call the universe of texts. It is an abstract object, but none the worse for that. Every existing text and any imaginable text, including all those that will be written but have not yet seen the light of day, and all those that are possible but will never be written, is represented in the universe of texts. It's a difficult idea to get to grips with but we shall see that thinking of texts in this purely syntactic way gives us some important information about the nature of literacy. Perhaps the best way to think of the universe of texts is as an endless repository of vehicles for carrying meanings which literate humans can create or discover. This is what makes literacy such a powerful technology.

7.2 A syntactic perspective on minds

Having taken the meanings out of texts, I now propose that we need to do the same for minds. This is a more difficult idea to get to grips with. At least with texts we are familiar with those written in languages we don't understand, but minds are rather different in the sense that each of us occupies the centre stage, as it were, of our own mind with a powerful consciousness of self and this affects how we think about minds. Nick Humphrey, whose work on the social functions of the intellect was discussed in Chapter 6, has described consciousness as 'soul dust', in a recent book (Humphrey, 2011). He argues that consciousness is an evolutionary adaptation providing a sort of mental glue which holds our lives together.

Consciousness is what makes the life of the mind meaningful to us, so it is especially difficult to think of minds in purely syntactic terms. However, for the purposes of understanding Turing machine theory we need to do just that. The task is made somewhat easier by the fact that the context in which we need to think syntactically about the mind is in its dealings with texts. Since we have already reduced these to purely syntactic objects, we are going to be concerned with minds in the very special circumstances in which they are 'reading' and 'writing' meaningless binary texts. We don't have to bother with meanings because we're supposing, at this stage, that there aren't any. We are exploring the purely mechanical operations that are involved in working with meaningless texts.

Let's take a simple example. Suppose I give you a sheet of paper and a pencil. Written on the paper is the binary text 01101011. I ask you to use it to generate a new text in which every 0 becomes a 1 and vice versa. There are many ways in which you could do this, assuming you agree to take on the task, but let's suppose you decide to start at the left and work from left to right on a symbol-by-symbol basis. The first symbol is 0 so you choose a blank place on the sheet to write the corresponding 1 of the new sequence. Then there is a 1 so you write 0 next to your 1, giving 10. The third symbol is another 1 which you transform, extending your new text to 100. Further steps extend the sequence to 1001, 10010, 100101, 1001010, and finally 10010100, at which point you are done. How might we describe your states of mind as you work through this process of transformation? When you read the first symbol we might say that this puts you in a 'zero' state of mind because the symbol read is a 0. Given the task, you write down 1. Moving to the next symbol, which is a 1, changes your state of mind to a 'one' state and you write down 0 because that's what the task specifies. The third symbol leaves you in the 'one' state and you write another 0. The fourth symbol changes your state to the 'zero' state again and so on. The 'zero' state at different points of time is essentially the same state and likewise the 'one' state. This means that we can describe your mind as needing just two distinct states in order to carry out the process of turning 0s to 1s and vice versa. Whenever you find yourself in the 'zero' state as a result of perceiving the next symbol to be 0, you write down 1 because that is what the task requires, and whenever you find yourself in the 'one' state as a result of perceiving the next symbol to be 1, you write down 0 because that is what the task requires. Mathematicians talk about functions which transform one sequence of symbols into another and we can adopt this terminology to talk about states of mind. The states 'zero' and 'one' are functional states of a mind engaged in the process of transforming 01101011 into 10010100.

The 'zero' and 'one' states can be given different functional definitions for different tasks. Suppose I asked you to copy the sequence 01101011 rather than to transform it. Then, the appropriate action in the 'zero' state would be to write 0 and the appropriate action in the 'one' state would be to write 1. Further possibilities are also easy to imagine. I could ask you to double the sequence so that it became 0011110011001111. In that case the appropriate response in the 'zero' state would be to write 00 and the appropriate response in the 'one' state would be to write 11. I could ask you to transform and double, in which case the response in the 'zero' state would be 11, and that in the 'one' state would be 00. As a final example, I could ask you to delete all the 0s. In that case the appropriate response in the 'zero' state would be to write nothing and you would end up with the sequence 11111. What we are doing in each case is considering the syntactic form of a text and deciding on a set of functional states which will bring it about. The definitions of functional states of mind are, therefore, task specific.

There are plenty of more familiar examples which may help to show that the definition of processes using functional states of mind really is as simple as I hope it seems. Consider the case of cookery. Lots of recipes use eggs for various purposes. One might begin with the statement 'Take two eggs'. By analogy with the 'zero' and 'one' states we might describe someone following a recipe who has just read that statement as being in the 'Take two eggs' state of mind, or 'tte' to use a convenient abbreviation. The 'tte' state could have various actions associated with it according to the recipe. The eggs might be separated, or beaten, or fried in butter, or whatever. States of mind in cooking, just as in literacy, are task specific and we have no difficulty in imagining different uses of eggs in different recipes. Similarly, our approach to the mind here involves using the same symbols in different ways to produce different sequences.

The functional states of mind discussed so far can be described as syntactic because they describe processes which are simple enough to be followed without needing any explanation of what the sequence produced is for, and they don't require any decision making. The 'zero' and 'one' states always have exactly one, fixed action associated with them even if that action involves writing more than one symbol. They also involve nothing more than simple acts of recognition such as perceiving 0 or 1. An appropriate criterion for calling a state or process syntactic, about which I shall say more shortly, is the possibility of mechanical execution. We will say that a process is syntactic if it is simple enough to be carried out by a machine which has no intelligence, no forethought, no hindsight, and no need for access to meanings.

All the examples so far have involved transforming one sequence of symbols into another, but an equally important kind of activity involves generating new symbol sequences. Most of the everyday writing we do is of this kind; jotting down a shopping list on a piece of paper, making an entry in a diary, and writing a letter or email are familiar examples. When we write in this way we rely solely on our mental resources. In the binary world we are exploring; we can define sets of functional states to carry out processes which generate binary sequences rather than copying or transforming them. Before we explore the details it may help to illuminate the discussion by considering the kinds of stages literacy learners need to go through when learning to write. First they need to be able to form letters and digits. Then they need to learn how to position them relative to each other. When we write English, successive symbols are positioned to the right of what has already been written, not on the left, not above, and not below, at least not until we reach the end of a line. Thus, when we have written a symbol, there is an implicit blank space, immediately to its right, where the next symbol will be written. When we use a word processor, the cursor moves to the right as symbols are typed indicating the blank space where the next symbol will go. We can model this activity in a purely syntactic fashion by defining one or more 'blank space' functional states. These can be used to specify actions when there is no symbol to copy or transform. Since each functional state can have only one action associated with it, we will need to define more than one blank space state if we want to specify more than one action. This sounds a bit complicated, but it's actually quite straightforward and best illustrated with a table. Consider Table 7.1.

The table defines a syntactic process which constructs the sequence 010101...The ellipsis...indicates an endless continuation. The table contains two 'instructions' one in each row. Each instruction specifies a current functional state in the first column, a perception in the second column, an action in the third, and a 'state transition' to the next state in the final column. The symbol # in the perception column represents the perception of a blank space. Now let's play a simple writing game. Take a clean sheet of paper and a pencil. Assume that your 'current state' is **bs1**. Fix your attention on an appropriate part of the sheet of paper; the top left hand side is a conventional starting point. You see nothing on the paper so your perception is of a blank space, represented by #. This means that the first instruction of the table applies. To follow the instruction, write down a 0 and consult the final column, which says that the next state is **bs2**. This means that the next instruction to follow is the one in the row with **bs2** in the current state column. The state transition is like the everyday changes in our mental states which accompany our ordinary activities. (Let's briefly revisit the cookery example. If you are a breakfast chef, different customers will want their eggs cooked in different ways. The 'take two eggs' state may have the action 'fry' associated with it or the action 'boil'. To specify the difference syntactically we would need to specify two different states 'tte1' and 'tte2'. One would have the action 'fry' associated with it, the other the action 'boil'. Functional state transitions for constructing symbol sequences have the same sort of character; they enable us to define sequences of different actions for the same input by using different states. Now shift your focus of attention to the implicit blank space to the right of the 0 you have just written and you are ready to take the next step. Your current state is now **bs2** and you are perceiving the blank space to the right of the 0, so the conditions for the second instruction are fulfilled. The action specified is to write a 1 and make a state transition to state **bs1**. This means that the first row applies again and so on, ad infinitum.

It's easy to see that if you follow it slavishly the table instructs you to write out a potentially infinite sequence 010101...Naturally you wouldn't

Table 7.1 Functional states to construct thesequence 010101...

Current state	Perception	Action	Next state
bs1	#	0	bs2
bs2	#	1	bs1

go on for ever but the point to note is that the syntactic specification does not include the possibility of halting and thus describes an endless construction sequence. Notice also that if I had asked you to start with functional state 'bs2' you would produce the sequence 101010... That, in a nutshell, is the syntactic perspective on minds and mental states that we need for the study of literacy. We're not dealing with minds and mental states in general, but with the very particular circumstances involved in constructing sequences of symbols. The interesting question is whether we can generalise this simple technique to more meaningful cases. Let me draw your attention, if you have not already thought of it, to the fact that 010101...and 101010...are members of the universe of binary texts discussed in the previous section. One question we might want to consider is how many texts from the universe we can construct using systems of functional states of the kind just described. Suppose we could construct them all. That would mean that we had at our disposal a way to construct binary representations of all the meaningful texts that have been written or that could be written.

There are two more points that I want to make here. The first is that we can take the entries from Table 7.1 and combine them in a string to give the sequence bs1#0bs2bs2#1bs1. We can then use the technique from the previous section to translate this sequence into binary. If we do that we get the binary sequence

011000100111001100110001001000110011000001100010011110011
001100100110001001110011001100100010001100110001011000010
0111001100110001

There are several interesting things to think about here. The binary sequence just produced is a perfectly good member of the universe of texts. Moreover, because we know how to interpret it, we see that it can serve as a finite representation of the infinite text 010101...It's a recipe for, or description of, that infinite text. This is hugely important for reasons that I shall discuss in the next section.

The second point that I want to make concerns the possible sizes of sets of functional states that we might use to construct binary symbol sequences. Thus far we've only encountered systems with two states, but we shall come across larger ones in due course. The question is, how large might they be? Could they, like binary texts, be infinitely large? Could there be a system with infinitely many functional states? To answer this question we need to think about brains, the physical systems that give us our minds. The brain is immensely complicated with billions of neurons, the nerve cells that make thinking possible, but for all its complexity it is a finite organ. That gives us the answer. The syntactic representations of minds as sets of functional states have to be finite because we want the model to reflect the constraints of the real system it models. We can define sets of states as large as we like, but a set has to be finite in size and can't be changed once it has been defined. Each set is a functional model of a mind which generates, copies, or otherwise transforms a particular binary text.

7.3   Turing machines

We now have the elements needed to understand the basic ideas of Turing machine theory. We have a universe of binary texts, whose members may be infinitely long, and we have systems of functional states which must be finite. A Turing machine is a finite set of functional states (with associated inputs and outputs) designed to produce a particular binary sequence. As we shall see, there are lots of possible Turing machines. The important point, for the purposes of studying literacy, is that any Turing machine is a syntactic model of the mind of a person engaged in the task of producing the sequence in question.

The term 'machine' is important here. I said in the previous section that a syntactic description of a functional state is one which is simple enough to be carried out by a machine with no intelligence. A Turing machine is a system which can produce a binary sequence automatically in just such an unintelligent way. The table in the previous section was almost defined tightly enough to do the job, but not quite. If you look over the description again, you will see that it needs some intelligence to decide where on the paper the sequence should begin and also that it fails to specify that symbols should be written next to each other. We've assumed the normal convention that symbol sequences are extended to the right, but there's nothing in the table that stops symbols from being written one on top of the other. We can sort these problems out quite easily. First, (as in section 7.1) we're going to imagine our binary texts being written out on one-dimensional strips of paper divided into squares. A strip of paper of this kind is called a 'tape'. We imagine the tape being fed through a machine which is called a 'finite automaton' (FA). It's finite because it serves as a model of a finite mind, and it's an automaton because it works automatically once started. We can think of it as a box containing various parts. The analogy is with the skull that contains the machinery of the brain. The tape is fed through the FA in such a way that a single square is inside the box at any time. This square is called the 'scanned' square. The machinery of the FA is set up to enable it to tell whether the scanned square is blank or whether it has a symbol written on it. It might do the job by having a camera focused on the scanned square sending images to an optical character recogniser. In the human case, of course, eyes are used to read symbols. The parts of the machine are organised in such a way as to carry out the actions needed to implement the functional states with additional actions specified to control the movement of the tape in and out of the machine. The system will also contain a print head which can print a 0 or a 1 on the scanned square, and

Table 7.2   A Turing machine to compute the sequence 010101...

Current state	Input	Output	Move	Next state
s1	#	0	R	s2
s2	#	1	R	s1

an eraser which removes a printed symbol if that is what the instruction specifies. Other parts of the machine serve to determine the current state. The exact specification for the physical construction of the machine is not important. What is important is that it is a machine, however organised, and that it carries out instructions as specified in what is appropriately called a 'machine table'. Here's one for the sequence 010101...

The table is very similar to Table 7.1. The functional state names have been simplified to s1 and s2 and we assume that the machine will always be started in state s1. The perception and action columns have been relabelled as input and output. An extra column has been added to the table to show how to move the tape. The instruction R means that the tape is to be moved so as to make the next square to the right become the newly scanned square. It's not hard to see that an appropriately constructed machine set up in the way specified in Table 7.2 and started in functional state s1 with access to unlimited supplies of tape and ink would output the sequence 010101...in the same way as a person following the instructions in Table 7.1. Such a machine is an example of a Turing machine.

A Turing machine has no idea of what it's doing because it's simply a dumb machine. It's all syntax and mechanics, no semantics. Theoretically, however, it's one of the most important inventions of twentieth century mathematical logic, and it has the added distinction of being the ancestor of the digital computer. The most important theoretical point about the Turing machine is not the possibility it holds out for the mechanical construction of texts, significant though that is, but what it tells us about the general possibilities inherent in literacy. I'm going to focus on two particular instances, one which describes why revision is a key process in the construction of texts, and one which describes how literacy opens up the world of texts via interpretation. These are not the only possibilities that the syntactic theory opens up for us, but they are among the easiest to understand and both are very powerful.

7.3.1   Revision

The revision of written texts is a possibility that distinguishes literate uses from oral uses of language. Spoken language is enormously versatile and serves innumerable human purposes but one thing you can't do with it is to revise or revisit an utterance. Once something has been said it has gone, as the energy of the sound wave dissipates. Everyday speech is fundamentally evanescent; its sounds die away almost as soon as they are spoken, and none of us is at all good at remembering exactly what we have said. This situation changes completely once we can write things down. Texts are durable in a way that speech is not. We can use an existing text as the basis for improvement and extension.

Much of what happens in educational contexts can be understood in terms of commentary on existing texts and revisions to them. My students write essay plans which set out how they propose to tackle an assignment. I provide feedback on those plans, which are then revised and extended to produce the finished essay. The more substantial the finished work is going to be, the more important it is to redraft and revise. Almost nobody has the capacity to produce a coherent, finished, text from scratch without revision, starting on page one, line one, and going straight through to the end. Some students find it hard to produce plans; others are reluctant to revise, and it is almost always students with one or other of these issues who find it hardest to produce high quality work. Revision is a highly significant process because it spreads the cognitive load of composition (Kellogg, 1994; McCutchen, 2008). The possibility of revision allows us to make a provisional first version of a text; we just write down what we think we think. Then, once there's something on paper, the revision process is used to clarify, to extend, to move, to lengthen, and to shorten. Revisions of revisions are frequently carried out and revisions of revisions of revisions. Programs like Microsoft Word, which I am using to construct this text, allow us to track the changes we make to texts in the course of our revisions and in this way add further possibilities to the process. The biographer Michael Holroyd, in an interview reported in *The Guardian* newspaper, described his perspective on revision:

> What I really like is rewriting, but you cannot rewrite until you've already written, and that is terrible. And then rewriting the rewritten text, and so on, up to 10 times, hoping always to get it shorter, more condensed, pack more energy into it. Even if it's a sad thing, you want to get the essence of the most dolorous phrases and connect them in some way, [and] so in that way try to perfect something. You have the energy from the first draft, the momentum, the "go", but then you try to shape it more. (*The Guardian,* 26.03.2011, Review, p. 4)

It's clear, then, that revision is an important practical process that leads to better texts. I suspect, though, that many writers harbour the wish to be able to write the perfect text the first time. We've probably all heard stories about writers whose minds are so clear that their first draft needs no revision and there's something obviously attractive and efficient about writing in this way. It suggests that revision is unnecessary in principle, that it's essentially just a strategy for muddled thinkers. As a prelude to thinking about this in detail, let's distinguish two processes. One is the process of re-writing, which changes what was written before. The other is the process of re-reading, which uses what was written before but does not change it. Let us call these revision and review. A revision involves the production of a new text, whereas a review does not. The model of 'perfect first time writing', typically implies, I think, that neither revision nor review is needed. The mind of the writer is so clear about what needs to be written that once the text is inscribed it does not even need to be reviewed, never mind revised. The question I wish to consider is whether there are texts which cannot, even in principle, be written without review. Are there texts which could not be written in a simple linear fashion starting with the first symbol and finishing with the final symbol without any going back? If this is so, it shows that texts are not just records of speech and that writing things down with the possibility of review adds something new to what can be represented. In answering the question we start to see the power of the Turing machine model because we can translate the question about review into a question about the texts it is possible for Turing machines to write using different strategies. Review implies going back to something that was written earlier and this means, in the Turing machine case, a machine which can move its tape in both directions. The question about review can thus be reformulated as follows: Are there texts which can be written by a Turing machine which can move its tape in both directions and review earlier writings, which cannot be written by a machine which can move its tape in one direction only? The answer is that there are texts of this kind; there are texts that cannot be constructed by a finite machine which can only ever move one way relative to its tape and hence cannot revisit, reuse, or revise its earlier writing. This is a fundamental logical result which proves conclusively that revision opens up a new class of written structures.

I'm going to demonstrate this with a simple example. Consider the sequence of numbers 0,1,2,3,... This is an infinite sequence. How much of it could any human write down without revisiting earlier parts of the sequence? The answer is not very much. To see why, consider that at a precise point in the sequence the number 1,393,796,574,908,163,946,345, 982,392,040,522,594,123,776 occurs. This is the number of binary tweets that we encountered in section 7.1. Although it's a big number, it's also obviously much smaller than many numbers we would have to write down in the course of putting the sequence 0,1,2,3,... on paper. Writing down the sequence of numbers without revising or revisiting an earlier part of the text means having to remember this number while writing it in order to be able to write the next one correctly. Could you do this? The average memory span is much shorter than the 43 digits needed in this case. The further on in the sequence you get, the worse the problem becomes because the memory load keeps increasing. Eventually, no matter how large the memory, if it is finite as human memory is, the task becomes impossible. It's the increasing memory load which distinguishes a task like this from producing the infinite, but repeating, sequence 010101 ... which we've already considered.

Let's consider a binary analogue of the counting task. The binary sequence 0010110111 ... is a representation of the decimal sequence 0, 1, 2, 3, ... Each number n greater than 0 is represented by 0 followed by n 1s. The point in the binary sequence analogous to the example considered above is going to require 0 followed by 1,393,796,574,908,163,946,345,982,3 92,040,522,594,123,776 ones. Suppose we allowed 5,000 characters per page and 1,000 pages per volume. We would still need trillions of volumes just to write down the binary representation of this one number. A Turing machine with a finite memory which could only move its tape rightwards would eventually run out of memory no matter how many functional states it had and could not write out the sequence in full. By contrast, a Turing machine which can revisit earlier parts of the sequence and use them to assist the construction can easily be designed to write out the whole infinite sequence. Indeed, the task can be carried out by a Turing machine with just four functional states. Here's a machine table for it:

You can see from the move column that the machine moves the tape both left and right. That's what makes its task possible. You can also see that the machine uses an extra symbol X in the course of its activities. X is used as a marker. The binary representation of each new number is achieved by copying every 1 from the previous number and adding an additional 1. The marker is used to tick off the digits of the previous number as it's copied. I've included the table for the interest of those readers who might like to understand fully how it functions. The important point, however, is not

Table 7.3   **A Turing machine to compute the sequence 0010110111 ...**

Current state	Input	Output	Move	Next state
s1	#	0	R	s2
s1	0	0	L	s2
s1	1	1	L	s1
s2	#	0	L	s2
s2	0	0	R	s4
s2	1	X	R	s3
s2	X	X	L	s2
s3	#	1	L	s1
s3	0	0	R	s3
s3	1	1	R	s3
s3	X	X	R	s3
s4	#	1	R	s2
s4	0	0	R	s4
s4	1	1	R	s4
s4	X	1	R	s4

the technical detail but the demonstration that revision and re-use of parts of a text are key processes which extend the powers of Turing machines and literate minds in quite specific ways. In fact, the process that we are talking about is something intermediate between revision and review. It does not require rewriting of the existing text but it requires more than just review. The earlier text is revisited and copied and it is this that makes its indefinite extension possible. Review, copying, and revision are processes that provide additional structure for the literate mind which is not available in purely oral processes. I am not claiming that the syntactic analogues of revision and reuse that we find in the Turing machine of Table 7.3 are anything like a full model of the semantic purposes to which revision and review are put, but I do want to say that without the syntactic support of existing text, the semantic processes of revision and reuse that we value in our everyday literate activities would not be possible. The difference made by revisiting and re-using parts of an existing text is massive. In the case of the counting number sequence it turns an impossible task into one which is essentially a matter of bookkeeping and there are many other tasks which are similarly transformed by the capacity to reuse and revise. Literate processes involving revision offer new possibilities for human minds which are as significant for travel in mental space as the invention of the aircraft has been for physical travel.

7.3.2 Interpretation

The other key literate process I am going to explore via the Turing machine model is the process of interpretation. Again, because Turing machines are purely syntactic we will only be able to demonstrate a syntactic analogue of interpretation, but it will illuminate our perception of some crucial aspects of the semantic interpretive processes that we value. Let's start by considering everyday understandings of textual interpretation. Perhaps the first and most basic aspect of interpretation is comprehension. To interpret a text is to understand it, to comprehend what it means. It's because comprehension is so basic that it is rather startling to read Primo Levi's description of a reader he encountered in a prison camp in World War II whose reading was little more than syntactic.

> He was a small man, about forty, thin and sallow, almost bald with an absent-minded expression. He spent his days stretched out on his bunk, and was an indefatigable reader. He read everything that came to hand: Italian, French, German, Polish newspapers and books. Every two or three days, at the moment of the check, he told me: 'I've finished that book. Have you another one to lend me? But not in Russian: you know that I have difficulty with Russian.' Not that he was a polyglot: in fact, he was practically illiterate. But he still 'read' every book, from the first

line to the last, identifying the individual letters with satisfaction, pronouncing them with his lips and laboriously reconstructing the words without bothering about their meaning. (Levi, 1979, pp. 239–40)

Another facet of interpretation is the capacity to transmit an understanding of a text to others either verbally or by making a written commentary on it. Some written works contain deep meanings and are so highly valued that the commentaries on them far exceed the original texts in size. In English literature the works of Shakespeare are a well known example. Some texts may be hard to understand. In such cases interpretive commentaries may be the best way for new readers to tackle them. Criticism and commentary are the lifeblood of academic work and lie at the heart of many of the uses of literacy. Many literary works are read in different ways by successive generations of readers and interpreted in specific ways that suit the particular zeitgeist. Re-reading and re-interpretation tend to go together. Seasoned readers often have texts which they admire and love, to which they return time and again for fresh understanding and enjoyment. Religious scriptures are key literate works whose readings and interpretations are often embedded in important social practices.

The Turing machine analogue of interpretation is a fascinating process which holds a number of deep lessons for students of literacy. I am not going to go into the maze of technical details but I will try to give a broad description of the major features. Readers who wish to understand the process in detail will find a full account in my book *Rethinking Cognitive Computation*. To understand what interpretation means in the Turing machine context, let us start by reconsidering the simple machine of Table 7.2 which produces the binary sequence 010101 ... The information in this table can be expressed as a string of symbols s1#0Rs2s2#1Rs1 and as a binary sequence

0111001100110001001000110011000001010010011100110011001 10010
0111001100110010001000110011000101010010011100110011000 1

Each representation contains the same information so it doesn't matter which we use to illustrate the interpretive process. Since we're dealing with Turing machines, which work very well with binary representations, let's choose the latter. What we have in these 112 symbols is a binary description of a Turing machine. The first 56 symbols tell us what the machine described does in functional state 's1' and the second 56 symbols tell us what the machine does in functional state 's2'. Suppose we were to write the 112 symbols on the tape of a Turing machine and use the sequence as its input. We already know that we can easily specify a set of functional states to copy the symbols or to transform the 0s into 1s and vice versa. The key question in the current context is this: Can we specify a set of functional states which will interpret the binary description and carry out its instructions by writing out the sequence it describes? The answer is that we can, and the fact that we can is hugely important. Moreover, because the format in which the description is written is one that can be used to describe any Turing machine, we can, with a little care, build a Turing machine which can interpret and execute the description of any other Turing machine. Let's be clear about what this means. It means that we can build a physical machine with a fixed set of parts and a fixed pattern of functional states. We can write the description of a Turing machine on the tape of this machine and set it going. If we give it the binary description of the machine in Table 7.2 our machine will produce the output 010101 ... If we erase that description and instead write the binary description of the machine in Table 7.3 our machine will produce the output 0010110111 ... The one physical machine when given different inputs produces different outputs. That's the syntactic model of the interpretive process in a nutshell.

The process of specifying a machine which interprets and executes the description of other machines is the syntactic analogue of the human process of learning to read a text and to write an account of what the text says. It is thus a model of one of the core processes of literacy. One way of describing, at a very general level of analysis, what happens when we learn to read and write is that new functional states of mind are organised in our brains which enable us to interpret strings of symbols and also to produce them in systematic ways. These new functional states are in addition to what our minds are already able to do. In that sense, learning literacy is like learning to ride a bike. When you learn to ride a bike you acquire a new skill that you previously lacked. So it is with learning literacy.

> As children grow up, they interact with a variety of people and other living creatures as well as a diverse range of physical objects. They also grow up surrounded by a particular type of visual marks intentionally created to transmit different messages. These marks appear on a particular types (sic) of artefacts that include pamphlets, road signs, labels, calendars, and books. They belong to different notational systems used, for example, in mathematics, logic, chemistry, and writing and perform a diversity of functions from the mundane to the sacred. In a sense, becoming literate means learning how to interpret and create these marks. (Tolchinsky, 2009, p. 468)

The interpretive Turing machine is called a 'universal' Turing machine because it can read and use the description of any other Turing machine. These machines may be carrying out processes with interpretations in mathematics, logic, chemistry, or writing and with diverse functions across the spectrum as described by Tolchinsky. This makes a universal machine exceptionally versatile and quite unlike any other kind of machine. Indeed, we can think of the universal machine as changing and enlarging our concept of what machines are like. This is one reason why it was such an important invention. The machines of Table 7.2 and 7.3 are fixed in what they do. The first can only write the sequence 010101 ... and the second can only write the sequence 0010110111 ... The universal Turing machine can write out both of these sequences and many others besides. How many? The simple answer is infinitely many. There are infinitely many different Turing machines whose descriptions can be expressed as finite binary sequences, and a universal machine can interpret all of them. Thus the interpretive capacity of a universal Turing machine is infinitely greater than that of fixed, non-interpretive machines like the two whose operations we have looked at.

The profoundly important implication for humans is that literacy is a skill which gives its possessors unlimited interpretive capacity. Naturally we are mainly interested in semantic capacity rather than syntactic capacity, but the universal machine model shows that a literate human has access to syntactic vehicles, i.e., texts that can express an infinite number of different meanings. Thus literacy provides, in principle, an infinite enlargement of intellectual capacity. By contrast, lack of literacy can be considered an infinite deprivation. Chapter 8 develops these points. The 'in principle' nature of the argument is important in part because it serves to direct attention to fundamental practical issues. It shows, for example, that it is not sufficient just to teach people to read and write. For them to be able to use this capacity they must have access to texts and this may require substantial investment in infrastructure. Literacy without texts is equivalent to a universal machine with no descriptions to interpret. The theoretical argument thus provides a powerful focus on the practical needs associated with literacy. The ordinary business of living generates physical hunger; the ordinary business of literacy generates a hunger for texts.

7.4   The co-design of functional states and symbol structures

The Turing machine model was based on the example of a human working with paper and pencil and it is widely agreed among logicians and computer scientists that the model captures the essential features of paper and pencil calculation. One of the striking features of Turing machines generally is that they demonstrate a tight coupling between structure in the environment, i.e., symbol structures on a tape, and structure in the mind, i.e., systems of functional states. It is appropriate to say that functional states and symbol structures are co-designed. The machine of Table 7.3, which demonstrates the fundamental importance of revision, is a good case in point. The set of four functional states that implements the machine is designed to start on a blank tape and produce an expanding symbol structure which starts with 0, from which 001 is generated, followed by 001011, etc. If the functional states were differently organised, the symbol structure would be different and if the symbol structure were different, a different set of functional states would be needed to achieve an equivalent output. The coupling of symbol structure and functional state structure needed to produce a universal machine is considerably more complex but also demonstrates exactly the same kind of interdependence. Universal machines can be designed to work with any finite alphabet but the details of their construction will vary according to the alphabet. There is also substantial variability in the methods by which universal interpretation is achieved. The important point to bear in mind when we consider humans is that literacy learners are born into specific literate environments with specific alphabets and scripts. Humans do not come into the world equipped to read and write; they have to learn the details of a particular system and internalise them. The learning involves explicit skills. Recognition of basic symbols and the forms of symbol structures are essential. We learn literacy for its semantic richness but the ability to exploit semantic resources depends on the mastery of specific syntactic skills. The process of meaning making in the human case involves interdependence between texts and minds exactly as it does in machines, but it is the human mind that has to be trained to understand the syntactic principles of existing languages and writing systems. The mind is remarkable for its ability to comprehend the meanings of texts despite the barriers to understanding posed by poor handwriting, poor spelling, and poor grammar for example, but the fact that comprehension is possible in the face of poor quality symbol structures does not diminish the importance of syntactic skills. Indeed, one might argue that the better developed syntactic skills are the better able the reader is to cope with poor quality scripts.

7.5 Summary

A syntactic perspective on texts leads to the idea of an infinite universe of symbol structures, each of which could serve as a carrier of meaning. A syntactic perspective on minds engaged in symbol processing shows that finite systems of functional states can produce infinite outputs. Bringing texts and minds together, at a purely syntactic level of analysis, allows us to understand the universal Turing machine, a syntactic device with infinite interpretive capacity. The human instantiation of this capacity demonstrates the unlimited power of literacy to enhance human lives. Perhaps paradoxically, the theoretical nature of the argument also focuses attention on the practical needs of the literate.

Chapter 8

The Scope of the Literate Mind

In Chapter 1 I proposed that all literate activities have two things in common: they are human, and they involve external symbol systems. In Chapters 3, 5, and 6, I have proposed that we should understand and analyse human literate activities in the light of what we know about the immense evolutionary history of our species and the consequences it has had for our individual and social selves. In Chapter 7 I have proposed that we should consider literacy from the standpoint of Turing machine theory, which provides a purely syntactic account of the capacities of systems that can use external symbol structures to augment finite memories. In this chapter, the evolutionary and computational strands of thinking are brought together to provide a conceptual framework for studying literacy skills, social practices, and the interactions between them. The framework describes the scope of literate activities, what it is possible, in principle, for literate minds to do.

The human mind is formed in part by the immense evolutionary history of our species and in part by the social and cultural conventions of the times and places in which individual human lives are lived. The natural endowment of adapted functions with which every individual mind is equipped has been outlined in terms of human universals. The universal functions are shaped and augmented by the material and intellectual tools which communities develop and refine over lengthy periods. Writing systems and literacy are powerful instances of such tools.

8.1 Literacy separates syntax from semantics

For the sake of clarity it is important to maintain the theoretical distinction between syntax and semantics when studying literacy even if, in real literate lives, the distinction is inevitably blurred. There is a fundamental difference between the letters, words, sentences, and larger textual units which make up the material features of a writing system and the meanings which the symbol structures convey. This is most obvious in the case of homonyms such as 'bank' where a single syntactic form has multiple meanings but it is generally true. In computers and in formal models like the Turing machine there is nothing but syntax, whereas in human minds meanings are dominant and it can be hard to separate the meaning of a text from its form. The

142

distinction between syntax and semantics helps us to navigate some difficult terrain and to re-examine key assertions about the nature of literacy. One of these is the idea, already discussed in Chapters 1 and 3, that literacy is best conceptualised in terms of social practices rather than in terms of skills. The concern that I have about this point of view is not that the focus on social practices is wrong but that it tends to underplay the importance of syntactic skills. An influential book by Brian Street, *Literacy in theory and practice*, is one of the key texts in this area. Street begins the book in the following way:

> I shall use the term 'literacy' as a shorthand for the social practices and conceptions of reading and writing…I shall contend that what the particular practices and concepts of reading and writing are for a given society depends upon the context; that they are already embedded in an ideology and cannot be isolated or treated as 'neutral' or merely 'technical'. I shall demonstrate that what practices are taught and how they are imparted depends upon the nature of the social formation. The skills and concepts that accompany literacy acquisition, in whatever form, do not stem in some automatic way from the inherent qualities of literacy, as some authors would have us believe, but are aspects of a specific ideology. (Street, 1984, p. 1)

Reflection on this quotation from Street leads me in two directions; I want to agree with much of what he says, and I also want to disagree. It is entirely clear, I think, that what literacy practices are taught and how they are taught do indeed depend on the 'social formation', that is on local, social practices. It is also clear, I think, that the practices of reading and writing in a given society are embedded in an ideology, although, in a pluralist society such as that in Britain today, it is not obvious that there is a single, dominant ideology or exactly what the effects of British life are on literacy acquisition. I also agree that literacy skills and concepts do not 'stem in some automatic way from the inherent qualities of literacy'. This is true for at least two reasons. First, the acquisition of literacy skills is an effortful process, not automatic. The effort is temporally and spatially extensive and it is shared among the members of literate communities involving parents, teachers, and literacy learners themselves. Second, it is far from clear what it could mean to say that literate skills and concepts flow automatically from the inherent qualities of literacy, whatever those might be. What Street has in mind here, I imagine, is the kind of idea that supposes literacy acquisition automatically to transform the supposedly irrational, pre-literate mind into the supposedly rational, literate mind.

However, having found myself in agreement with much of what Street says, I also find much to question. I do not know what it means to say that literacy skills and concepts are 'aspects of a specific ideology' nor is it clear why the ideological perspective should be treated as an alternative to the so-called 'autonomous' view. I am also puzzled by the use of the expression 'merely technical' which has, to my understanding, a slightly pejorative evaluation of technique. Technique is certainly not everything but it is hugely important. In music, in art, in sports, and in literacy secure technical ability is the foundation of success. There is nothing 'mere' about it at all. Literacy depends on the acquisition of the technical skills needed to work with a particular writing system. If the system is alphabetic, the skills involve symbol recognition, word recognition, letter-to-sound correspondences, and so on. I cannot see that there is anything 'ideological' about these skills, unless we use the term in a sense which is devoid of its normal political connotations. The acquisition of literacy skills in English, for example, is not associated with any specific political ideology, nor are those skills restricted in their application to any particular ideology. There is a big difference between the claim that literacy skills are embedded in an ideology and the claim that they are aspects of an ideology. Consider, as an example, research done by Anna Robinson-Pant in Nepal who discovered that adult literacy classes were positioned by men in a way which reinforced existing gender divisions:

> I found that these men saw adult literacy classes as 'women's domain' – as an appropriate form of education for women quite distinct from the school education that they had received. They assumed therefore that literacy instruction at these classes should be in Newari or Nepali rather than in English. (Robinson-Pant, 2008, p. 787)

The women to whom she spoke were anxious to learn English, ostensibly for practical reasons but also, and more importantly, in order to feel educated and, presumably, to redress the imbalance they felt in relation to the opportunities available to men. Very clearly, in the local context, literacy skills were embedded in an ideology. However, in order to make sense of the fact that instruction in English was more highly valued than instruction in Newari or Nepali, it has to be treated as separable from the local ideology and therefore not just an aspect of it.

The separation of syntax from semantics provides a way to navigate this difficult terrain. The syntax of a writing system is essentially a matter of technique. There are, of course, different views, some ideologically based, about what skills are needed for literacy and how best to teach them, but the skills themselves are not ideological in any ordinary sense of the term. At my first primary school, writing was taught using a copperplate script. There may well have been ideological reasons for the choice of this script but the daily practice in forming the letters was drill rather than ideology. A change of school brought a change to italic script and a new form of drill which, as a left-hander, I found even more difficult than the loops of the copperplate I had previously struggled with. The literate human has to have basic technical skills in order to generate texts as vehicles for meanings and to understand the meanings of texts produced by others.

It is at the semantic level of analysis that ideology comes into play. The purposes for which literacy is taught, or the reasons for denying it, are ideological. It is also a matter of ideology whether whole populations are educated in the same way or whether populations are stratified and their members taught differently according to the social stratum to which they are assigned. These are hugely important matters but no good purpose is served by conflating them with the underlying skills that individuals have to acquire if they are to become skilled readers and writers.

The great merit of the Turing machine, and other formal systems, is that they demonstrate absolutely clearly that there is a fundamental distinction between syntax and semantics. When the distinction between syntax and semantics is firmly in place we can see that both the technical skills of reading and writing and the social practices within which those skills are embedded are essential for an adequate theoretical account of literacy. In order to emphasize the importance of the distinction, I propose two principles.

8.1.1   The syntactic unity of literacy

Numerical calculations, word processing, spreadsheets, databases, images, videos, sounds, games, and programs are implemented in computer memories as binary texts. The binary representations of all of them are members of the infinite universe of texts described in Chapter 7. This commonplace fact illustrates a principle which I shall call the syntactic unity of literacy. The principle expresses the idea that underlying the multiplicity of uses of literacy and the multiplicity of modes of presentation is a common symbolic framework within which all literate works of every size and kind can be located. It says, in effect, that all literate productions are related to each other because every one of them is (or can be) represented in the universe of binary texts. It is a theoretical principle because no one reads binary texts in practice, but it serves to focus attention on what literate activities have in common and it is also helpful for thinking about computers and the internet.

8.1.2   The semantic diversity of literacy

The other, equally fundamental, principle I shall call the semantic diversity of literacy. This principle expresses the idea that the meanings of texts can be as diverse as the people who use them. There is no such thing as 'the' meaning of a text. Texts, in and of themselves, do not have meanings. They are purely syntactic entities. The examples in Chapter 2.8 illustrate the point. It is, perhaps, easier to see this with short, simple texts than it is with longer ones, which often have meanings which are shared and, in some cases, normatively enforced. Legal and religious texts are often of this kind. The two elementary binary texts 0 and 1 do not have intrinsic meanings of their own, although they can easily be given them. They may be used to represent the yin and the yang, the good and the bad, black and white, presence and absence, or innumerably many other pairs of opposites or relations. Semantic diversity exists because people have different understandings of what they read and write and engage in literate pursuits for a variety of purposes. Semantic diversity does not imply that the sharing of meanings is unimportant.

The syntactic and semantic principles taken together can help us to maintain a balanced view of what literate activities are really like. A focus on purely syntactic concerns may lead to an overestimate of commonalities; conversely, a focus on semantics may lead to an overestimate of diversity. The universal Turing machine model captures the syntactic underpinnings of fundamental interpretive processes but says nothing at all about the meanings of texts. By contrast, an extreme focus on the meanings and uses of literacy associated with a specific social practice may have nothing to say about the underlying syntax. Any real literacy event has both semantic and syntactic components and the principles remind us that this is the case.

8.2   The literate mind is infinitely powerful

A key proposition of the framework outlined here is the idea that a literate mind is infinitely more powerful than a non-literate mind. It has unlimited scope. This idea is based on the syntactic approach to literacy outlined in Chapter 7 in which the possibilities of revision and universal interpretation are identified as key properties of minds interacting with external symbol systems. Power in this context means computational capacity. It is not directly related to political or personal power, nor is there any moral evaluation. The idea of infinite power does not, in any way, support the idea that literate people are morally superior to those who are not literate or that non-literate people are deficient. The concept of infinite computational capacity indicates the vast scope of knowledge and enquiry which is opened up to those who have full command of the resources, both personal and institutional, needed for unrestricted reading and writing. Someone who can read and write can, in principle, engage in an infinite number of different literate processes. This extraordinary capacity of the fully literate mind should be considered a privilege by those who enjoy it, particularly because it is still refused to many or unavailable to them for lack of resources. Literacy is recognised as a universal human right in the United Nations declaration and it is listed as a core human capability by Nussbaum (2006, p. 76). It is to be hoped that the strong characterisation of literacy as an infinite gain will help to show just how sharp a loss the lack of literacy is for those deprived of it. Indeed, one might argue that illiteracy is an infinite deprivation. This is not to say that non-literate people cannot and do not lead worthwhile, happy, or fulfilled lives. It is, rather, to suggest that those lives should be able to reap the additional benefits to be had from access to the universe of texts.

The analysis of Chapter 7 can be extended to make four specific propositions about literacy. The propositions describe different kinds of process capabilities. They are simply stated here without any technical detail. See *Rethinking Cognitive Computation* (Wells, 2006) for an in-depth treatment of finite automata and Turing machines. Proposition L1 describes the capacities of finite automata, which are systems of functional states which may be able to read but cannot write. L2 describes the capacities of systems which may be able to write as well as read, but which cannot revise or reuse what has already been written. L3 describes the capacities of systems like task-specific Turing machines, which can revise and reuse their written output, but which do not have the capacity to interpret the descriptions of other machines. L4 describes the capacities of systems which have the interpretive powers of universal Turing machines.

L1: Non-literate minds and minds which can read but not write have the processing capacity of finite automata.

L2: Minds which can read and respond by writing a finite output, but cannot revise what they have written have the processing capacity of finite automata.

L3: Minds which can revise what they have written and can generate outputs of unlimited complexity have the processing capacity of task-specific Turing machines.

L4: Minds which can interpret and act upon sets of written instructions have the processing capacity of universal Turing machines.

The four theoretical propositions taken together suggest that important distinctions can be made about the nature of literate competences independently of the meanings of texts or of the surrounding institutions within which real literate lives are embedded. The propositions are concerned specifically with syntactic capabilities, as was the analysis of Chapter 7, but it is clear that the syntactic capabilities have corresponding semantic consequences. Revision and interpretation, for example, are key requirements for the generation and comprehension of complex meanings. The fundamental contrast embodied in the set of propositions is not that between literate and non-literate minds if literacy is defined simply in terms of the basic capacities of reading and writing. The important distinction is that between the powers described in L1 and L2 and those described in L3 and L4. This distinction rests on the ways in which reading and writing are used. Completely non-literate minds and those with the restricted literate capacities described in L1 and L2 have the processing capacity of finite automata. Literate minds with unlimited capacity to generate outputs and revise them have the capacity of task-specific Turing machines described in L3, and those which have universal interpretive capacity as described in L4 have the processing capacity of universal Turing machines. Reading alone does not serve to discriminate non-literate from literate minds in terms of formal powers, nor does it discriminate among the different types of literate capacity. It is writing with the possibility of revision that makes the important difference. Revisiting what has been written earlier and modifying the record so as to facilitate further steps in a literate process are the key capacities. One consequence of propositions L1 – L4 is that they highlight the inadequacy of definitions of literacy which consider only low-level reading and writing abilities.

In theoretical computer science, universal machines constitute the top of the machine hierarchy because they are the most general form of computing machine. The capacity to act on different sets of instructions gives a universal machine infinitely more capacity than a task-specific Turing machine, when capacity is described in terms of the transformation of inputs into outputs. Modern digital computers are, essentially, universal Turing machines because they can be programmed. A computer program is a set of instructions and, from the perspective of Turing machine theory, also a task-specific Turing machine. When a computer user switches from word processing to search the internet, or to watch a film recorded on DVD, or to calculate statistics using a software package, or to do any of the other things that can be done with a modern computer, the process is equivalent to switching from one task-specific Turing machine description to another.

In the context of literacy it is appropriate to think about the capacity to follow arbitrary sets of instructions as described in L4, in a cautious way and not to think of it as the most important literary capacity. The reason for caution can be appreciated when it is understood that a universal machine is itself a task-specific Turing machine, albeit one that can be described as a second order machine. The specific task that a universal machine carries out is instruction interpretation and execution. A universal Turing machine originates nothing. Without the description of a task-specific machine to interpret and act on, a universal machine is powerless and inert. It requires a machine description as input and can do nothing without it. Unlike a task-specific machine whose activity is internally generated, a universal machine started on a blank tape (analogous to a clean sheet of paper) would be unable to do anything because its processing is driven by an external machine description.

In terms of real world literacy the key capacities are those described by L3 and L4 together, not by either alone. A literate person with L3 but not L4 capacity might be someone who has learned to read and write but has no access to the world's literatures and has to rely solely on imagination and what can be learned through non-literate perception. The capacities described by L3 are intrinsic capacities of the minds of individuals. A poet who writes a new poem, for example, is exercising an intrinsic L3 type of capacity. We imagine the poet starting with a blank sheet of paper and producing a new, creative output from the resources of the imagination. An example that illustrates the point is by the musician/poet Paul Taylor:

> *Night Shift*
>
> it was a cracker a corker
> that cackled me awake
> in the dark morning
>
> the best joke ever dreamt
> was scribbled down for posterity
> and I smiled back to sleep
>
> re-awakening hours later
> I remembered writing
> reached for the notebook
>
> there it was
> the golden one-liner:
> hit the egg with the hammer!

To say that a poem such as NIGHT SHIFT results from the intrinsic resources of the poet does not deny that it may also be a response to external events and circumstances. The point, rather, is that the poem is not the result of a formula following exercise but springs from the complexities of experience and feeling that accumulate during a lifetime. The capacities described by L4, by contrast, are only partly intrinsic. They require the literate person to have mastered the techniques of reading and writing but do not require the exercise of creativity. They provide a window into the minds and thoughts of other people. Both kinds of literate activity are enormously valuable but there is a clear sense in which L3 activity requires an active exercise of the mind of the individual, whereas L4 activity does not. A literate person with L4 but not L3 capacity would be able to read the world's literatures (given suitable translations) and to act on any set of written instructions, but would be totally dependent on existing texts and unable to engage in any independent, creative literary activity. It is not hard to think of practical situations in which either L3 or L4 capacity might be present without the other. If, for example, one teaches children or adults to read and write but is unable or unwilling to provide them with any texts, they can be said to have L3 capacity alone. If, on the other hand, one were to inculcate an attitude of dependence on texts and to discourage creative writing and independent thinking, the result might be considered L4 capacity alone. What we would naturally think of as full literacy requires the development of both L3 and L4 capacities.

8.2.1   The Library of Babel

The relationship between syntactic and semantic properties can be further elucidated with the help of *The Library of Babel*, a famous short story by the Argentinian writer Jorge Luis Borges. The Library he describes is composed of an indefinitely large set of hexagonal galleries containing bookshelves, connected to each other by passages and staircases. The Library contains all the books that can be created with an alphabet of 25 symbols, when each book has 410 pages, with 40 lines per page, and 80 characters per line. The construction principle is essentially the same as that of the universe of binary texts. The Library, being finite, is smaller than the universe but is vast for the same combinatorial reasons. In the story, Borges described the interpretations of some of the books that the Library has to contain by virtue of its size.

> *All* – the detailed history of the future, the autobiographies of the archangels, the faithful catalog of the Library, thousands and thousands of false catalogs, the proof of the falsity of those false catalogs, a proof of the falsity of the *true* catalog, the Gnostic gospel of Basilides, the commentary upon that gospel, the commentary on the commentary on that gospel, the true story of your death, the translation of every book into every language, the interpolations of every book into all books, the treatise Bede could have written (but did not) on the mythology of the Saxon people, the lost books of Tacitus. (Borges, 1999, p. 115)

The striking thing about the story is its illumination of the fact that, as a consequence of the combinatorial, syntactic properties of the symbol system, the Library contains all the arrangements of symbols that can be interpreted as meaningful texts, including the exotic products of Borges' imagination which make the story so fascinating. It is a formal property of the Library that it includes texts which map exactly, symbol for symbol, the books described and, of course, countless others besides. It is a semantic, not a formal, property that one of the texts can be interpreted as the faithful catalogue of the Library and others as the lost books of Tacitus. Another formal property with semantic interpretations of interest to me is that the Library includes vast numbers of exact copies of the text of this book with strings of symbols on their covers which can be interpreted as the names of many different authors, and publishers for that matter! It is clear that the formal, combinatorial properties of the Library are of interest primarily because of the striking semantic interpretations that Borges' imagination created from them but the syntactic properties are needed to provide the underlying variability.

8.3 Literacy augments the powers of the non-literate mind

The analysis of Chapter 7 shows that it is possible to characterise the functional states of mind needed to interact with symbol systems abstractly and to explore the purely syntactic possibilities of symbol manipulation. Interactions that allow for revision and the interpretation of symbol structures as sets of instructions provide the syntactic foundations for literacy. Writing provides durable and stable access to the infinite universe of texts. Powerful though it is, however, the Turing machine model tells us nothing about the purposes for which these powerful symbolic tools are likely to be exploited. In order to approach these issues we need to consider the human side of the equation, in particular the question of what human minds are for and where human energies are most likely to be directed. In this book answers to these questions have been sought in evolutionary theory, which suggests that the competitive and co-operative demands of social living are among the primary motivators of human conduct. It is clear from the list of universals at the end of Chapter 3 that the concerns of literate and non-literate peoples overlap to a huge extent and it is thus more appropriate to think of literacy as augmenting rather than transforming the non-literate mind. For us to understand what this might mean we need to know what kind of a system the non-literate mind is.

Two major perspectives can be found in the history of psychology. The first treated the mind as a general purpose learning machine which has no particular proclivities at birth. This perspective is sometimes summarised as the idea that the mind is a blank slate or *tabula rasa* (Pinker, 2002). The slate is written on by the experience of living and becomes inscribed with the rules and conventions of the culture in which the individual is raised. For example, every normal human learns a natural language but the language learned depends on the place of birth and the linguistic environment. The blank slate view of the mind was popular through much of the twentieth century as a result of the influence of behaviourism which promised, among other things, a powerful technology for behavioural control (Watson, 1913; Skinner, 1974). The idea was that a set of behaviours could be chosen and stamped into the organism by a system of rewards for behaviours which were desired, and punishments for those which were not. Over time it was expected that the organism would learn to produce rewarded behaviour and to curb punished behaviour. The behaviourist programme foundered when it was discovered that organisms were not indefinitely malleable. It turned out not to be possible to choose an arbitrary set of behaviours for an organism and to write them on its slate by carefully chosen rewards and punishments. It was found that different animals were predisposed to learn certain kinds of things but not others. Rats and pigeons, for example, the experimental subjects in many behaviourist laboratories, cannot learn exactly the same kinds of things. With hindsight this is hardly surprising given the very different conditions of life they experience. The programme was by no means a complete failure, however. All complex creatures have some capacity to learn from experience, to have their behaviour shaped by life experiences, but this learning is constrained by the pre-existing architecture of the mind which is much more structured than the blank slate idea supposes.

The other major perspective on the mind understands it as a system which is pre-structured at birth. There are many variants on this perspective but an important line of thinking going back to Darwin has proposed that the pre-structuring results from adaptation taking place over millions of years (Darwin, 1871; Campbell, 1972; Hockett, 1973; Brown, 1991; Barkow, Cosmides, and Tooby, 1992; Pinker, 1994, 1997). Human universals are evidence for this adaptive structuring of the mind. Whereas the behaviourist perspective saw the mind as a general purpose learning mechanism, the evolutionary perspective sees the mind as a mosaic of special purpose mechanisms, some with relatively fixed behaviours, others capable of learning. A popular way of summarising the approach is to think of the mind as a 'modular' system (Fodor, 1983; Hirschfeld and Gelman, 1994; Mithen, 1996). The modularity approach has itself been controversial (Franks, 2011) but the idea that human minds are structured in significant ways as a result of evolution is well established.

8.4 Stable, durable texts provide new opportunities for human minds

The syntactic analyses of Chapter 7 and the previous section show that external symbol systems extend the powers of the finite mind. In the case of Turing machines it is assumed that texts are infinitely durable and stable. The tape of a Turing machine suffers no wear or tear. A symbol once written on it remains in pristine condition until it is erased or replaced by a different symbol. Real texts, of course, are more vulnerable to the ravages of time and circumstance but they typically last long enough to serve many practical functions even if they do not have the limitless durability of their theoretical counterparts. One interesting phenomenon which illustrates the significance of the durability of external symbols is lucid dreaming. Lucid dreamers are aware of the fact that they are dreaming and this awareness can be harnessed in various ways which have proven useful for the study of both sleeping and waking consciousness. One thing that lucid dreamers can typically do, only poorly if at all, is to read books or other texts in their dreams. When they try to read, the texts tend to change or become incomprehensible. Green and McCreery (1994, Chapter 10) discuss psychological and biological factors which may help to explain the difficulties. To these we might add the simple fact that dream texts do not have the external grounding of real texts. It would be interesting to know if people who have particularly good verbatim memory for texts might succeed more often in reading during lucid dreams.

The discussion of social evolution in Chapter 6 suggests that a significant factor in human evolution has been the need to respond rapidly to changing social situations and to modify goals and tactics as the consequences of interactions with other strategic agents become apparent. Evidence in these circumstances, as Nick Humphrey says, is 'ephemeral, ambiguous and liable to change' (Humphrey, 1976, p. 309). Lengthy reasoning processes are unlikely to be socially valuable because the premises on which they are based may change while inferences are being made. Texts have a stability and relative durability which allows reasoning to take place in a more leisurely and secure fashion. Literacy provides a completely new, stable, source of information which does not bite back (immediately at least!) and which doesn't change. Because the elements of a text can be assumed not to change once written down, it becomes possible to make the calculations of their formal properties from which the concept of the universe of texts is derived. Stable representations make formal reasoning possible on a scale which is impossible or useless in the quicksilver arena of everyday social life. Texts provide a fixed starting point for chains of reasoning. Naturally, if changing circumstances invalidate the assumptions with which a text-based reasoning process starts, its outcomes will be unhelpful but the practical successes of text-based reasoning suggest that many general processes can be understood and powerful conclusions reached about them.

It would be hard to overestimate the importance of the stable space for reflection and reasoning provided by texts. Indeed, the whole mode of operation of Turing machines may be considered a consequence of this stability. The literate capabilities identified in propositions L3 and L4 depend on the stability of representations. If the text being created during a specific literacy process were not stable, it would not be possible for systematic revisions to be made or for later parts to build on earlier ones. If the instructions followed by a universal literacy processor were not stable then its activities would become random rather than related to the task described by a specific literacy process. Thus the systematicity of literate processing is a consequence of stable textual representations and it would not be possible without them. This marks a definitive distinction between the types of processing that are possible with durable texts as opposed to those which are possible without them.

The durability of texts has some interesting corollaries. The Turing machine model is specifically concerned with the dynamic processes of reading and writing which occur while texts are being created. It pays no attention to the independent history that a text has after it has been written, although the interpretive capacity of the universal machine depends on access to elements of the universe of texts. However, in the real world, once a text has been created, it becomes an object with which others can engage and with which authors can engage in new ways. The novelist, Lionel Shriver, who wrote *We Need To Talk About Kevin,* a widely discussed novel about a young serial killer first published in 2003, described how her readers had contributed to her own understanding of the work:

> I am grateful to an astonishingly sophisticated audience for defying the condescending assumptions that people only want to read happy-clappy, mindless pap. I'm especially grateful for the application of many strangers' imaginations to a set of characters who don't exist and events that never happened. A novel is able to tap into its readers' brain power, much as a project like climate-change calculation can enlist the computing power of individual laptops around the world. Thanks to a smart, creative audience, *Kevin* has become more vivid, more complex and, well, more real to me, and thus constitutes as much an achievement of its readership as of its author. (*The Guardian*, 17 May 2008).

A paper by Gabrielle Cliff Hodges (2010) discusses the importance of imaginative engagement in literature for school-age readers. Her research was framed by a context of concern that pressure to meet nationally set curriculum objectives in England had reduced opportunities for independent reading for pleasure in schools. Without readers who have been encouraged from childhood to engage deeply with literary texts, the mutual achievement described by Shriver would not be possible. Cliff Hodges draws on the work of Rosenblatt (1994) and Iser (1978) to emphasize the situated dynamics of readings of texts and the subtle interplay they encourage between real and imagined worlds.

As a further illustration of the complexity of the relationship that can exist between a literate mind and a text, consider the fact that poets sometimes describe their creations as achieving a kind of independence. The Nobel prize-winning poet Seamus Heaney has described a form of transcendence in the relationship between a poet and a poem:

> [I]f a poem is any good, you can repeat it to yourself as if it were written by somebody else. The completedness frees you from it and it from you. You can read and reread it without feeling self-indulgent: whatever it was in you that started the writing has got beyond you. The unwritten poem is always going to be entangled with your own business, part of your accident and incoherence – which is what drives you to write. But once the poem gets written, it is, in a manner of speaking, none of your business. (Heaney and O'Driscoll, 2008, p. 197)

One way in which I think such experiences might be understood is in terms of the distinction between task-specific and universal machine processes.

The act of writing a poem is a task-specific process, creative rather than interpretive. The act of reading it, after it has been finished engages a process which is interpretive rather than constructive and it is quite plausible that the writer should feel somehow freed from the work when reading it as a complete, achieved, piece. The possibility of acting as one's own critic when reading and revising a text is another instance which may be related. The consequences of stable texts are discussed further in Chapter 12.

8.5   Symbol systems have objective properties

The combination of realism with an understanding of the universe of texts as structured by the combinatorial properties of the binary system provides the basis for an account of mathematics and its privileged role in natural science. Binary notation is clearly a human invention. Another human invention of huge importance is the 'principle of position' as Dantzig (2005) describes it. I have been using the principle without describing it as a crucial literate invention. It is the principle by means of which indefinitely large numbers can be represented in a systematic way. Thinking just for the moment in terms of the more familiar decimal notation, ten different numbers can be represented by a single digit, 0,1,2,3,4,5,6,7,8 or 9. It now seems obvious to us because of the way we learn elementary arithmetic in school that larger numbers can be represented by using places for units, tens, hundreds, etc. This is 'positional numeration'. The number 999 means 900 + 90 + 9 because the rightmost position indicates units, the second from the right indicates tens, and the third from the right indicates hundreds. The value given to the digit in a particular position depends on the base of the number system, ten in the case of the decimal system, and two in the case of the binary system.

Positional numeration is so common and obvious to us now that we typically do not appreciate what a fundamental invention it was. Dantzig, reflecting on the limited nature of arithmetical achievement prior to its invention, suggests that it 'assumes the proportions of a world event' (p. 30). We have, then, two distinctly human inventions, binary notation and positional numeration. These, we may confidently assume, were the products of human minds whose subjectivity was much like our own, turbulent and subject to conflicting motivations. They give rise, however, or provide access to an objective realm which really is independent of that subjectivity. The simplest demonstration of this, and it is extraordinarily simple, comes from thinking about the properties of the patterns of marks with which we are already familiar. If one place holder or position is available, there are two possible marks, 0 or 1. If there are two positions, there are four possible patterns of marks, 00, 01, 10, and 11. This is an objective fact about the binary system and it is objectivity of this kind which lies at the heart of mathematical methods in science and elsewhere. It would, I think, be difficult to overstate its importance as the basis for the possibility of objectivity in science. Binary notation and positional numeration are both human inventions but the system of patterns which results from putting them together has completely objective characteristics. The appreciation of the fact is ontologically subjective but epistemically objective.

All sorts of further objective consequences flow from the simple facts just described. If we have three positions then there are eight possible patterns to fill them: 000, 001, 010, 011, 100, 101, 110, and 111. These sets of possibilities can be described as 2 raised to the power of the number of positions. The numbers are completely objective properties of the positional system of binary numeration. It doesn't matter what you or I think about them or how emotionally involved or separate from them we are, they remain objective truths about the system. They have practical applications. If you want a computer memory of a particular size you may specify it in terms of megabytes or gigabytes, or even these days, in terabytes. Each of these words has a unique, objective interpretation in terms of the binary system. Two more ideas which have already been used in the book also stem from positional numeration.

First, consider the fact that any binary sequence can be transformed by changing 0s to 1s and vice versa. This operation, encountered in Chapter 7 is known as complementation. Every sequence of binary digits, no matter how long, has a unique complement which is arrived at by changing 0 to 1 and 1 to 0 as described. The complement of a given sequence is an objective relation between sequences. Complementation has significant practical applications in computer arithmetic. It leads to the design of hardware in which calculations can be made much more quickly than would otherwise be possible.

Second, consider a binary sequence of a given length, taking eight as an example. Suppose each digit is selected by a random procedure, for example by tossing a fair coin (cf. Chapter 2.8.3). What is the probability of ending up with a given sequence, for example 00110100? It's clear that there is one chance in two of getting 0 in the first position, one chance in two of getting 0 in the second position, one chance in two of getting 1 in the third position, and so on. How are these chances to be combined? Well, since each choice is, by definition, independent of the others, either of the two possibilities for the first choice could be combined with either of the two possibilities for the second choice. So there must be four possibilities i.e., $2 \times 2 = 4$ for the outcome of the first two choices. Since only one of these can be realized there must be one chance in four that we will arrive at a given combination of two binary digits, i.e., the probability is $1/(2 \times 2) = 1/4$ or 0.25. The logic extends to eight choices and we find that there is a probability of $1/(2 \times 2 \times 2 \times 2 \times 2 \times 2 \times 2 \times 2) = 0.00390625$ of getting a particular binary sequence eight digits long when each digit is chosen independently and at random. It also becomes apparent, on reflection, that the ideas discussed are related to each other. The operation of complementation and the concept of probability are both derived from the same basic combinatorial possibilities which flow from arranging binary digits in positional sequences. It took human ingenuity and creativity to discover these different properties of the system which is very rich in consequences. They were not all discovered at the same time and they were not equally obvious. Thus there is a clear sense in which mathematical developments are products of human creative imagination but the discoveries thus made have completely objective properties which are independent of the minds of their discoverers as well as of everybody else. There are undoubtedly other equally interesting properties which have yet to be discovered despite the simplicity of the fundamental underlying structures. Kitcher (1984) has given an account of mathematical knowledge which recognises both its objectivity and its roots in the activities of human communities.

8.6   Mathematics underpins objective science

The application of the objective properties of mathematical systems to scientific questions about the nature of the external world is a hugely complex topic which goes well beyond my expertise, competence, and understanding. However, there are some elementary points which demonstrate that scientific objectivity is a real possibility. The ordinary decimal number system has objective properties whose investigation is part of pure mathematics. Extensions of the whole number system to include operations with rational fractions and complex numbers also have completely objective properties despite the fact that these extensions and notations to handle them were invented by human mathematicians. Complex numbers are particularly important because it turns out that they have fundamental applications in physics (Penrose, 2004). Geometry is a system which contains objective truths about the properties of lines, angles, and the abstract objects which can be constructed from them. The linear domain of geometry deals with constructions that can be built and analysed by the use of a straightedge alone; the circular domain deals with objects that can be constructed with compasses, and the classical domain comprises both the linear and the circular domains (Dantzig, 2005, pp. 229–30). Analysis of the properties of the abstract objects contained in the circular domain led to some startling discoveries, including the objective fact that there are numbers, pi being a primary example we have already considered, which cannot be expressed as rational fractions. These so called 'irrational' numbers are not subjective or illogical; the word 'irrational' in this context simply means that such a number cannot be expressed as a ratio of whole numbers. Irrational numbers have objective properties which can be discovered, some of which, like those of pi, have practical applications. The existence of such numbers was, in itself, a profound discovery which led to the exploration of the domain of real numbers and to the development of a whole range of concepts associated with mathematical infinity.

8.6.1   Euclidean geometry as a model of physical space

An early and profound scientific thought was that the objective properties of three-dimensional Euclidean geometry describe, perfectly, the nature of the physical space of the universe. The productivity of this thought is striking and it continues to have practical applications today in disciplines such as engineering, surveying, and cartography. The point was that if accurate measurements could be made of some characteristics of real objects such as lengths, heights, or volumes, other values such as areas and weights could be calculated from the measurements. Accurate measurements plus the objective truths of the system of geometrical inferences would provide accurate values for previously unknown quantities. Naturally the system is only as good as the measurements made and these can be faulty by accident or by design but in principle good measurements allow a degree of precision which is simply unavailable to guesswork and which result in objective truths about the physical systems being measured. Human failings can, of course, lessen the value of the work done but do not, in any sense, damage the principle.

It is a commonplace observation, sometimes made by those wishing to argue that science is just one knowledge system among many that the Euclidean hypothesis about the nature of physical space turned out to be incorrect. Perhaps the most extreme conclusion that has been said to follow from this is the claim that any description of the world is as good as any other and thus the most accurate stance one can take is one of complete relativism. The first thing to be said about this is that the Euclidean model works extremely well at the kinds of scales that have practical consequences for human life and technology. It is incorrect and leads to errors when the spatial scales involved are extremely large or extremely small, but the approximations it gives for many practical purposes are extraordinarily precise. The second point to make is that the only reason we now know the hypothesis to be false is because the objective characteristics of the mathematics involved plus the extremely accurate measurements that have been made led, as the methods became more sophisticated, to discrepancies between the results expected from theoretical calculations and those derived from experiment. What this shows is not that objectivity is impossible but that certainty is not something that can be claimed even for the most accurate theory available and the most careful measurements that can be made.

It is worth saying a little more about the nature of the systems of geometry involved. Classical geometry, as developed by Euclid, rests in part on something called the 'parallel postulate' an assumption about parallel lines which is less intuitive than the other principles underpinning the system. It turns out that consistent geometries can be constructed in which the truth of the parallel postulate is not assumed. These are called 'hyperbolic' geometries. Hyperbolic geometries, just like Euclidean geometry, have objective features which are independent of their human inventors. The real universe is probably best modelled by a hyperbolic geometry and it appears definitely to be the case with regard to the treatment of velocities: 'the space of *velocities*, according to modern relativity theory, is certainly a three-dimensional hyperbolic geometry... rather than the Euclidean one that would hold in the older Newtonian theory.' (Penrose, 2004, p. 48)

8.7   Literacy promotes objectivity in nonmathematical disciplines

The objectivity of mathematical systems stems from the nature of their elements and the combinatorial operations prescribed. Once these have been chosen, the characteristics of the resulting symbolic expressions are fixed. However, not all objective science is mathematical in character. It is, therefore, possible for those who wish to dispute the objectivity of science to focus on nonmathematical disciplines. Literacy is a source of objective techniques in these disciplines as well because durable records of experience can be made and shared. Such records arise not from the objective properties of the symbol system as in mathematics but from the objective properties of environments and personal experience.

When I walk from my house to Hampstead Heath, the pattern of streets and houses is the same from one day to the next and, with minor changes, from one year to the next. The same is true of what I see as I walk round the heath and of the view over London from the summit of Parliament Hill. The contours of the ground, the layout of paths, the ponds and streams and the trees remain much the same from one visit to the next. Against this background of relative permanence there are regular changes. The grass grows and dies back, the trees shed their leaves in the autumn and produce fresh growth in the spring, the birds to be seen change as the seasons change, and the ponds are sometimes icy. The population of human visitors comes and goes in predictable ways. On a wet winter's day there will be joggers and dog walkers and a few hardy souls; on a hot summer's day, particularly at weekends or on public holidays, there will be teeming crowds with picnics and games. The Heath with its flora and fauna is independent of my perceptions of it. It was there long before I was born and it will be there after I have died. One of the reasons I know this is because I have read written accounts of events on the Heath that predate my birth.

I know the Heath well and can find my way around it by day or night but this does not mean that I can describe accurately the physical layout or the precise locations of the various places in the surrounding urban environment like Highgate or Gospel Oak. Maps are two-dimensional representations which complement and extend one's familiarity with an area. A map is an objective representation of aspects of the layout and cartography is an essentially literate discipline because it requires an external, symbolic medium (Barber, 2005). To represent on a map at a scale, say, of 1:50,000 is to make subjective choices about what to focus on, but the subjectivity has limits or the resulting object would not count as a map. A scale map shrinks the large so as to make relative locations comprehensible at a glance. A consequence of the shrinkage is that small objects are no longer visible but the choice of which objects to represent is not random. At a given scale there is a minimal unit of size such that objects smaller than the scale unit will not be represented. The concept of scaling deserves careful attention. Scale models were made before literacy was invented, particularly figurines and other representations of animals and humans, not to mention cave paintings. These artefacts demonstrate the perception of spatial relations which lies at the heart of scaling but not the abstraction of the idea of representation at a particular scale. To derive the concept of representation at a given scale there is a need for examples. It is, therefore, to be expected that later cartographic techniques will extend and improve upon earlier ones.

The contour is an interesting example. A contour is a line which joins points of equal value. On many maps, contours are used to represent areas of land at equal heights above sea level. The contour has been used on maps since the eighteenth century. A contour map is an approximation for at least two reasons; the elevations of areas between the lines are not mapped and the lines themselves are formed by interpolation between points which have been surveyed. Interpolations have a degree of subjectivity and that produced by one cartographer may differ from that produced by another. The inescapable presence of subjectivity does not compromise the concept of objectivity in maps. It does not mean that any map of a terrain is as good as any other. It does imply that one map may be more accurate than another. The concept of accuracy of mapping itself requires that there be something independent of the map against which it can be compared. If there were no objective facts of the matter it would not be possible to say that one map is more accurate than another. Any serious map user knows that maps do differ in their accuracy.

Another literate technique which helps to create an objective record of events on the Heath is the use of a field notebook to record sightings of birds and other creatures. Unaided memory is a fallible thing but with a written record, even if it contains mistakes, an understanding can gradually be built up of the species to be seen and the times of year when they are found. If observers pool their records, a more comprehensive picture can be constructed. With respect to birds, for example, the systematic recording of species makes it possible to see if there have been marked changes over time. Systematic reports from different parts of the country can be collated to provide a national view of bird life and ecology. Naturally such a picture is not perfect. There are mistakes and omissions, there may be some deliberately fraudulent records, and observation is not always complete. However, it is important, theoretically to distinguish relative accuracy from subjectivity. The presence of subjective factors does not mean that a degree of objectivity cannot be achieved. Most observers are honest and wish to make accurate records.

8.8   Literacy transforms the social ecology

Thus far in this chapter I have focused on the micro-ecology of literacy at the level of the individual. Analytical separation of the functional core from the surrounding institutions is not intended to suggest that literate individuals can, in practice, be separated from the society and circumstances in which they find themselves. The major thrust of the substantial body of work devoted to socio-cultural analysis of literacy makes it clear that actual literacy practices, as opposed to the theoretical possibilities of literacy, depend on a wide range of factors such as economic and social status, ethnicity, and gender. Before discussing any of these it is appropriate to say a little about physical infrastructure and institutions.

For theoretical purposes it is interesting and important to be able to discuss the infinite range of possible texts but the idea of an infinite library is an abstract conception. The power of literacy stems from the fact that it is based on real, symbolic records which constitute a form of external memory supplementing the unaided human memory which is limited, both physically and psychologically. The important point about an external symbolic record is not that it should be permanent but that it should be sufficiently lasting to serve its purpose. This may be achieved in a matter of minutes or seconds, as when one jots down a number for immediate use, or it may be that the record is intended to be permanent. Permanence, if required, can generally be assured by making multiple copies and renewing them as necessary. Fortunately for scholarship concerning the earliest texts, in the Middle East they were inscribed on clay tablets rather than written on paper and thus there are survivors from the dawn of literacy. Robson (2009) provides a concise introduction to the world of clay tablet books.

It may seem trite and obvious to point out that libraries and archives are the principal stores of symbolic records but they are not simply warehouses or stockpiles, although collection is an important and significant function. More important is the fact that libraries and archives are central to the systematisation and classification of literate works. Our ways of understanding are derived in part from the nature of the subject matter that is explored but they are also derived from the social institutions which we develop to aid classification and analysis. The United States Library of Congress, for example, is responsible for a widely used classification system which determines textual relations by subject matter. Judgements of the importance of different kinds of material are also explicitly or implicitly made by decisions about collections policies and these can have substantial effects on the literate resources of societies. Although the universe of texts is limitless in principle, in practice even the largest collections have active policies concerning what is retained and what is discarded. Explicit collections of the everyday writings of ordinary people, for example, are rarely made, whereas the writings of academic and other elites are more likely to be kept. The Mass Observation Archive in Britain is an interesting exception. Sheridan, Street, and Bloome (2000) describe the project from the standpoint of literacy studies.

The internet is changing fundamentally the range of possible interactions between individuals and texts. Prior to the development of the internet, an individual who wished to have access to texts had to go to a library or to buy or borrow the materials they wished to read. The infrastructure constraints placed barriers in the way of many potential users. Good libraries are not universally available and many people had insufficient purchasing power to buy books for themselves. Infrastructure costs remain in place now, of course, but the expenses involved in acquiring a computer or electronic book reader and access to the internet are rapidly falling in many parts of the world. Once a user has the physical means of access, internet resources make enormous collections of material freely available on a scale previously unimagined. Publishing models are changing as the opportunities for widespread dissemination of texts become more apparent. Costs are still a barrier in many domains but from the early days of the net there have been ventures such as Project Gutenberg (http://www.gutenberg.org/wiki/Main_Page) which are making large collections of texts freely available. Equally important is the drive to achieve uniform standards for the presentation of digital documents. TEI, the Text Encoding Initiative, (http://www.tei-c.org/index.xml) is a non-profit organisation which has developed and maintained guidelines for the representation of texts in digital form since 1994. Standardisation is of both theoretical and practical significance. The internet and World Wide Web are discussed further in Chapter 9.

The extent to which the invention of the printing press was responsible for the development of mass literacy has been a matter for debate but there is no doubt that multiple copies of texts have consequences for social communication. Christian missionaries, for example, have been responsible for the dissemination of huge numbers of copies of the Bible worldwide in a vast number of languages in pursuit of the goal of mass conversion. Organisations like the Gideons (http://www.gideons.org/) continue this project both online and in print, and political leaders, including Mao and Gaddafi, have had their thoughts printed and distributed throughout the populations they govern. The imposition of doctrines, both political and religious, and the suppression of creativity and dissent are facilitated by multiple copies of texts as much as are individual liberation and the freedom to think for oneself. Standardized curricula in schools may likewise have both stimulating and deadening effects. Very few texts are copied on the scale of works like the Bible and it is important to ask why a vanishingly small proportion of the universe of possible books is privileged in this way. Whose interests do they represent? How are those interests maintained?

A simple answer to these questions is that the interests of the powerful and the energetic are represented and they are maintained by control over and dissemination of resources. These issues are much more readily integrated with a Darwinian perspective than might initially appear. Darwinian thinking, as described in Chapters 5 and 6, focuses on scarcity, competition, cooperation, conflict, and sex differences as important mediators of social structure. Darwinians will readily understand the following:

> [B]ecause material resources are always limited, discourse communities produce and struggle over cultural tools, resources, and identities (both within and across communities) that provide them access to Discourses and thus, to the material goods. Some participants in discourse communities may have better access to or control of tools, resources, and identities necessary for full participation and control of Discourses and material goods. This access or control is not only an artifact of expertise (newcomer versus oldtimer), but also of qualities of difference such as race, gender, sexual orientation, or economic status, depending on what aspects of difference matter most or are most marginalized in a given discourse community.
>
> If one accepts that learning is always situated within discourse communities or is about gaining access to communities, as well as that discourse communities struggle over access to resources and that people within discourses (sic) communities are not always viewed or treated equally, one must then acknowledge that learning is shaped by and mired in power relations. (Moje and Lewis, 2007, p. 17)

The book from which this quotation was taken does not refer to Darwin, biology, or evolution in its index, nor have I found any mentions in the text. However, although Darwinians tend not to talk about discourse communities, referring rather to in-groups and out-groups, the issues discussed are familiar. If we substitute 'statuses' for 'Discourses' and 'groups' for 'discourse communities' the quoted passage could easily have been written by a Darwinian for the simple reason that the phenomena of human interactions are essentially the same regardless of the vocabulary in which we choose to describe them. Where Darwinian thinking scores is in the comprehensiveness of its explanatory power. Taking the reality of evolution as a starting point for the study of literacy does not commit us to genetic or biological determinism. It does not abolish human freedom or responsibility. It does, though, suggest that human reasoning has particular propensities and biases. The list of human universals in Chapter 3 includes the fact that the UP overestimate the objectivity of their thinking. Brown reports that 'it is particularly unobjective when they compare their in-group with out-groups' (Brown, 1991, p. 134). However, at least partly, and perhaps largely as a result of the invention of literacy, we have begun to understand the evolutionary sources of some of the less desirable aspects of our human nature. It is perhaps no accident that one of the most interesting books I have encountered which discusses the nature of evolved rationality (Stanovich, 2004) is by a distinguished scholar of reading.

The task of understanding the social institutions and practices surrounding literacy from a Darwinian point of view is not a focus of contemporary literacy theory but I hope that the perspective presented in this book will persuade readers of its potential. Its particular value, I believe, is that it opens up a way to achieve much stronger integration between social and cognitive factors in the study of literacy than is currently evident. Contemporary academic publications about literacy continue to manifest the assumption that social and cognitive factors, although related, can be separated for investigative and analytical purposes. The simple use of the two terms 'social' and 'cognitive' makes the point forcefully. It is almost as though there is an assumption that cognitive factors operate within the skin of the individual and that social factors operate in the wider environment. I am aware that the distinction between functional core and surrounding institutions that I make in this book could be thought to perpetuate such a division but that is not what is intended. The point about contemporary Darwinian understanding of humans which bears on this issue is that a fundamental distinction between social and cognitive factors is simply not tenable because management of social life is a plausible explanation for the evolution of the intellect in humans. The human capacity for culture is the primary demonstration of this point. Human minds are tuned to social life but it is still possible to make a fundamental distinction between minds and texts. It is this distinction whose importance is minimised in social practice theorising about literacy.

Because the elements of the functional core, texts, and individual minds, are separated from the surrounding institutions for analytical purposes in the theory proposed here, it actually becomes easier to see how important those institutions are and how far reaching their effects can be. If we make social institutions and practices constitutive of literacy then it becomes difficult to make cross-situational comparisons of a given text, because what constitutes a text is, in part, the institutions within which it is embedded. Consider, for example, some of the different institutional settings within which the Christian Bible has been used. In some settings the Bible is considered to be the revealed word of God and may be treated as the literal truth. In other settings, such as university departments of theology or biblical studies, the text may be treated with rather more caution, still considered as divinely inspired, but not necessarily as literally true. In still other settings, the Bible may be treated as a set of stories, arising from the human tendency to seek transcendental explanations. The text in all these cases is broadly the same but the institutions are very different and the social practices associated with them are different. The text may be the subject of uncritical veneration in one context, of detailed historical exegesis in another. It may be treated as an object of scorn and derision elsewhere. What changes from situation to situation is not the meaning of literacy itself but the goals and purposes of the literate agents involved.

8.9   Summary

Literacy is the means by which a species of hyper-social primate, *Homo sapiens*, has begun to achieve a scientific understanding of the world and the place of humanity in nature. Literacy provides finite minds, evolved to live complex social lives, with access to a potentially infinite universe of texts. A single mind may, in principle, have an indefinitely complex interaction with a single text. Fully literate minds have symbolic processing capabilities which, in theory, infinitely surpass those of minds without them. Literate capacities require surrounding institutions for their realization. If the institutions provide appropriate support then individuals can flourish as unfettered literate agents. Unfortunately, in many parts of the world for many reasons, adequate support is not available. The withholding of support is best understood as a consequence of the Darwinian nature of literate creatures. Darwinian analysis, far from being deterministic, suggests that humans respond flexibly to their physical and social environments. The infinite capacities of literate processing can be made available universally if we can find ways to build institutions which promote our pro-social rather than our selfish instincts.

Chapter 9

Literacy in the Age of Computers and the Internet

Many twenty-first century studies of literacy emphasise the transformational impact of computers and the internet on literacy (Kress, 2003; Knobel and Lankshear, 2007; Coiro, Knobel, Lankshear and Leu, 2008; Sheridan and Rowsell, 2010; Dalton, Proctor, Uccelli, Mo and Snow, 2011; Zammit, 2011). There is no doubt about the impact that digital technology is having. Young people, at least in developed countries, are growing up in an age where instant access to the nternet via computers, smartphones, and other devices is an everyday phenomenon. Digital technology is augmenting literacy practices partly by the ease with which different modalities can be deployed together (text, images, and audio, for example) and partly by the variety of reading systems and formats through which digital media are available. Developing adequate theory to understand these ongoing transformations is a challenging task. In this chapter, I use the theoretical framework of earlier chapters to explore some of the remarkable changes that have been initiated by the invention of computers and the internet. An important point I wish to emphasise is that although computers and the internet do indeed change the external symbol systems with which literate humans interact, they do not change human nature. We should not, therefore, expect too much from the new technological opportunities. The idea, for example, that they will help to decrease the social and economic inequalities that are manifest across the world rests on hope rather than on solid evidence.

9.1 Computers and the fundamental syntax of literacy

In Chapters 2 and 7 I have referred to the binary alphabet as the basic alphabet, one in which all other alphabets can be represented. The digital computer has transformed literacy theory and practice because it gives us access to this fundamental syntactic system in a practical, flexible way for the first time ever. We could say that literacy has finally come of age and is fully mature as a result of the invention of the computer. The computer enables us to transcend many of the limitations of traditional symbol systems as basic syntactic vehicles for literacy. It enables us to use binary representations of texts for practical as well as theoretical purposes. For almost all of its 5,000-year history, literacy has existed in one or another specialised representational form. Different symbol systems have been used to represent words, numbers, images, and sounds. Theoretically, all of these symbol systems can be translated into the binary system but, until the dawn of the computer age, the binary system was just a theoretical possibility and a somewhat exotic one at that. The development of computers and the internet has led to the construction of cyberspace. Cyberspace is the electronic medium in which computer mediated communication takes place. The concept of cyberspace is a way of thinking about the information content of electronic communication rather than about the hardware which supports it. The fundamental syntax of literacy has become a reality in cyberspace which contains a tiny but growing fraction of the universe of binary texts.

Theory and technology converge in the computer in ways which are of pivotal importance for literacy. The impact of the computer will be at least as great as that of the printing press, probably greater. The computer is the ultimate writing system, the last word in flexibility and formal representational power. It exploits what was called the syntactic unity of literacy in Chapter 8. Internally and in communication with others, computers manipulate and communicate strings of binary symbols. Texts, images and sounds are all represented internally in this way. The simplicity of binary representation is partly responsible for the speed with which digital computer technology has developed since it was invented in the 1940s and for the relative ease with which it is possible for computers all over the world to communicate with each other. Binary representation is the key to the multimodal functioning of computers, and hence can be seen in a sense to underpin the suggestion that computers have made traditional print literacy obsolete. That, I believe, is an overstatement. Computers and the internet extend the practical but not the theoretical power of the literate mind beyond what is possible with the traditional means of paper and pencil. New literacies are indeed new and much remains to be learned about their social and pedagogical consequences, but they can be understood with theoretical tools we already have at our disposal. An important need is to understand how to cope with the enormous mass of information that is generated and how to use computers to harvest useful material from the mass.

9.2   Computers are practical versions of universal Turing machines

The theory of Turing machines, introduced in Chapter 7, provides a bridge between literate humans and computer technology. The theory of Turing machines was developed specifically to give an account of all and only those syntactic processes that a literate human, working with paper and pencil, could carry out in constructing a text. The model would not have been deemed successful if it had included syntactic processes that could not be carried out by a human reader/writer or if it had failed to include syntactic processes that a human could carry out. The original work was done by the mathematician Alan Turing in a famous paper published in 1936, and it is widely agreed that the model does what it was intended to do. Other formal systems for studying symbol processing have been devised but they have all been found to converge on the same set of processes and most of the alternative formulations are intuitively harder to grasp than Turing's system. The Turing machine is, in other words, as good a syntactic account of fundamental literacy processes as we are likely to get and it is based on how people work with paper and pencil. It is for this reason, if for no other, that computers and the internet do not render traditional literacy obsolete.

Turing's paper was purely theoretical and it was designed, in part, to solve some challenging problems in the foundations of mathematics. However, because Turing developed his theory in terms of abstract machines rather than mathematical functions, it turned out to have practical implications for the design and understanding of real computers. Indeed, Turing himself was involved in early efforts to build computers in the 1940s and 1950s and parts of a machine inspired by his work are on display in the Science Museum in London. In effect, a digital computer is a practical version of a universal Turing machine. The core components of a digital computer are the central processor and the memory. The CPU is analogous to the finite automaton of a Turing machine and the memory of a computer is analogous to the tape of a Turing machine. Given the design history of the Turing machine there is also an analogy with literate humans. The CPU is analogous to the literate mind and the memory is analogous to a textual medium such as paper. We thus have a tripartite set of correspondences. Mind stands to text as finite automaton stands to tape and as CPU stands to computer memory. The CPU of a computer is a machine which carries out syntactic transformations of elements of binary texts stored in its memory. It works on larger chunks than the single symbols that Turing machines process but that is a practical, rather than a theoretical, difference.

One point of the comparison is to make clear that there is nothing magical about the nature of the fundamental operations of computers. They are doing the same sorts of things that literate humans do when they carry out instructions to generate binary texts such as the infinite texts 01010101 ... and 0010110111 ... examined in Chapter 7. The apparent magic comes in the speed with which computers carry out their fundamental operations and the extraordinary miniaturisation of their components. Both of these things are hugely significant for practical purposes. Speed makes almost instant communication possible and miniaturisation has allowed for the development of hand-held computing devices which have greater power than early computers which required whole buildings to house them.

Another point of the comparison is that it helps us to see clearly that meanings are still the exclusive domain of humans. Computers are hyper-fast syntactic processors and that is all. They do not do semantics. Any meaning that is found in an electronic text, image, or audio file results from the activities of the minds that engage with them. The lightning fast speeds of computer processes and the complexity of the programs that have been written sometimes give the illusion of understanding but at present that is what it is, an illusion. To say this is not to rule out the possibility of future computers that 'mean' what they say. However, while there are still huge gaps in our understanding of what makes life meaningful for us, it is premature to suggest that computers understand anything of what they do or mean anything by the processes that they carry out.

9.3   Stand alone computing

Let us now consider briefly the sorts of things that can be done with individual computers. This will serve to highlight the transformations wrought by the development of the internet and the World Wide Web. Historically computers were thought of as tools for doing numerical calculations that were too large and time consuming to be carried out by hand, even with the assistance of mechanical calculators. It gradually became apparent that they could also be used for data processing more generally and functions such as payrolls and corporate records were computerised. In the early years of the personal computer revolution, word processing, spreadsheets, and games became available on a large scale. From the standpoint of literacy the word processor was an obviously important development. It added text manipulation and revision to the legibility of the mechanical typewriter. Most of those who, like me, are old enough to have done a significant amount of writing prior to the availability of word processors will, I think, tend to see both advantages and disadvantages in word processing with the advantages generally outweighing the disadvantages. Easy revision and rearrangement of texts are key advantages for me, as is the increase in legibility. Revision, as we have seen, is a key theoretical aspect of literacy and the word processor makes it much easier in practice than it used to be. Perhaps there has been a loss of spontaneity and decisiveness in the construction of texts as a result. What one writes feels provisional until it appears frozen in print because it can always be fiddled with a bit more. If this is a disadvantage, for me at least it is a minor one. I was an early convert to the word processor, having been an enthusiastic user of the typewriter beforehand.

Another fundamental arena opened up by the invention of the computer is programming. A computer program is the symbolic specification of a task, usually with accompanying data. The program uses the data to accomplish its task which usually involves the production of more data. In terms of the universe of texts we can think of a computer program as a text which produces further text. According to the definition offered in Chapter 1, computers are not literate because they do not understand what they do, but computer programs can and do produce interesting and complex texts at extraordinary speeds. Because this is so we can think of computer programs as second order texts. From the standpoint of literacy theory computer programming should be of great interest but there seems to be relatively little direct linkage at present between the study of literacy and the study of computer science. That may change as the internet revolution continues apace. Facility with a programming language is an important skill, but anyone who interacts with a computer is providing data for a program and thus potentially changing the behaviour of that program.

Some far-seeing pioneers may have glimpsed the possibility of the digital future that is now becoming a reality, but for most computer users prior to the development of the internet, from the standpoint of literacy, the computer functioned as little more than an electronic version of the typewriter, very useful but hardly revolutionary. Even the concept of hypertext, which is one of the key aspects of communication over the internet, is of relatively limited significance in the context of a single computer.

9.4   The internet revolution

The impact of the internet has been revolutionary in large part because of the social nature of the human animal. Rapid dissemination and sharing of materials through cyberspace are hallmarks of the internet era. Communication between computers was not, originally, an important consideration. Indeed, one of the principles of early computer design was quite specifically to make a computation independent of communication with the external world by equipping machines with memories large enough to store everything needed to carry out their tasks (Aspray and Burks, 1987, Ch. 1). In this way the speeds of electronic media could be exploited to the full. The internet era has changed this picture fundamentally, largely because communication between, as well as within, computers is now possible at electronic speeds. Networking is among the most important features of computer design, and computers have become adjuncts to social life. The extremely rapid spread of social networking sites is an indication of the societal significance of networked computers. To understand the range of possibilities it is helpful to know some basic things about the organisation of the internet and the services such as the World Wide Web which run on it. The terms 'internet' and 'World Wide Web' are sometimes used as synonyms but they should be distinguished. The internet provides the hardware via which the software of the Web is disseminated. The distinction is a bit like that between a book and its contents. It is particularly apt if we think in terms of e-book readers. A device such as the Kindle provides the hardware which makes the text of a book available. So it is with the internet and Web. The internet is a system of interconnected computer networks, located all around the world. The World Wide Web is a set of documents, images, sound files, etc., which are stored on the networked computers of the internet and accessed by users. These documents, images, and other files constitute cyberspace, the things that we find when we go online. A computer which provides information is known as a server and one which uses it is a client.

From the perspective of literacy, it is the organisation of the World Wide Web which is of particular interest. In keeping with the approach taken in this book, we can think of the WWW in terms of the universe of texts. The materials that are available on the Web are elements of the universe of texts. However, whereas up to now we have mainly considered individual texts in isolation, the Web provides powerful tools for linking them and for using one text to gain access to others. The key concept that we need to relate the universe of texts to the WWW is the concept of hypertext.

Hypertext exploits the possibility of using binary texts both as information and as addresses (See section 2.8.6). Hypertext is text displayed on a computer or other electronic device which includes usable references to other texts. These references are hyperlinks. An example is a link to the Wikipedia article about hypertext which can be found on the Web at http://en.wikipedia.org/wiki/Hypertext. An electronic version of this book with hyperlinks would enable the reader to access the Wikipedia article immediately, and to return to the text of the book later. The Wikipedia article itself contains further links to other related texts. Links offer ways of reading text which depart from the linear process of starting at the beginning and working through to the end, which is assumed to be the normal way in which printed texts are read. The syntactic principle, which emphasises the common framework of binary representation underlying all literate production in principle and all electronic literacy in practice as well, helps to explain the logical extension from hypertext to hypermedia. Hypermedia exploits representations of binary texts such as images, videos, and sounds. Thus a 'reading' of an electronic text with hyperlinks may involve watching video and listening to audio as well as traditional absorption of print. The extraordinary achievement of Tim Berners-Lee, who invented the Web, has been to make flexible, practical access to multiple representations of large numbers of elements of the universe of binary texts a real possibility for an increasing proportion of the global population. The growth of interest in, and consumption of, hypermedia may be one of the most salient phenomena of literacy in the twenty-first century. The extension of syntactic possibilities beyond traditional print literacy enabled by hypermedia is matched by an extension of semantic possibilities. Considerable attention has been paid to screen-based modes of presentation, to the nonlinear patterns of use of hypermedia and to its literary possibilities (Aarseth, 1997; Landow, 2006; Ensslin, 2007; Sheridan and Rowsell, 2010).

Hypermedia and multimodality extend the possibilities of traditional literacy but it is too early to say whether or not they will lead to a terminal decline in the use of more traditional forms. The opportunities they offer also have costs associated with them. The use of hyperlinks creates navigational challenges and the use of multiple modes may, if not well handled, lead to distraction rather than illumination. Research to understand the advantages and disadvantages of hypermedia in pedagogical environments is booming but is, as yet, still in its infancy and there is a shortage of well designed randomised trials to assess the claims made for and against hypermedia-based educational practices. In principle, the flexibility of computer-based literacies makes it possible to envisage a time when educational programs are designed specifically for individual students with substantial control exercised by those individuals, but this implies a better understanding of the needs of individuals than we have at present and a better understanding of the societal dynamics that are likely to accompany the burgeoning possibilities of the new literacies.

9.5   The added value of the internet

The fundamental theoretical proposition of this book is that literacy, construed primarily in traditional terms such as access to books and other durable printed materials, augments the powers of the non-literate mind. In Section 9.1 I have suggested that literacy has finally come of age because the computer makes it possible to use the binary universe of texts in a practical way. Access to the internet and the resources of the World Wide Web can be thought of as adding further value to the gains of traditional literacy. This, I think, is true in a huge variety of ways, and new ways of using the internet and the Web for literacy purposes are constantly being developed, so much so that even relatively recent texts seem obsolete and out of date. Donald Leu has suggested that literacy has become deictic, meaning by this that it is undergoing processes of continuous redefinition and development (Leu, 2000; Coiro, Knobel, Lankshear and Leu, 2008). If this is so, then much of what we currently think of as important may soon come to seem trivial and many important developments may be missed until they are almost upon us. One case which seems to demonstrate the point is the Facebook phenomenon. Facebook is a social networking site. It was started as recently as 2004 but by January 2011 had attracted more than 600 million users. Facebook is a very interesting instance of a 'new' literacy, but it has as yet attracted relatively little serious study from literacy theorists.

Because the possible developments in literacy are almost boundless, it would be imprudent as well as fruitless to try to survey them. Instead, I propose to consider two internet-related developments which are already well established but have attracted relatively little notice from theorists of literacy. Each of them relates in its own way to the task of achieving a better understanding of the functional core of the literate ecology, that is, a mind interacting with a text. The added value of the internet will, I believe, enlarge our vision of both.

9.5.1   Text mining

One of the key motivations for this book was the idea of a Turing machine, working through the eons, self-sufficiently generating an infinite text spun out of its finite set of functional states and the burgeoning symbol structure already created. The vision was, and is, an individualistic one, and in my view it is none the worse for that. It captures, for me at least, the focused dedication that has been needed over the centuries by the authors of abiding classics in all domains of intellectual inquiry. The vision is defective, however, in one crucial respect. A human who really behaved like a Turing machine would be a strange person indeed, reclusive and obsessive; whereas great authors in almost all domains have built on the cumulative efforts of those who went before them and have often had extensive networks of informants and access to well stocked libraries. Indeed it has been said that you cannot be a great writer unless you are also a great reader.

The status of the individual text in the internet era is subject to numerous challenges. The existence of hypertext challenges the idea that a text has a clear beginning, a clear end, and a clear sequential structure (Landow, 2006). The existence of hypermedia challenges the idea that print is the dominant mode of representation. Some theorists have suggested that these challenges undermine the authority of the single text as a locus of high-quality information.

Not all developments point in this direction, however, and one particularly intriguing aspect of the computer/internet revolution derives jointly from the vast mass of information available on the Web and from the specific capacities of computers. It underpins the possibility that authoritative texts can continue to be produced. It suggests that the internet can be used to produce order out of chaos rather than introducing chaos into the ordered world of libraries and academic disciplines as some cloistered academics may fear.

The scale of the universe of texts creates a problem. However assiduous a human reader may be, the proportion of texts that can be read in a lifetime is vanishingly small. This was true before the development of computers and the internet, but it has become more obvious now. However, the universe of texts in the electronic form in which it is now coming to exist is the natural terrain of computer programs which, as Turing explained, can be construed as syntactic analogues of human readers and writers. They don't understand what they do, but they can be structured to look out for complex patterns of all kinds and, given the connectedness of texts on the Web, they can be set to roam through that portion of the universe which currently exists in cyberspace, absorbing and systematising what they find there. Moreover, they are so fast at what they do that the scale of the universe of texts becomes less of a liability and more of an advantage. Imagine then a situation in which a program or Turing machine is generating a text, not simply from the resources of its own functional states but from patterns it finds in texts already out there in the universe. That is the domain of text mining and it contains endless possibilities. These are an important part of the value that the internet and the Web add to the traditional outputs of literacy.

In discussion of members of the universe of texts thus far, I have considered them principally in terms of their syntactic and structural properties. For example, it is a structural property that there are eight different binary texts of length three. Many other properties of binary texts have been discovered via mathematical investigation. The mathematical properties of symbol strings apply to the entire universe and are, therefore, very general in character. However, cyberspace now contains large numbers of texts which have been written by human authors and these have syntactic properties which encode the meanings of the texts. In the pre-computer era, the meanings of texts were compared, if at all, by individuals reading them, making notes and observing commonalities. The process was laborious and painstaking, and still is so for the large numbers of texts not available in cyberspace. For those which do exist in electronic form, text mining is becoming a real possibility, although the technology is still new and relatively undeveloped.

Text mining is a generic name for a class of syntactic processes by means of which computer programs compare electronic texts and extract patterns from them which express semantic properties. The enormous scale of the data in cyberspace means that these patterns could not be observed without programs that sift data at electronic speeds. However, computer programs have no understanding and thus could not use the patterns or interpret them in practically useful ways. Text mining programs thus provide, as it were, electronic eyes and ears on patterns in cyberspace which can then be understood by human observers. This is a fundamental new departure in the possibilities for literate exploration. It represents a genuine collaboration between humans and programs or, if a different metaphor is preferred, text mining programs constitute a totally new form of electronic tool for large-scale literate surveys of cyberspace. Text mining tools make it possible for new relationships between bodies of knowledge to be discovered and for greater coverage of complex domains to be achieved. Text mining has been deployed in a range of disciplines, not just in the natural sciences but also in the humanities and social sciences (Dozier et al., 2003; Plaisant et al., 2006; Dey and Haque, 2008; Gelernter and Lesk, 2009; Hoblitzell et al., 2010).

An example which demonstrates the power of text mining for discovering new relationships is reported by Swanson and Smalheiser (1997). Their starting point was the poor communication that often exists between domains of expertise. In order to become an expert in a given domain it is necessary to concentrate on research in that domain. This inevitably implies a relative narrowness of focus. The narrow focus carries with it the risk that information developed in one domain may be of relevance to another domain without specialists in either domain knowing that this is the case. A particular example discussed by Swanson and Smalheiser is the link between migraine and magnesium deficiency which is now known to exist as a result of text mining. Prior to the discovery of the link, there was an extensive literature on migraine and a similarly extensive literature on magnesium deficiency. Experts in migraine were typically not knowledgeable about the effects of magnesium deficiency and vice versa. However, detailed and systematic searching of the two literatures using text mining techniques discovered common factors. For example, migraine specialists knew that spreading depression in the cortex, a particular form of brain activation, was associated with migraine attacks. Quite separately, experts in magnesium deficiency knew that it could inhibit spreading depression in the cortex. The obvious inference, that magnesium and migraine might be linked, was unknown until the linkage was discovered and explored for its possible therapeutic potential.

A more recent example, reported by Michel et al. (2011), has investigated cultural trends using a digitised collection of more than 5 million books. The corpus contains books in seven languages, the oldest of them dating from the 1500s. Computers are essential to analyse collections of this size:

> The corpus cannot be read by humans. If you tried to read only English-language entries from the year 2000 alone, at the reasonable pace of 200 words/min, without interruptions for food or sleep, it would take 80 years. The sequence of letters is 1000 times longer than the human genome: If you wrote it out in a straight line, it would reach to the Moon and back 10 times over.
>
> (Michel et al., 2011, p. 176)

All sorts of interesting results have emerged from the analysis. The evolution of grammar can be seen in the changing frequencies with which different word forms appear. Collective memory for past events appears to be declining faster than it used to. Perhaps this has something to do with the increased pace and media-saturated nature of daily life. Fame can be measured by tracking the number of times specific names occur. It appears that fame now comes earlier in life than it used to but that it is also more transitory. Like other aspects of collective memory, the famous are forgotten more quickly than used to be the case. It has also proven possible to track the effects of censorship and suppression in different countries at different times, again using frequency of mention as the basic datum. The suppression of Jewish writers and artists in Nazi Germany can be seen through the lower citation rates for them and their works that are found in books published in Germany as opposed to those published elsewhere.

9.5.2   Mapping the human genome

The second example of how the use of cyberspace augments existing literacy practices is the mapping of the human genome and the ongoing efforts to understand the complex structure that underpins human life and experience. It is a particularly apt example given the evolutionary orientation of this book. It shows how the extraordinarily powerful tools of digital literacy have enabled the genomics research community to turn an investigative spotlight on the building blocks of human nature. It demonstrates the search and pattern recognition powers of digital technology and also the enormous gains to be had from collaboration and free sharing of information. McElheny (2010, p. xiii) says that 'work on genomes has grown more heavily computational and more intricately collaborative than ever before in the history of biological and medical research.' Thus we can see both the technical and social gains of digital literacy. Without computers the genome could not have been sequenced and without the information sharing and collaboration made possible by the internet it would be impossible to understand what the sequence means. Skills and social practices are both exhibited in the processes that led to the construction of the text of the human genome.

The fundamental information to build a human being is stored in the genome. The genome is not a text in the ordinary sense of the word; it is a set of macromolecules of DNA. However, we can think of it as a book, a version of the book of life perhaps, because it can be represented as a linear sequence of symbols. The syntax of the book has been discovered as a result of the Human Genome Project. This has established the basic text of the genome. A full copy is contained in every cell of the human body except for the gametes, sperm in males and ova in females. The genome is far too small to be read by the naked eye but the scale of it can be understood by visiting the Wellcome Collection in London, which has a printout of the human genome sequence, an actual copy of the book of life. The printout consists of 120 substantial volumes each with about a thousand pages of text recording, in tiny print, the sequences of the 22 autosomal chromosomes and the X and Y sex chromosomes of the human genome. The genome alphabet has only four letters, A, C, G, and T which represent the bases Adenine, Cytosine, Guanine, and Thymine. To the untrained eye, the human genome sequence appears random; there is no obvious punctuation just page after page, volume after volume, of sequences of letters, some 3.2 billions in total. Most of the text is in lower case but occasionally there are sequences in capital letters. These sequences, some 2 per cent of the total, indicate those parts of the genome which are known to code for proteins. The non-coding parts of the genome are sometimes referred to in a rather disparaging way as 'junk DNA' but this now seems premature as possible functions are being suggested (Kapranov et al., 2007; Gingeras, 2009).

The text of the human genome is without doubt the most important literate product of the twenty-first century so far. The printed version in the Wellcome Collection is mainly of symbolic value but electronic versions of the text have profound practical significance in a wide range of domains. Medical science, evolutionary science, and biology have seen the most immediate effects, but we can expect that psychology, and social science more generally, will in due course be transformed by better understanding of genes and genomes. Genetic influences on literacy are starting to be understood (Bishop, Adams and Norbury 2004; Byrne et al., 2008) but here I want to consider something different. The process of sequencing made it possible, for the first time, to construct textual representations of the human genome. These texts have powerful consequences for the development of biological science in particular but also illustrate the power of textual representations more generally.

The first important point is that textual representations of the genome provide a durable basis for comparison and study. Prior to the sequencing of the whole genome, scientists had nothing but short excerpts to work with. Trying to understand these excerpts was rather like trying to understand single paragraphs from a long book. A paragraph can make sense locally, but without knowledge of the rest of the book or where the paragraph is located it is impossible to understand its implications for the wider context. One of the many challenges faced by the teams which sequenced the genome was that of putting together the whole book from a huge number of paragraphs, many of which had significant similarities. Two different teams were involved in a competitive effort to be first with a whole text and the ensuing race got the job done more quickly than had initially been expected. Each team announced the completion of its draft at the same time in June 2000, and papers describing their work were published the following year (Venter et al., 2001; Lander et al., 2001).

The two initial versions of the genome were deservedly referred to as drafts. Both were known to be incomplete and inaccurate in some ways. However, the simple fact that drafts were available and could be studied and corrected by the wider community quickly led to an improved version which was both more complete and more accurate (Collins et al., 2004). Since 2004, significant further improvements to the accuracy of genome sequencing have been achieved. These improvements provide an illustration of the power of revision, one of the key possibilities inherent in literacy, in both traditional and digital forms. The accuracy of genomic texts is important for a number of reasons. Perhaps the most important reason is the need to distinguish between sequence differences that arise from individual variation and those that arise from inaccurate determination. The human genome is almost identical across individuals. At the level of single nucleotides, humans differ on average by about 0.1 per cent or about 1 in

1,000 locations (Tishkoff and Kidd, 2004). However, since the genome is so big, even a 0.1 per cent difference amounts to about 3,000,000 differences in sum between individuals. Accurate determination of these differences is informative, among other things, about susceptibility to illnesses and other health-related factors. More accurate textual representations of genomes also mean that patterns of similarity and difference among human genomes and between humans and other creatures can be studied.

Successful sequencing of genomes is the beginning, rather than the end, of the process of understanding them. Genomes carry within them a record of the evolutionary history of their species and they also provide the basis for understanding the development and functioning of individuals. Genomic texts are thus an inestimably valuable resource for the human community. In the 10 years since the first genome sequences were achieved, a vast amount of information has been gathered and much of it is freely available on the internet. One example is the Ensembl genome browser, http://www.ensembl.org/index.html, a joint enterprise between the European Bioinformatics Institute and the Wellcome Trust Sanger Institute. The browser supports an international community of researchers and students in ways that could only have been dreamed about in the pre-internet era. The sequencing of the genome and the subsequent developments in representing it accurately have led to a better appreciation of the complexity of living things and the challenges of understanding them.

9.6 Summary

Computers and the internet have made access to the binary universe of texts a reality with the invention of cyberspace. Projects of enormous complexity have been made possible and information sharing on an unprecedented scale has started to occur. Digital literacy is a transformational force, but it does not imply that traditional literacy is now obsolete. There is still a need for durable, authoritative texts as the basis for further development. Many of these texts may be kept primarily in electronic form, but durability and accuracy are still fundamental characteristics. Indeed, the complexity of the processes enabled by digital forms of literacy is likely to have increased, rather than decreased, the value of durability and accuracy. One of the most striking products of digital literacy is the textual representation of the sequence of the human genome. This text makes manifest the structural foundations of human life. If a better understanding of the human condition is one of the principal goals of literacy it is clear that the text of the genome offers powerful opportunities for pursuing that goal. Similar progress in other domains of knowledge and enquiry will also be facilitated by computers and the internet.

Chapter 10

Grounding the Literacy Episteme

Up to this point, most of the book has been devoted to setting out the background material needed for the theoretical framework outlined in Chapter 8, although I have tried to indicate some points of contact with existing literature. This chapter addresses some of the ideas of the existing literature more directly and suggests how the approach proposed here might make contact with them. The starting point is a wide ranging paper by Brockmeier and Olson (2009) which discusses the concept of the literacy episteme.

10.1   The literacy episteme

An episteme is defined as 'the cultural order of ideas and concepts that define, at a given moment in history, what knowledge is and how we gain and transmit it' (p. 6). Brockmeier and Olson follow Foucault, from whom the notion of the literacy episteme is derived, in describing it as an historical a priori. The juxtaposition of 'historical' and 'a priori' is striking and somewhat disturbing because the term 'a priori' normally denotes a form of justification or grounding which is taken to be independent of experience and thus stands outside history. Foucault offers a direct challenge to this view. The aim of his enquiry is

> to rediscover on what basis knowledge and theory became possible; within what space of order knowledge was constituted; on the basis of what historical *a priori*, and in the element of what positivity, ideas could appear, sciences be established, experience be reflected in philosophies, rationalities be formed, only, perhaps to dissolve and vanish soon afterwards. (Foucault, 2002, p. xxiii)

Brockmeier and Olson suggest that understanding literacy as an historically conditioned episteme brings two important ideas to the fore: first, that writing is 'a peculiar form of language and not simply a secondary representation of speech' (p. 8); and second, that particular forms of written language

179

are historical, contingent, and subject to change. Thus answers to the question 'What is literacy?' will depend on the thinking of the specific historical period within which the question is posed. As a means to illustrate the changing conceptions of literacy over time and to document its emergence as a domain of study in its own right, the literacy episteme is a valuable concept but its fundamental relativism, including the idea inherited from Foucault that sciences can form, dissolve, and vanish, fits poorly with the ideas explored in this book.

10.2   Against relativism

Culturally relative discourse is obviously important, but I propose that we also need to recognise deeper realities in a way that contradicts Foucault. The point bears on the possible scope of social constructions. These appear, in Foucault and elsewhere, to be more powerfully constitutive of reality than I think we should accept for the sorts of reasons discussed in Chapter 2. Social construction of institutions in the context of realism is plausible, social construction as constitutive of physical reality is not. For there to be thought at all, there has to be a creature that thinks. It may be that conscious thought is needed for a creature to know that it thinks, and it may be that conscious thinking is largely framed by the overarching cultural discourse, but those are epistemological concerns. Epistemology presupposes a something which can know as well as a something which can be known. These presuppositions are matters for ontology, the study of what there is. Ontology is prior to epistemology.

The computational and evolutionary concepts proposed in the book as groundings for the study of literacy are consistent with a wide range of approaches but also build on lasting foundations. Brockmeier and Olson suggest that we need the concept of the literacy episteme because it is only within such a cultural, historical trajectory that the wide range of activities considered as literacy can 'take on an epistemic form and become subjects of thought and theoretical curiosity as well as public attention' (p. 5). I think the implied relativism is too high a price to pay and that the structure proposed in this book has the requisite scope. Some literacy theorists may worry that grounding the study of literacy in logic and biology leads inevitably to scientism and a reductionist approach to moral issues. If readers share this concern, I think it is misplaced.

Natural science tells us about the mechanisms of the world, both physical and biological, and literacy is one of the conditions of possibility for the flowering of natural science, but science does not, and cannot, tell us how to act. In the absence of a transcendental being or plan, there are fundamental choices to be made. How should humans behave? What actions should they take? Is there such a thing as an objectively good life? Scientific knowledge does not mandate particular forms of social action. It is incumbent on humans to create their own future. The institutions and concepts that we develop to manage this future may be based on the best science we have but that science cannot determine how we ought to act. It may, for example, be prudent to limit carbon emissions in order to minimise global warming, but science cannot dictate that we follow the prudent course. For literacy understood using the general theory described in this book, questions about human action are not resolved by the mechanisms of natural selection or the theorems of mathematical logic. There are solid foundations in these forms of knowledge for understanding the power of literacy but nothing follows specifically from them about how we should behave. The radical contingency of the moral domain is always a pressing issue.

10.3   Literacy scholarship in the 1960s

Brockmeier and Olson describe the emergence of the literacy episteme as a predominantly twentieth century phenomenon although they acknowledge, of course, the contributions of earlier writers going back to Plato and Aristotle. They suggest, however, that profound changes in the cultural matrix of ideas about literacy and social institutions relevant to literate practices became established in the 1960s. They single out four publications as having outstanding significance: Havelock's *Preface to Plato*; McLuhan's *The Gutenberg galaxy*; Levi-Strauss's *La Pensée Sauvage*, and Goody and Watt's *The Consequences of Literacy*. Brockmeier and Olson also refer to the work of Unesco and the emergence of concern for literacy as a global phenomenon and as an engine for economic and political change.

Among the issues brought into prominence in the 1960s were the relationship between orality and literacy, the impact of literacy on societal organisation, the possibility that writing creates a new psychological mentality, and the revolutionary nature of mass media and technologies of communication. The key figures in the emergence of the literacy episteme were mainly working in the humanities and social sciences but Brockmeier and Olson also cite the work of the biologist Ernst Mayr, the palaeontologist André Leroi-Gourhan, and the psychologist Lev Vygotsky whose book *Thought and Language* was published in English for the first time in 1962.

Brockmeier and Olson pay particular attention to the works of the economist Harold Innis and the philosopher Jacques Derrida. Including their work widens the time frame for the emergence of the literacy episteme to include the 1950s when Innis's two books were published and the late 1960s and early 1970s when Derrida's primary works on writing were published. Innis is credited with understanding the practical impact of literacy on economic, social, and political development. He proposed that more permanent media for writing, such as parchment, clay, and stone made the concept of time more salient, whereas less durable media such as papyrus and paper emphasised the concept of space with correlative effects on forms of social institutions. An emphasis on time was said to favour decentralisation and hierarchy, whereas an emphasis on space favoured centralisation and less hierarchical institutions. Derrida is credited with placing writing at the centre of philosophical concerns in a new way and for rescuing it from consistent neglect in the Western philosophical tradition. Derrida and Innis are taken to have a common interest in issues of power and violence within society and for bringing together the material and conceptual orders.

> Both scholars aim to fuse two orders that traditional academic discourse has always tried to keep apart: the order of material (i.e., political, economic, and social) interests and the order of thoughts and concepts. (Brockmeier and Olson, 2009, p. 13)

One of the compelling reasons for construing literacy in terms of Turing's theory of computation is that it also fuses the material and the conceptual in a model of the individual mind interacting with a text. It is this theoretical model that underlies the technology of digital computers which have, of course, been of huge significance for modern societal organisation. Turing's model is not directly concerned with natural language and thus also underscores the point that writing is not simply a secondary representation of speech.

10.3.1   Derrida and Turing

There are some striking parallels to be found between Derrida and Turing, evident commonalities of interest which I think have not been remarked on before and there is a scholarly exercise waiting to be done to understand and document them more fully. I shall give just one illustration here. In a substantial paper called *Typewriter Ribbon*, dealing among other things with the relations between human events and machines, Derrida makes the point that for something to be considered a human event it has to include consideration of its organic effects on bodies and their sensitivities. This he contrasts with the workings of a machine.

> The machine, on the contrary, is destined to repetition. It is destined, that is, to reproduce impassively, imperceptibly, without organ or organicity, received commands. In a state of anesthesia, it would obey or command a calculable program without affect or auto-affection, like an indifferent automaton. Its functioning, if not its production, would not need anyone. Moreover, it is difficult to conceive of a purely machinelike apparatus without inorganic matter. (Derrida, 2002, p. 72)

Derrida's starting point is thus the apparent incompatibility of thinking and machinery. Turing, in a speculative paper of 1948, republished in his collected works, which explores the possibility of constructing intelligent machinery, started from the contrary assumption of the compatibility between human minds and machinery but came to interestingly similar conclusions:

> All of this suggests that the cortex of the infant is an unorganized machine, which can be organized by suitable interfering training. The organizing might result in the modification of the machine into a universal machine or something like it. This would mean that the adult will obey orders given in appropriate language, even if they were very complicated; he would have no common sense, and would obey the most ridiculous orders unflinchingly. When all his orders had been fulfilled he would sink into a comatose state or perhaps obey some standing order, such as eating. Creatures not unlike this can really be found, but most people behave quite differently under many circumstances. However the resemblance to a universal machine is still very great, and suggests to us that the step from the unorganized infant to a universal machine is one which should be understood. When this has been mastered we shall be in a far better position to consider how the organizing process might have been modified to produce a more normal type of mind. (Turing, 1992, p. 120)

Contemporary cognitive neuroscience demonstrates that the mind of the infant is, in fact, highly organised, contrary to Turing's suggestion, but it is still a system which needs suitable 'organisation' or training if it is to become capable of meaningful interaction with external symbol systems (Blakemore and Frith, 2005; Geake, 2009).

Brockmeier and Olson suggest that somewhere 'between Innis and Derrida' the dam which had kept literacy back from widespread intellectual consideration was breached and numerous attempts to understand it were launched which explored the institutional realities within which literacy was produced as well as its technological effects. Issues of power came to the fore with a focus on 'the mega-institution of schooling' (p. 15) and wide recognition of the significance of institutional knowledge and power. The electronic media revolution, whose theory Turing played a significant part in creating, has also been a powerful force with far reaching effects that were first powerfully understood and documented by McLuhan (1962).

10.4   Autonomy and ideology revisited

Brockmeier and Olson end their survey of the literacy episteme with the conclusion that literacy can never again be ignored, although one might think that the construction of the literacy episteme as an historical a priori ought to lead to a more cautious conclusion. Literacy they say,

> has become a part of the discourse in all of the human sciences. It is not surprising that as the concept has been assimilated by various disciplines and social movements, the entire notion of literacy itself has changed. We can no longer simply compare the literate with the illiterate, the spoken with the written, the word with the text, the primitive with the civilized as some of the pioneers of the literacy episteme did. Literacy today is understood in many different cultural configurations. It has a place in countless social practices and activities, in institutional settings, and on political agendas as well as in many theoretical perspectives and empirical research paradigms. (Brockmeier and Olson, 2009, pp. 17–18)

Despite the breadth of this characterisation, studies across the spectrum of literacies continue to be divided by questions about the relations between skills and social practices and the extent to which literacy skills are context-free and independent of the ideologies of the societies in which they are learned and used. Brockmeier and Olson tentatively suggest that there are significant areas of literate skill which have general applicability and are therefore to some extent context-free:

> It is widely assumed, perhaps optimistically, by educators that literacy skills are generalizable and that the skills involved in creating and using texts are sufficiently important that they justify an enormous investment in education ... there does seem to be a consensus that at least some forms of competence are sufficiently general that they can be taught and learned in such a way that they may be applied to any domain, whether in science or literature, economics or politics. (Brockmeier and Olson, 2009, p. 18)

It appears obviously true, to me at least, that highly developed writing skills can be applied in science, in literature, in economics, in politics, in physics, in biology, in philosophy, in religion, and in countless other contexts. Writing skills really are generalisable across domains and hence 'autonomous' of context to a considerable degree. The Turing machine model supports this claim for autonomy by showing that different classes of literacy processes can be defined with reference only to readers and texts. However, in the same volume, Brian Street reiterates a critique of the concept of autonomy that he has maintained since the appearance of *Literacy in Theory and Practice* (1984):

> The autonomous model ... I have argued, disguises the cultural and ideological assumptions that underpin it and that can then be presented as though

they are neutral and universal. Research in the social practice approach challenges this view and suggests that, in practice, dominant approaches based on the autonomous model are simply imposing Western (or urban, e.g., conceptions of literacy on other cultures) (Street, 2009, p. 337)

Elsewhere, Street and Lefstein have put matters slightly differently but offer essentially the same message:

> A central debate … is about the alleged positive effects of literacy for individuals, societies and cultures that acquire or develop it. On the one hand, a number of authors advocate a 'literacy thesis', according to which literacy is a key factor in the development of rational, scientific thought … On the other hand, others argue that the effects of literacy cannot be disentangled from the social, cultural and historical contexts of its use … Proponents of the first approach tend to talk about literacy and its consequences as being *autonomous* of the historical or social contexts of its development or use, while their critics insist upon the *ideological* nature of literacy practices and debates. (Street and Lefstein, 2007, pp. 9–10)

Other writers have taken a rather similar line. Collins and Blot (2003) make the link to ideology explicit in the title of their book *Literacy and Literacies. Texts, Power, and Identity*:

> The title of this book itself presents a dichotomy – literacy/literacies – which it initially develops, then complicates and reformulates. At issue will be a distinction between universalist or "autonomous" models (Street, 1984) of *literacy* – which conceive it as a uniform set of techniques and uses of language, with identifiable stages of development and clear, predictable consequences for culture and cognition – and relativist, sociocultural or situated models of *literacies* – which conceive literacies relationally, that is, as intrinsically diverse, historically and culturally variable, practices with texts. (Collins and Blot, 2003, pp. 3–4)

The puzzle in all these cases is to understand why the skills and social practice approaches should be thought of as alternatives when a balanced view appears to require us to acknowledge the importance of both. A number of factors may be involved in addition to those already discussed in Chapters 3 and 8.

10.4.1   Description and evaluation

The distinction between literacy skills and the social practices within which they are embedded tends also to involve a distinction between description and evaluation. Emphasis on the technical, 'autonomous' aspects of literacy leads to theories which try, in the main, to be descriptive and explanatory of the phenomena with which they are concerned. Emphasis on social practices and ideology leads rather naturally to theories which are less descriptive and more evaluative. Questions about whose interests are being served and about who should or perhaps should not be trained to become literate are emphasised. The distinction between description and evaluation has, I think, contributed to the disputes which are evident in the literacy domain. To oversimplify, a descriptive emphasis on the cognitive skills associated with literacy can seem to ignore or undervalue the inequalities and inequities associated with literacy training and education and it may attribute failure to acquire skills to individual shortcomings rather than to social factors. Conversely, an evaluative emphasis on social factors can seem to ignore the distinctive technical skills which are universally required for adequate performance in advanced domains such as mathematics and literature and to privilege instead the specific understandings associated with particular local social practices.

One of the major theses of the book has been to defend the claim that literacy skills can be treated separately from the social practices within which they are embedded. The formal analysis in terms of Turing machine processes has been developed with that independence in mind. I have also tried to exhibit some of the foundations for the strategic and ideological uses to which literacy gets put by framing literacy in the context of evolved human nature. In both respects the intention has been primarily descriptive and explanatory rather than evaluative. It is a matter of fact that a universal Turing machine is computationally more powerful than a task-specific Turing machine. It is equally a matter of fact that evolution has equipped individual humans with propensities for both conflict and co-operation. I have tried to recognise and set out some of the fundamental contours of universal human nature which appear to bear on literacy in a non-evaluative fashion. Readers will reach their own conclusions about the extent to which I have succeeded in doing this.

However, my reasons for writing the book stem not just from an academic, purely theoretical, interest in literacy but from concern about the manifest inequity and injustice of literacy and education provision in the contemporary world. It strikes me as scandalous that it appears certain that the modest 2015 targets of the Education for All initiative will be missed. I think it is equally scandalous that women and girls continue to be particularly disadvantaged and that poverty and social immobility are characteristic even of the most advanced societies on the planet. Nevertheless, although I think these inequities need to be tackled, an emphasis on literacy as social practices rather than as skills sometimes seems to lead to a characterisation of its benefits as little or nothing more than illusions foisted on the unwary by power players and ideologues, typically Western ones. Such a view tends, I think, to undervalue literacy in precisely those circumstances where it should be of greatest benefit, i.e., among the poorest and most deprived members of the global community. The point is not that it is wrong to be concerned with injustice but that it is muddled to be so concerned with social practices and ideology that one is no longer able to see the theoretical principles and practical advantages of literacy with a clear eye.

10.4.2   Scribner and Cole on social practices

A further factor, I think, has been an over-reliance on, and a tendency to misinterpret, the results of an influential study by Scribner and Cole (1981) which used experimental methods to separate the effects of literacy from those of schooling. They studied a Liberian people, the Vai, who had developed a script which was learned and used outside the context of formal schooling, thus enabling an examination of the effects of script use independently of school contexts. Scribner and Cole found, as they put it, 'the first direct evidence that literacy makes some difference to some skills in some contexts' (1981, p. 234). However, they reported that their results could not be understood purely in terms of cognitive effects but also required reference to the settings in which they were used. Thus they concluded that

> Literacy is not simply knowing how to read and write a particular script but applying this knowledge for specific purposes in specific contexts of use. The nature of these practices, including, of course, their technological aspects, will determine the kinds of skills ("consequences") associated with literacy. (Scribner and Cole, 1981, p. 236)

This passage describes literacy as involving both skills and social practices. Literacy is 'not simply knowing how to read and write' but it certainly requires those skills, to which must be added the 'specific contexts' in which they are used. Some commentators have tended to privilege references to contexts over those to skills. Here are three examples:

> Scribner and Cole (1981) have found that the cognitive consequences of greater control over mental processes and symbolic information, attributed to literacy alone, may in effect be attributable to schooling itself. (Cook-Gumperz, 2006, p. 45)

> Their book (1981) is a very readable account of their work. In it we can see how they shift their ideas from the notion of literacy as a set of skills with identifiable consequences. They are edging towards their alternative notion of a **practice account** of literacy, arguing that literacy can only be understood in the context of the social practices in which it is acquired and used. (Barton, 2007, p.25, emphasis in original)

> The Scribner and Cole research clearly indicates that what matters is not "literacy" as some decontextualized "ability" to write or read, but the social practices into which people are apprenticed as part of a social group, whether as "students" in school, "letter writers" in the local community, or members of a religious group. (Gee, 2008, p. 80)

The effect of these commentaries, taken as a whole, is to underestimate the significance of the technical skills associated with literacy. Cook-Gumperz implies that schooling rather than skills is the significant factor; Barton suggests that social practices provide an alternative theoretical account of literacy rather than adding the contexts in which literacy skills are used to the theoretical picture; and Gee appears to deny any importance to the skills component of literacy. That all these commentaries underestimate the skills aspects of the original research is evident not just from the quotations but also from a recent reappraisal of Goody's impact on literacy studies by Michael and Jennifer Cole, in which it is reported that in the third stage of their work using a variety of experimental tasks,

> Scribner and Cole (1981) routinely found what they considered cognitive consequences of literacy. Vai who wrote letters in Vai dictated more complex oral descriptions as letters to a friend about the unfamiliar game. They were more facile in rebus reading and writing tasks, and they showed a greater ability to segment text by syllables. (Cole and Cole, 2006, p. 319)

As one of the original authors, Michael Cole is in a position to know. In the years since 1981 a mass of experimental evidence has been accumulated demonstrating distinct cognitive consequences of the acquisition of literacy skills. A significant contribution to this body of work has been made by Keith Stanovich and his colleagues (Stanovich, 1993, 2000, 2003; Stanovich, West and Harrison, 1995; Cunningham and Stanovich, 2001). Stanovich (1993) is of particular interest because the work was explicitly intended to build on the contribution of Scribner and Cole.

> In choosing which variables to focus on in our initial investigations, my research group was again influenced by the outcomes of Scribner and Cole's investigation. In a sense, we started where Scribner and Cole finished. (Stanovich, 1993, p. 142)

It is a sorry reflection on the divided nature of literacy studies that a reader of Cook-Gumperz (2006), of Barton (2007), or of Gee (2008) will find no references to Stanovich and his colleagues or to any other part of the body of subsequent research which shows clearly that both cognitive consequences and social practices need to be taken into account in a comprehensive, balanced theory of literacy.

10.4.3   Overvaluation of skills

The subsections above have indicated what seem to be denials of the value or reality of autonomous literacy skills by researchers starting from a social practice standpoint. Conversely, one can also find numerous instances of research in which the significance of social factors is underestimated or discounted by research considering the skills base on which literacy rests. I shall briefly consider the logic of one recent study in the United States to make the point. The study by Pierce, Katzir, Wolf, and Noam (2010) reports technically sophisticated research using structural equation modelling to examine the construct of reading among dysfluent urban children. The introduction to the study describes a number of social, cultural, and economic factors linked to poor reading performance in urban cohorts. For example, a study of national performance in the U.S. showed that 50% of fourth grade students eligible for free or reduced-price school lunch failed to read at the basic level, whereas only 21% of those ineligible for free lunch fell below the basic level in their reading. In a later section of the paper other conditions associated with poverty including hearing problems, ear infections, lead exposure, and poor nutrition were identified as 'pernicious to cognitive development' (p. 133). It is therefore puzzling to find that the study focuses not at all on the social and cultural determinants of poverty but solely on details of the cognitive processes of poor readers from impoverished backgrounds. The rationale for this focus is as follows:

> By focusing solely on these at-risk students as opposed to an undifferentiated sample of elementary school students, analyses can target the variation in reading ability displayed by poor readers, to evaluate the hypothesis that subgroups of poor readers may require different kinds of reading intervention targeting different facets of reading. (Pierce et al, 2010, pp. 127–8)

The point I want to make is not that there is anything wrong, in principle, with wanting to understand the details of cognitive deficits but that one might think it more important to try to make such studies unnecessary by focusing on the removal of poverty and other types of social disadvantage first.

At the risk of caricaturing a serious study, let me offer a thought experiment for comparative consideration. Let us suppose that I have concluded, on the basis of numerous observations and wide acquaintance with the literature, that children from impoverished backgrounds typically take longer to run 100 metres than do those from more affluent backgrounds. The children from impoverished backgrounds are less well nourished than the more affluent and suffer from a variety of other poverty-related health deficits. I have also observed, however, that the impoverished children display a variety of technical deficiencies in their running performance. They respond more slowly to the starting gun, they are less attentive to lane discipline, and they rapidly lose their motivation to improve as they constantly lose races. I decide, on the basis of my observations, to study a chosen sample of poor runners who fail to achieve the basic time for the 100 metres. The rationale for this focus is as follows:

> By focusing solely on these at-risk runners as opposed to an undifferentiated sample of elementary school runners, analyses can target the variation in running ability displayed by poor runners, to evaluate the hypothesis that subgroups of poor runners may require different kinds of running intervention targeting different facets of running.

That, of course, is not how running is studied, nor is it how reading should be studied. There is no doubt at all that there are individual and group differences among both runners and readers but in order to determine what they are and how they function we need, first of all, to remove the obvious environmental differences. Thus, we first make sure that our runners and readers are all adequately nourished and motivated. Then, when we have a secure basis for comparison, we can begin to make systematic studies of different subgroups. The methodology of Pierce et al (2010) appears to be focusing on relatively minor cognitive differences within the target group of poor readers while ignoring the major societal and environmental factors that place them in the target group in the first place. In the final section of the paper the significance of social and motivational factors is recognised but somewhat as an afterthought. Let me reiterate that I am not, in any sense, attacking the need for well planned studies of the cognitive factors that affect reading performance, nor am I attacking the need for equally well planned studies of social and cultural factors. I am, rather, making a positive plea for studies which integrate both and try to tease out the causal as well as correlational links between them.

10.5   The capabilities approach

What is needed to tackle inequity is the understanding that mastery of the basic skills of literacy is not automatically followed by the acquisition of its potential benefits because adverse personal or social circumstances may prevent further progress. The capabilities approach to human development includes a distinction between capability and achieved functioning, which can be used to make exactly this point. It thus becomes possible to discuss what one can, in principle, do as a literate person in the context of a broad approach which sets out what one ought to be able to do to live a full and satisfying human life.

The capabilities approach was pioneered by Amartya Sen and further developed by Martha Nussbaum (Sen, 1999; Nussbaum, 2000, 2003, 2006; Drèze and Sen, 2002; Robeyns, 2005). It offers a normative framework within which the links between literacy, human development, and social justice can be explored. It seems to me to offer a more secure grounding for the literacy episteme than the relativism inherent in a Foucauldian perspective and it can be applied equally to issues arising in highly developed and in developing countries. As its name implies, the focus of the capabilities approach is on what people are able to do.

> The core characteristic of the capability approach is its focus on what people are effectively able to do and to be; that is, on their capabilities. This contrasts with philosophical approaches that concentrate on people's happiness or desire-fulfilment, or on income, expenditures, or consumption. (Robeyns, 2005, p. 94)

There has been interest in the application of the capabilities approach to education (Nussbaum, 2003; Saito, 2003; Unterhalter, 2003, 2005; Robeyns, 2006; Walker and Unterhalter, 2007; Young, 2009) and some attention has, of course, been paid to literacy within the educational context, but Maddox (2008) is the only paper I have found which deals specifically with literacy as a capability.

The capabilities approach fits rather well both with the Turing machine model of literacy and with the evolutionary emphasis on human universals taken in this book. The capabilities approach is focused on individuals and what they are able to do, as the best way to evaluate human well being and functioning. The focus on individuals fits with an evolutionary approach which emphasises the genetic uniqueness of humans (identical twins excepted), and also with the analytical concept of the functional core which I have used to designate a reader/writer interacting with a text. The normative character of the capabilities approach makes an interesting contrast with, and addition to, the descriptive character of evolutionary theorising and the analytic character of Turing machine functionalism. Consider, for example, the situation of women and girls with respect to literacy. The capabilities approach says that women and girls must be given the same access to literacy as men and boys if justice is to be done; evolutionary theory explains that there are natural differences between males and females which may help to explain (but not to justify) why women and girls suffer persistent disadvantage. Turing machine functionalism is blind to sex differences and demonstrates that the infinite differences in computational power between literate and non-literate people apply equally to women and girls as to men and boys. Deprivation of the capability for literacy is thus an infinite deprivation whether those deprived are male or female.

Sen and Nussbaum take slightly different approaches to the delineation and use of capabilities, although there is much about which they are in agreement. Nussbaum, but not Sen, endorses a list of central capabilities. The list is provisional and revisable. The most recent version I have found from Nussbaum (2006) includes literacy as a part of the capability for sense, imagination, and thought.

> 4. *Senses, Imagination, and Thought.* Being able to use the senses, to imagine, think, and reason—and to do these things in a "truly human" way, a way informed and cultivated by an adequate education, including, but by no means limited to, literacy and basic mathematical and scientific training. Being able to use imagination and thought in connection with experiencing and producing works and events of one's own choice, religious, literary, musical, and so forth. Being able to use one's mind in ways protected by guarantees of freedom of expression with respect to both political and artistic speech, and freedom of religious exercise. Being able to have pleasurable experiences and to avoid nonbeneficial pain. (Nussbaum, 2006, p. 76)

The notion of 'truly human' functioning is a normative framing of what is desirable in human life, emphasising the pro-social rather than the anti-social instincts of humans. Nussbaum, in an earlier work, described it thus:

> The core idea is that of the human being as a dignified free being who shapes his or her own life in cooperation and reciprocity with others, rather than being passively shaped or pushed around by the world in the manner of a "flock" or "herd" animal. A life that is really human is one that is shaped throughout by these human powers of practical reason and sociability. (Nussbaum, 2000, p. 72)

From an evolutionary standpoint it is clear that this is an aspiration rather than a currently realised vision of what human life is like. We may very well endorse the vision as both humane and necessary for the longer term stability and peace of global human society, but to make it real will require the development of institutions which enable us to manage and limit the effects of our instincts for conflict and out-group derogation which, unfortunately, are as real and as persistent as those for cooperation.

10.5.1   Literacy from the capability perspective

The capability perspective focuses on what individuals are effectively able to do and to be. This immediately raises the question of what kinds of things literate individuals are able to do and to be. It is clear that literacy as a capability implies much more than simply being able to read and write. Reading and writing are merely the entry points to a literate life rather than definitive of it. The extension of the concept is already present in Scribner and Cole's idea that literacy is not simply the capacity to read and write but the application of reading and writing 'for specific purposes in specific contexts of use'. I think it is useful to try to make a distinction between contexts and purposes which are internal to literacy and those which are external. The point of doing this is to make it possible to explore both intrinsic literacy capabilities and non-literate capabilities which make use of literacy. There is an existing distinction in the literature between literacy events and literacy practices (Street, 1998; Barton, 2007, Chapter 3). A literacy event is, essentially, any particular communicative situation in which literacy plays an integral part. A literacy practice is a socially defined way of utilising literacy which is drawn on in literacy events. Festivals of readings and carols at Christmas, for example, are instances of a literacy practice which is characteristic of the Anglican community in England. A particular festival on a given day, in a given place, is a literacy event which instantiates the practice. Certain kinds of things tend to happen; carols are sung, the scriptures are read, mulled wine and mince pies may be available after the service. Certain kinds of things tend not to happen. Political addresses are not usually made during carol festivals; lists of lots for the next local auction are not usually read out between carols.

The distinction I want to make is one which has a different focus. When I think of specific contexts that are internal to literacy, I have in mind, for example, the distinction between prose and poetry or that between formal inference and speculative reasoning. It is true, of course, that prose and poetry tend to be used in specific, external contexts and thus to be involved in different cultural practices such as political meetings and poetry readings, but that is not what I have in mind. The context of poetry, if I can describe it thus, is different from the context of prose and it is this kind of difference that I have in mind as an internal difference of literacy context. Poetry is concerned with rhyme, meter, and line length in ways that prose typically is not. Prose is concerned with narrative structure in ways that poetry typically is not. The question, then, regarding internal contexts from the capabilities standpoint is what sorts of different things can a literate person do within literacy? The point is important because social practice theorists have, in my view, typically privileged external contexts over internal ones and thus have not explored the structure of the universe of texts and the various genres which are found within it. In one way this is entirely understandable. If a child is prevented from learning to read and write because she is female and local literacy practices are reserved for males, then questions about what she might like to read and write cannot arise for her and one may think that there is an urgent need for the local practices to be changed. However, if we reach a situation in which not just primary, but secondary and tertiary education become widely available then explorations of internal contexts and genres will become more important. A child who is passionate about poems may want to explore quite different aspects of the universe of texts from one who is passionate about sums, but it will be desirable to ensure that as many children as possible have as wide as possible an appreciation of the various internal contexts of literacy so as to keep open for them the possibility of access to literate ways of functioning which are poorly explored and may be seen as elitist or esoteric. Studies of genres and specific contexts of use have not, I think, considered genres specifically from the capabilities standpoint (Devitt, 2004; Donovan and Smolkin, 2006; Tardy and Swales, 2008; Biber, 2009; Snow and Uccelli, 2009; Norris and Phillips, 2009).

The capability approach distinguishes capabilities from achieved functionings. The distinction is between what one is able to do in principle and what one chooses to do in practice. The distinction is fundamental in the human development context because it makes it possible to focus on giving people the freedom to do and to be in ways which they have reason to value, without forcing them in any particular direction (Sen, 1999). The point applies equally to literacy (Winter, 2000). A person who is literate and numerate has capabilities which make her free to read a book, to write a poem, or to solve an equation, should she choose to. A person who is literate but not numerate would enjoy the first two capabilities but not the third, and a person who is neither literate nor numerate would enjoy none of them. Some internal literate contexts and genres require more advanced capabilities than others. Most literate people have the capability to write a short letter should they wish to do so, but relatively few have the capability to review an academic journal article or to follow a complex technical argument in a scientific paper. Nussbaum's definition of the capability for senses, imagination, and thought quoted above says that it should be 'by no means limited to, literacy and basic mathematical and scientific training'. This raises the interesting question of what literacy as a capability should ideally involve. The millennium goal devoted to education has as its target to 'Ensure that, by 2015, children everywhere, boys and girls alike, will be able to complete a full course of primary schooling.' (UN, 2010, p. 16). Exactly what this means varies from country to country but it is, at best, an extremely modest goal. It is clear, however, that even such modest provision, when properly made can have profound effects on the quality of life for individuals, although such positive effects are not in any sense guaranteed and may be undermined by continuing poverty, political repression, and prejudice. What, we might wonder, would the world be like if completion of secondary education and the possibility of tertiary study became a reality for everyone?

10.6   Summary

What, then, of the literacy episteme for the twenty-first century? We will, I hope, continue to understand literacy as the primary intellectual technology but we will come to see that it has its roots in the capabilities of evolved humans, amplified by the objective properties of the infinite universe of texts and the ways of recording thinking that are enabled by writing. We will need to develop powerful social institutions to allow us to harness the cooperative possibilities of literate disciplines while trying to minimise the natural tendencies that humans have for conflict, aggression, and strategic manipulation. The curriculum for modern schools should include evolutionary biology because we cannot hope to manage our own future development without an understanding of the selective forces that have shaped our species.

Chapter 11

The Limitations of the Literate Mind

The account of the literate mind outlined in this book describes literacy in terms of processes of interaction between the finite, evolved system of the non-literate mind, and symbol sequences sampled from an infinite universe of possible texts. The mental processes involved in these interactions have been described in terms of the functional states of Turing machines. In real minds these functional states are superimposed on areas of the brain evolved for other purposes by the learning processes that most literate people experience through their schooling. Literacy can be learned at any point during a lifetime and the effects of practice accumulate with experience (Stanovich, 2000, Chapters 9 and 10). Literacy is a systematic way to construct and interpret strings of symbols. The nature of the universe of texts demonstrates that the scope for literate discovery and creative invention is limitless. It is for this reason that the literate mind has been described as infinitely more powerful than the non-literate mind.

It might appear that a system with infinite power would, by definition, be unlimited but that is not the case. Literate minds are constrained by two classes of limitations. There are formal limitations arising from the syntax of symbol systems, and there are natural limitations arising from the fundamental characteristics of the evolved mind. Formal limitations are principally of interest to mathematicians and logicians but they are fascinating and may indicate limitations to what it is possible for humans to understand. Natural limitations are of more practical significance. They constrain the human capacity to use literate skills and knowledge to act for the good of all and for the good of the planet. They make it hard for us to co-operate with each other and they tend to produce gross inequalities of opportunity.

11.1 Reasoning cannot be captured fully by formal methods (but without literacy we would not know this)

The list of human universals presented and discussed in Chapter 3 provides a broad brush picture of the core capacities of non-literate humans. The list includes the following: conjectural reasoning; decision making; attempts to predict the future; the interpretation of behaviour; the core logical notions of conjunction, equivalence, negation, and identity; the distinction between parts and wholes; the concepts of truth and falsity. These universals show that non-literate people have the core capacities for reasoning that are deployed in formal reasoning systems such as the syllogistic logic systematised by Aristotle, and the much more recently developed propositional and predicate calculi (Quine, 1974; Boolos and Jeffrey, 1989; Machover, 1996). The list also makes it clear that non-literate humans have a range of tendencies which may colour the use of their reason, including a tendency to derogate out-groups and a tendency to overestimate their own objectivity. If the thesis of Humphrey (1976) is correct, as discussed in Chapter 6, it is likely that human reasoning was evolved to solve the pressing problems of social life rather than for the development of abstract chains of inferences linking premises to conclusions. Human reasoning may typically have more to do with rhetoric and argument than with abstract validity (Mercier and Sperber, 2011).

One of the claims of Goody and Watt (1963) was that the Greeks invented new kinds of logical methods which depended on writing. They did not claim that non-literate minds were irrational or pre-logical, although there was a substantial strand of thinking in the anthropological literature which considered rationality to be fundamentally linked to literacy. Harris (2009) provides a compact and trenchant review of this tradition. The new methods which the Greeks invented were, essentially, systematisations of existing principles of reasoning and they proved both durable and useful. Aristotelian logic, for example, was seen as the basis of sound reasoning until the nineteenth century.

11.1.1 Russell's paradox

Confidence in traditional methods of reasoning was shaken by paradoxes which emerged in the foundations of mathematics in the later years of the nineteenth century. Attempts to resolve the paradoxes led to the development of more formal systems of reasoning including meta-mathematics, the study of mathematics using mathematical methods. A particularly troublesome problem was identified by Bertrand Russell at the beginning of the twentieth century. Russell had been studying the work of the German mathematician Gottlob Frege who was trying to demonstrate that mathematics rested on logic, the science of sound reasoning. Russell discovered that Frege's system of logic, which represented the culmination of his life's work, contained an incompletely analysed assumption which led to a paradoxical conclusion. Rebecca Goldstein (2005), in her book *Incompleteness*, has described the situation beautifully:

> Russell's paradox concerns the set of all sets that are not members of themselves. Sets are abstract objects that contain members, and some

sets can be members of themselves. For example, the set of all abstract objects is a member of itself, since it is an abstract object. Some sets (most) are not members of themselves. For example, the set of all mathematicians is not itself a mathematician – it's an abstract object – and so is not a member of itself. Now we form the concept of the set of all sets that aren't members of themselves and we ask of this set: is it a member of itself? It either is or it isn't, just as the problematic sentence of the liar's paradox [*this very sentence is false*] either is or isn't true. But if the set of all sets that aren't members of themselves is a member of itself, then it's *not* a member of itself, since it contains *only* sets that aren't members of themselves. And, if it's not a member of itself, then it *is* a member of itself, since it contains *all* the sets that aren't members of themselves. So it's a member of itself if and only if it's not a member of itself. Not good. (p. 91)

Not good indeed! The nature of the problem can be further appreciated by considering how we understand what the expression 'the set of all sets that are not members of themselves' means. It seems to define a distinct collection of things in the way that the expression 'the set of all Nobel prize winners' defines a distinct collection of people. Consequently we are inclined to reason the same way in both cases. The things are people in one case and abstract objects in the other but that is not a reason for thinking that there is anything wrong with the definition. The concept of a set is clear (a set is just a collection of objects) and, as the quote shows, there is also a clear distinction between sets which are members of themselves and those which are not. Unfortunately, as we have just seen, Russell's paradox shows that 'the set of all sets that are not members of themselves' does not define a totality since there is at least one thing which both must and cannot be a member of whatever collection the definition indicates. Thus we have a case in which a definition in everyday language specifies a collection which is not a totality. The point is not that the total number of items in the collection is unknown in practice but that it is unknowable in principle. Very odd!

11.1.2   Formalism and meta-mathematics

Difficulties of this kind are not generally encountered in everyday reasoning and it may be hard to see why they should be a cause for concern, but for mathematics it is crucial that the methods of reasoning used are consistent and do not lead to contradictions of the kind embodied in Russell's paradox. Meta-mathematics was proposed by the German mathematician David Hilbert as a way to deal with the problems. Hilbert suggested that paradoxical results emerged because the meanings of the terms used in reasoning were not defined absolutely precisely. He proposed, therefore, that methods of proof and reasoning should be developed which were purely syntactic and which did not depend on the meanings of terms. Such systems are called formal systems.

11.1.2.1   *Formal systems*

The Turing machine is one type of formal system, computer programs are another. Formal systems consist of external symbol structures which mimic other systems in the real world and allow us to study the evolution of those systems and make predictions about how they will behave in the future. The fundamental syntactic point to make about these systems is that they are unthinkable without literacy. The fundamental semantic point to make about formal systems is that the meanings derived from them are related to precise rules of operation. Formal systems differ from the everyday uses of symbols for reading and writing because their operations are determined by exact rules. Formal systems are like games played according to rules. A formal system consists of a set of starting structures known as axioms or initial conditions and rules of inference which allow consequences to be derived from the axioms. The consequences are known as theorems and the derivation of a theorem from the axioms via applications of the rules is a proof. Consider the game of changing one word into another by single letter substitutions. We can think of the starting word as the single axiom of a formal system. The rules of inference specify how the starting word can be changed:

Rule 1: Only one letter can be changed in a single step. The change must be a substitution, not an addition or a deletion.

Rule 2: The result of any change made under Rule 1 must be an English word.

Rule 3: No other type of change is allowed.

Suppose that the axiom is the word ONE. We might ask if TWO is a theorem of the system. Here's a proof that it is. ONE, ORE, ARE, ART, AIT, TIT, TIN, TON, TOO, TWO. Proofs are not normally unique and the one given is not the only way to get from ONE to TWO. I'm not entirely happy with the proof because it uses the word AIT which is a less common word than the others. I wonder if I can find a proof which doesn't use AIT or any other uncommon word. One way to do this would be to exploit the partial results already achieved. I know that ART can be proved from ONE and I know that TWO can be proved from TIT. These part proofs are sometimes called lemmas. Given the existence of the two lemmas I will have a proof of the kind I want if I can connect ART to TIT without the intermediate use of AIT or any other uncommon word. Here's one proof: ART, ARM, AIM, AIR, FIR, FIT, TIT.

The example system is not entirely satisfactory for a couple of reasons. First, Rule 2 is very loose because there may be disagreement about what counts as an English word and the rules of formal systems should be unambiguous. One way to improve the system would be to define an appropriate list of words or to specify an official dictionary for consultation in cases of disagreement. *The Chambers Dictionary*, featured in Chapter 2, could be a candidate. A second weakness of the system is that it doesn't enable us to do anything very useful. I'll return to this matter shortly but it is worth pursuing the example a little further because it can be used to demonstrate some other features of formal systems in a relatively intuitive way. One question we might ask, in the interests of speed and efficiency, is about shortest proofs. What is the shortest proof of TWO given the axiom ONE and the rules as described? We know from the first proof that no more than nine steps are needed. We can also infer from Rule 1 that the shortest proof must be at least three steps long. We know this because ONE and TWO have no letters in common in a given position. Thus, even if non-word single letter changes were allowed we could do no better than ONE, TNE, TWE, TWO. Thus we can be certain, in advance, that the shortest proof of TWO from ONE has somewhere between three and nine steps. It is also possible to ask questions about the scope of proofs available in a given formal system. Suppose we wanted to know whether or not we could prove THREE, FOUR, FIVE, SIX, SEVEN, EIGHT, NINE, and TEN in the system given with the single axiom ONE. We can use the rules without generating any theorems to show that most of the putative proofs are not possible because six of the candidate theorems have more than three letters and there is no way to generate words longer than the axiom ONE which has only three letters. It's easy enough to prove that SIX and TEN are theorems of the system. We can either do this directly or use existing lemmas. The insufficiency of the axiom ONE for the proofs of all of TWO to TEN leads very naturally to a question about what would be the smallest system needed to prove all the desired theorems. Inspection shows that there are four- and five-letter words in the list of desired theorems so the obvious thing to try is to add new four- and five-letter axioms to the system. FOUR and THREE are obvious candidates. If we could prove SEVEN and EIGHT from THREE, and FIVE and NINE from FOUR, we would have a system in which all the desired proofs could be achieved. I have not done the work to establish whether the system with the rules as specified and ONE, THREE, and FOUR as axioms does indeed admit the proofs desired but I have my doubts. I can't immediately see how to get from THREE to SEVEN or EIGHT. Even if it is possible, the resulting system is still very limited. Suppose we want a system which allows us to generate all the number words in English as theorems of a formal system with just the single axiom ONE. We would plainly have to add one or more rules of inference to allow the addition of letters. More or less restrictive rules to do this can be specified. A rule might be added permitting the addition of a single letter anywhere or a more restrictive rule might specify that an addition can only be made to the end of an existing word. Different rules lead to different proofs with different patterns of inference. If we add a rule specifying that single letters can be inserted anywhere, we can prove THREE from TWO easily as follows: TWO, TOO, TOE, TEE, TREE, THREE. If, however, we allow insertions only at the end of words, the last two steps of the proof would be invalid and the task becomes more difficult. I have found a proof of THREE from TWO with the rule allowing insertions only at the end of words. It took thirteen steps and involved some work with *The Chambers Dictionary* and the use, among others, of a word for 'a cylinder with a helical groove or ridge (the *thread*) used as a fastening driven into wood...' Readers who do not think of themselves as the kind of people who prove theorems in formal systems might like to obtain a proof of their own. The activity differs from what logicians and other users of formal systems do only in terms of the familiarity of the elements of the system.

The example given is only a game but formal systems have applications in a range of contexts for the study of complex systems. Consider human reasoning as an example. People reach conclusions about all kinds of things on the basis of arguments of various kinds. In Britain there is an ongoing argument about the configuration of National Health Service hospitals in a time of financial austerity. The premise or starting point of one argument is the need to save money on specialist services. Some people argue that savings can be achieved if specialist services are concentrated in a small number of key hospitals, whereas others argue that they should be more widely diffused in smaller community hospitals and that savings should be made elsewhere. Evidence is adduced on both sides of the argument. A formal system might be used to model the arguments in one of two ways. First, it might be used descriptively simply to record the premises, the evidence presented, the inferential steps taken and the conclusions reached. Second, it might be used normatively to examine the arguments presented with a view to discerning their quality. Are the arguments valid? Are the premises true? If all the valid modes of reasoning are available as inferential rules in a formal system, and if all the premises of an argument are available as axioms of the system, then all the valid conclusions can be reached by application of the rules of inference. If it turns out that a conclusion reached via an intuitive chain of reasoning cannot be obtained via systematic application of the rules of inference, that implies that the intuitive argument is invalid. The formal system thus serves as a check on the quality of the reasoning. Since we know that human reasoning operates with biases which we find hard to detect, the use of formal systems can be a major step forward in the construction of rigorous arguments. Hardman (2009) provides an introduction to the study of human judgement and decision making.

In the computer age, formal systems can also be used for prediction. Weather forecasting is an interesting example. The atmosphere can be modelled by measuring important quantities like temperature, pressure, humidity, and so forth at a range of different locations. Data of this kind serve as the axioms of the system. The behavioural evolution of the system then uses differential equations rather than rules of inference to predict the future behaviour of the atmosphere. In Britain it is customary to treat weather forecasts with caution but their accuracy over the short term has increased substantially over the 50 years or so during which computers have been used to generate forecasts because the models used have become more sophisticated and detailed.

From a theoretical point of view the aim of a formal systems designer is to generate the maximum number of useful theorems from the minimum number of axioms. The expressive power of a formal system describes the theorems it can produce. The explanatory power of a formal system can be thought of, roughly, as the ratio of the size of the formal system to the range and interest of the theorems it produces. A highly explanatory system produces large numbers of interesting inferences from a small number of axioms and inferential rules, whereas a formal system with poor explanatory power needs a large amount of information to begin with.

11.1.2.2   Meta-mathematics

In the early decades of the twentieth century it was hoped that meta-mathematical reasoning using formal systems would guarantee the foundations of ordinary mathematical reasoning. Van Heijenoort (1967) contains a selection of fundamental papers from this period. The essential idea was to codify all the properties of reasoning in formal systems and thus to turn reasoning into a mechanical procedure. Hilbert expected that all mathematical reasoning could, in principle, be expressed formally although it would not be practical to do so for everyday mathematical purposes because formal inferences are lengthy and rather unwieldy. If Hilbert's proposal were correct, all of human reasoning could be captured syntactically; it could be generated automatically from a finite set of rules expressed in the form of a text. That would show, effectively, that literacy could transform human reasoning from an unreliable system which could lead to paradoxical results into a flawless, formal system which would always yield correct results.

11.1.3   Gödel's logical critique of formalism

In what is probably the most famous logical paper of the twentieth century, Kurt Gödel (1931) showed that Hilbert's formal program for the foundations of mathematics could not be carried through as he had hoped and expected. Nagel and Newman (1989) provide an introduction to Gödel's theorems and methods. Gödel proved that it was not possible to replace all aspects of human reasoning with purely syntactic symbol manipulation. If one tried to do so the results had either to be inconsistent or must fail to capture at least one inference. That is why his proofs are described as proofs of the incompleteness of formal systems. The details of Gödel's paper are intricate and hard to master but in outline he exploited the fact that particular syntactic arrangements of symbols can have more than one semantic interpretation, as described in earlier chapters. Gödel used this possibility to construct strings of symbols which could be interpreted both as numbers and as statements about numbers thus creating a form of self-reference. The specific self-referential statement he constructed said of itself that it was unprovable in the formal system which he used to express it. The important point about this was that the statement described itself as unprovable rather than as true or false. This left open two possibilities. Either the statement was provable in the system used to express it, in which case the system contained a contradiction, or it was not provable, as it maintained. If the latter were the case then the statement was true but there was no way of knowing this with the resources of the formal system used to express it. Its truth was evident only from outside the formal system, which was thus incomplete. From the standpoint of literacy this is profoundly interesting because it shows conclusively that human reasoning cannot be captured in its entirety by syntactic symbol manipulation. However, we could not have known this without the detailed syntactic construction that Gödel made and thus we see that literate means can be used to demonstrate some of their own limitations. It does not follow from this that everyday reasoning is superior to formal reasoning. The vagueness of everyday reasoning and the incompletely analysed meanings of the terms involved were what led to the crisis in mathematics in the first place. What does follow, some theorists propose, is that formal reasoning can never be a complete substitute for creativity in any literate field. Curiosity and imagination cannot be replaced by rote learning and formula manipulation. Technical competence and mastery are essential foundations but these need to be thought of as tools in the service of creative intellects (Chaitin, 2005).

11.1.4   The unsolvability of the halting problem

Five years after Gödel's paper was published, Turing published the paper in which the concept of the Turing machine was set out for the first time. As described in Chapter 7, he was able to show that a single machine, the universal machine, could be constructed which was capable of reading and acting on an infinite number of textual descriptions of other machines. The universal machine provides a syntactic model of the literate mind, which I have used to demonstrate the infinite increase in capacity which literacy makes available to those who can read and write. Turing's paper also contained proofs of several limitations on the powers of universal machines. The most famous of these is a proof of the unsolvability of what is called the halting problem. I have described the proof in some detail in Wells (2006). Turing machines can be divided into two classes, those whose computations come to an end after a finite number of steps, and those whose computations go on forever. The question posed by the halting problem is this: is it possible to specify a single procedure which can decide whether an arbitrary Turing machine with which it is presented is of the halting or the non-halting kind? Turing used the universal machine in a self-referential way to demonstrate that a single procedure of the kind could not be specified. His proof has some features in common with Gödel's. In both cases the proofs use self-referential constructions and in both cases the demonstration of limitations is shown to stem from the use of a fixed, finite system, a formal system of axioms in Gödel's case, and the fixed interpretive structure of the universal machine's processes in Turing's case. Turing's limitative results point in the same direction as Gödel's, I think. They indicate that there will always be a role for creativity and new ways of doing things. Turing was quite specific about the limitations of what could be calculated by a 'uniform process' and about the need for 'an essentially new method' to produce certain kinds of strings of symbols (Turing, 1936, p. 253).

11.2   Evolved limitations of literate processes

The formal limitations described in the previous section indicate that reasoning cannot be replaced in its entirety by syntactic symbol manipulation following fixed rules. It rests on human judgement and creativity as well. The enormous progress made in a vast range of intellectual endeavours in the literate epoch, in science, mathematics, literature, and the humanities demonstrates the fertility of the underlying evolved structures in which literacy has flourished. Progress has been enabled both by the co-operative and competitive instincts which are equally natural for humans. The general consensus, I think, if one were to ask, is that literacy is pretty much an unqualified good, although we have seen that there are theorists for whom the positive answer is not obvious. A more nuanced view requires us to consider the matter at different levels of analysis. At the level of individuals, given the state of the world in which we live, it is clear that literacy is essential to full participation in the kind of life that is most highly valued, thus for individuals literacy should be considered an unqualified good. It is for this reason, I think, that proponents of the capabilities approach to human development always consider literacy as a central requirement. At the level of communities there is also evidence of the importance of literacy. Doronila (1996) and Bernardo (1998) have both demonstrated the positive effects of literacy on small scale communities. If, though, one asks whether the invention of literacy has been a good thing for humanity as a whole viewed from an evolutionary standpoint, one would have to say that it is too early to tell. Trying to assess literacy overall is somewhat like trying to assess the effects of other powerful technologies such as nuclear power. In the latter case there are both benefits and dangers and the same may be true of literacy. It may be that literacy enhances capabilities of the evolved mind that do not have positive consequences.

11.2.1   Religious fundamentalism

I consider here the case of religious scriptural fundamentalism as a possible semantic analogue of the limitations on formal reasoning which stem from the following of fixed rules. The problem with religious, and other forms of fundamentalism, is that they exacerbate the conflictive tendencies of the human animal and may lead to violence and the destabilisation of society. Profound ideological differences between human groups on religious, political, or other bases are, I think, among the most pressing dangers that we face as a species and it is not clear that literacy is more of a help than a hindrance. Religious fundamentalism is, of course, not the only kind of fundamentalism that exists in the contemporary world but it is intrinsically interesting and it is appropriate for a book of this kind if only because religious fundamentalists frequently deny the relevance of evolutionary theorising to human minds and human nature. Schimmel (2008) has written a fascinating book comparing scriptural fundamentalism in Judaism, Christianity, and Islam and I have drawn substantially on his work in this section. Schimmel's book originated in his attempt

> to understand *why* modern Orthodox Jews believe that the Pentateuch (*Torah* or *Humash* in Hebrew) was revealed in its entirety by God to Moses at Mt. Sinai or during a sojourn of forty years in the wilderness in the late second millennium BCE, in the face of overwhelming evidence and logical arguments against such a proposition. (Schimmel, 2008, p. 3)

He documents the fact that scriptural fundamentalists tend to claim that the doctrines underpinning their beliefs are immutable, inerrant, and eternal despite evidence showing significant changes over time. It is clear that maintaining such a position in the face of strong counter-evidence requires significant mental gymnastics and Schimmel describes and discusses a variety of strategies that fundamentalist believers use to maintain their positions. Many of these strategies are common to Islamic and Christian fundamentalism as well as to Jewish orthodoxy, and Schimmel proposes that the underlying psychology is the same. This perspective fits well with the emphasis in this book on the universality of human nature.

Schimmel suggests that beliefs are retained in the face of opposing evidence because there are significant individual and communal rewards for so doing and because giving up beliefs can and does lead to alienation from community and family. These social psychological influences are reinforced by an unwillingness to consider other approaches to the subject matter. Thus Schimmel describes how biblical scholarship is treated with suspicion and hostility by some Orthodox Jews because it threatens the fundamental belief that the Torah is the word of God transmitted directly to Moses on Mt. Sinai. Schimmel's explanatory strategy is mainly psychological although he also draws attention to the importance of broader social and cultural factors to explain issues such as the resurgence of creationism in the United States.

Schimmel's book makes fascinating, if rather depressing, reading but he nowhere addresses the possibility that religious, scriptural, fundamentalism may be fuelled by the durability of the texts to which it relates. Texts provide stable reference points which may, if what they claim is wrong, function as perverse incentives to social solidarity at both individual and communal levels. A text provides a banner or standard which serves as the rallying point for a group which identifies with it. The primary fact is that a text is 'ours' or 'mine' and it is backed up by traditions of learning and study and by interpretations licensed by authorities that we respect. Comparison with other texts and testing of the text against other forms of evidence become secondary considerations at best.

The simple fact of its relative durability may give a text a spurious authority. What it says is there on the page and can be re-read, recited, and studied as often as one wishes. Olson (1994, p. 31) cites the writing of Karen Blixen about the Kikuyu, who appear to have been credulous with regard to news conveyed by writing while remaining sceptical of news conveyed orally. The medium, one might say, adds to the message. The Kikuyu were non-literate at the time but it is not hard to see how texts can encourage credulity among those who can read them as well. We are all enjoined not to trust what we read in the newspapers, for example, but it is notorious that it is much easier to set a rumour going than to stop one once started.

The analysis of literate capabilities in terms of Turing machine processes shows that an individual may have an indefinitely lengthy interaction with a single text. Reading the text gives rise to thoughts about it which may be set down as written commentary. Further reading of the original text and of the commentary may lead to further insights or to revisions or rethinking of earlier comments. There is, in principle, no limit to the processes of elaboration and refinement, of commitment and understanding which may be undertaken. If, in addition, the target text is treated as the inerrant word of the creator of everything, one can see why it might easily become the source of fierce, unrelenting, and uncritical approbation.

11.2.2   Education for All

Education for All is a global program, agreed to by the governments of the world, and managed by UNESCO which has been cited at various points in the book. The program was started at the turn of the century with a range of educational goals including universal primary education by 2015. It has achieved a certain amount of success but it is falling far short of the targets with which it began and it can serve as a large-scale example of some of the limitations of the human mind, literate or otherwise, and the failure to solve straightforward problems which a more optimistic era took to be soluble. The limited progress of Education for All provides evidence for criticism of the kind that proponents of the social practice approach to literacy tend to level at the more simplistic assumptions made by governments and other institutions about the societal benefits of education, including literacy training. One limitation that we see writ large is the inability of humans to care sufficiently about inequality. This is a deep-rooted consequence of our evolutionary history and it means that we fail to build social institutions which promote and guarantee equality and that we pay lip service to equality while continuing social practices which depend on and maintain inequality. The limitation, in this case, is not intrinsic to literacy. It is a limitation of human sympathy, but it suggests that education and literacy, in and of themselves have limited power to change human behaviour. A broad picture of the progress of Education for All can be had by reading the forewords to the reports which have, with one exception, been produced annually from 2002. The quotations taken from them speak for themselves.

EFA 2002: Is the world on track?

> The goals of EFA are of enormous significance. Without constant and steady progress towards them, development cannot be judged to be happening. The Report shows that the challenge faced by the nations of the world remains substantial. Although planning is under way, it needs to be strengthened. National commitment by both governments and civil society is the key to securing the goals, but costs and resources are crucial considerations, too. Although most countries will be able to meet these costs and find the necessary resources, the report shows that a significant minority will not if existing trends persist. In response, as yet, the international community has not adequately demonstrated its own commitment. In spite of grand promises, the aid record (both overall and for education) over the 1990s was both disappointing and worrying. Since Dakar, the question of education, especially basic education, has risen higher on the international agenda, but much remains to be done to ensure that aid flows are adequate, timely and well-targeted. Future practice has to be different from the past if our joint responsibilities are to be met and if the EFA goals are to be achieved. (p. 5)

EFA 2003–4: Gender and Education for All; The leap to equality

> As this issue of the Global Monitoring Report goes to press, the world is two years away from the date by which the gender parity goal is to be achieved. It is, then, timely that the report should pay particular attention to the progress being made with its implementation – and with that of the longer-term goal of achieving gender equality in education. The

report shows that, while many countries are likely to miss the 2005 goal, this circumstance could change quickly if appropriate changes in policy were made. However, achieving equality throughout education is more profoundly challenging. Educational inequality is caused by deeper forces in society that extend well beyond the boundaries of educational systems, institutions and processes. The report demonstrates that changes in a wide range of economic and social policies – as well as in education itself – will be needed if gender equality in education is to be attained. (p. 5)

EFA 2005: The Quality Imperative

This Report tells both a quantitative and a qualitative story. First, that the number of out-of-school children is declining too slowly to achieve universal primary education by 2015. Second, that despite progress, no country outside the developed word has achieved the four measurable EFA goals. Improving the quality of learning through inclusive, holistic policies is an overriding priority in a majority of countries. The Report highlights a number of urgent needs – for more and better trained teachers, for improved textbooks available to all learners, for pedagogical renewal and for more welcoming learning environments. While no reform comes without cost, better learning outcomes have been achieved in very diverse political contexts, and in societies with greatly varying degrees of wealth. (p.5)

EFA 2006: Literacy for Life

As in previous years, this Report examines progress towards the six EFA goals. The year 2005 has been particularly significant. On the one hand, it is now apparent, as the Report confirms, that the goal to achieve gender parity in primary and secondary education by 2005 has not been met, despite very rapid progress, especially in a number of low-income countries. We must renew our commitment and move forward. On the other hand, resources for basic education are increasing: public spending on education is rising in developing countries and the international community has promised to increase its support, especially to sub-Saharan Africa, as reflected at the G-8 summit in Gleneagles in July 2005 and the United Nations World Summit in New York in September 2005. The challenge now is to translate broad commitments into specific actions in developing countries and to step up the pace of change everywhere. We only have ten years left and we must not fail. (p. 6)

EFA 2007: Strong foundations; Early childhood care and education

This fifth edition of the EFA Global Monitoring Report assesses progress towards the first EFA goal, which calls upon countries to expand and improve comprehensive early childhood care and education, especially for the most disadvantaged children. Such interventions are crucial to improving children's present well-being and future development.

Yet the evidence suggests that young children in greatest need, who also stand to gain the most, are unlikely to have access to these programmes. Coverage remains very low in most of the developing world and few programmes exist for children under age 3. Even in the context of limited public resources, designing national policies for early childhood carries benefits for the country's entire education system. It is therefore vital that countries and the international community systematically make early childhood provision an integral component of their education and poverty alleviation strategies. This is essential for reducing extreme poverty and hunger, the overarching aim of the United Nations Millennium Development Goals.

A tone of urgency pervades this Report. While regions farthest from the goals are making impressive progress on enrolling new children into primary school, major challenges remain. Policies must address the barriers to education: household poverty, rural locations, poor quality, and lack of secondary schools and trained teachers, and not enough adult literacy programmes. (p. 5)

EFA 2008: Education for All by 2015; Will we make it?

We are steering the right course but the years ahead will require unwavering political will to consistently ensure that education from early childhood onwards is a national priority, to engage governments, civil society and the private sector in creative partnerships, and to generate dynamic coordination and support from the international community. Time is of the essence: for the 72 million children out of school, for the one in five adults without basic literacy skills and for the many pupils who leave school without acquiring essential skills and knowledge. (p. 5)

EFA 2009: Overcoming inequality: why governance matters

This seventh edition of the EFA Global Monitoring Report offers a warning to governments, donors and the international community. On current trends universal primary education will not be achieved by

2015. Too many children are receiving an education of such poor quality that they leave school without basic literacy and numeracy skills. Finally, deep and persistent disparities based on wealth, gender, location, ethnicity and other markers for disadvantage are acting as a major barrier to progress in education. If the world's governments are serious about Education for All, they must get more serious about tackling inequality. (p. 6)

EFA 2010: Reaching the marginalized

This year's Global Monitoring Report underscores that there is a long way to travel. There are still at least 72 million children who are missing out on their right to education because of the simple fact of where they are born or who their family is. Millions of youths leave school without the skills they need to succeed in the workforce and one in six adults is denied the right to literacy.

The 2010 Report is a call to action. We must reach the marginalized. Only inclusive education systems have the potential to harness the skills needed to build the knowledge societies of the twenty-first century. The international community has a determining role in supporting countries' efforts to protect and expand their education systems. We must not abandon them at this critical juncture. Promises to help poor countries out of the crisis must now translate into the financial resources that many governments so urgently need. (p. 5)

EFA 2011: The hidden crisis; Armed conflict and education

As this new edition of the EFA Global Monitoring Report makes clear, conflict continues to blight the lives of millions of the world's most vulnerable people. Warfare is also destroying opportunities for education on a scale that is insufficiently recognized. The facts are telling. Over 40% of out-of-school children live in conflict-affected countries. These same countries have some of the largest gender inequalities and lowest literacy levels in the world. I hope that, by turning the spotlight on what has until now been a 'hidden crisis' in education, the Report will help galvanize national and international action in four key areas. (p. 5)

Lack of commitment can be seen in the financing of Education for All both by the governments of developing countries and by provision of aid from wealthy donor countries. The 2002 report estimated that at most, the EFA initiative would cost some US $9.4 billion per annum of which 2.5 billion would be external aid. By 2007, it was clear that the costs had been underestimated and it was suggested that US $11 billion per annum in external aid would be needed to meet all the EFA targets. The 2009 report said that both developing countries and aid donors had failed to meet their commitments. The 2010 report estimated a funding gap of some US $16 billion and the 2011 report recorded that donors were not on track to meet their commitments. The sums required are considerable but they are minuscule when set against the US $10 trillion which the 2010 report estimates had been spent by advanced economies to shore up their financial systems. It is clear that this had to be done to prevent a worse global economic disaster from unfolding but it is equally clear that the financial crisis is simply one more chapter in a sorry tale in which the poor of the world suffer further from the systematic inequalities which pervade the global economic system.

From an evolutionary point of view, the global situation can be understood as human nature conducting its business as usual. We care most for those near to us but relatively little for those far away. We guard the resources we can garner for ourselves. Literacy, in and of itself, is powerless to transform this picture because most of us do not consider ourselves to have any serious responsibility for strangers, particularly not those living in distant lands. Modern technology has made physical travel to distant places possible but human psychology limits the empathic distances we are prepared to travel. There are, of course, individuals whose lives are transformed when they encounter the sufferings of the poor and oppressed but most of us in the privileged West are shielded from the brutal realities of life for those at the bottom of the heap and do little to inform ourselves. The point I am trying to make here is not a moral one, although of course there are morals to be derived from the global situation. The point is simply that the default settings of human nature are not transformed by literacy. The human mind is an ancient, highly sophisticated system evolved over countless generations for co-operation and conflict. Literacy adds intellectual tools to this potent mix of positive and negative impulses but it is not, by itself, capable of radically transforming them.

11.3 Summary

Literacy has both formal and evolved limitations. The formal limitations show that human reasoning cannot be captured in its entirety by syntax alone. Exercise of the imagination to create new meanings for symbol structures and to invent new, more powerful axioms will always be needed. The evolutionary process that produced the human mind suggests that literacy alone is not sufficient to transform societies and to remove the injustices and inequalities which characterise the contemporary world.

Chapter 12

The Consequences of Literacy

A quick search via Google Scholar in June 2011 revealed 120 citations since 2010 of Goody and Watt's classic paper whose title I have borrowed for this chapter's heading. The paper was first published in 1963 and it is itself evidence for the claim that literacy does have consequences. Without the durable record of the paper and the many copies of it which now exist, nearly 50 years of debate would not have happened. I have touched briefly on the paper and the controversy it has stimulated at various points in the book and I do not propose to reprise the arguments about it here. Goody (2000, Chapter 1) makes a considered response to some of the criticisms.

I want to make two points related to Goody and Watt's work. The first, in agreement with the broad thrust of their paper, is that literacy has had, and continues to have, profound consequences for *Homo sapiens*. Second, I want to suggest that their focus on literate versus non-literate societies is not the best way to approach the consequences of literacy in the contemporary world. The vast majority of human societies today are literate. It is thus more revealing now, I think, to consider the consequences of literacy within rather than between societies even though, as programs like Education For All make clear, there are still significant differences between societies in terms of literate achievement.

In keeping with the theoretical distinction between the functional core (an individual interacting with a text) and the surrounding institutions, I propose to consider the consequences of literacy separately at the individual and societal levels of analysis. The distinction does not for a moment deny the obvious fact that the surrounding institutions have powerful consequences for individuals. It shows, rather, that those institutions may promote or smother the possibilities of literacy that can be defined and understood at the level of the functional core. Supportive institutions make it possible for individuals to realise their literate potential. Unsupportive institutions may prevent people from having any chance of developing literate lives. Chapter 7 describes the consequences of literacy in terms of purely syntactic processing capacity increases. This chapter considers the meanings of the literate activities people engage in, extending the discussion in Chapter 8. Goody (1977) discussed the power that lists and tables have on our perceptions. In this chapter I consider the consequences of literacy in terms of two binary distinctions: individual/society, and positive/

Table 12.1   Consequences of literacy: a fourfold classification

	Positive	Negative
Individual	???	???
Society	???	???

negative. A tabular representation (Table 12.1) of these distinctions invites us to consider four classes of questions: What are the positive and negative consequences of literacy for individuals and societies?

It turns out, as might be expected, that it is often not straightforward to decide whether a consequence should be described as individual or as social and readers may disagree with some of my assignments. However, the point of the exercise is really to try to think things through in terms of a framework rather than to achieve an absolute, unambiguous partitioning.

The evolutionary perspective of the book emphasises the continuities rather than the differences between literate and non-literate humans because, large though the effects of literacy are, it is unlikely that they have led to fundamental transformations of adaptations for social living. Thus the discussion of the consequences of literacy is not intended as a comparison between literate and non-literate human groups but as a means of assessing the possible interactions between genetic resources and the new cultural resources derived from literacy. The point is to consider the literate epoch as a new stage in the lengthy history of our species. How have social relations been changed? To what extent have social adaptations proved resistant to modification by literacy? Are there selective advantages or disadvantages arising from literacy? Are there new opportunities for hierarchy construction, for the development of status differentials, for the creation of elite groups? Are there new opportunities for altruism, for cooperation, for developing systems of equality and equity?

12.1   The consequences of literacy are not automatic

Among the charges that have been levelled at Goody and Watt is the suggestion that they took the consequences of literacy to be automatic. They have been said to believe that literacy has its effects on societies independently of the social context. From my reading of their paper and Goody's later work on literacy, I cannot find evidence to support this critique. The consequences of literacy are nowhere claimed to be automatic in Goody's oeuvre. Nor am I claiming them to be automatic here. If they were, reading and writing would be much more powerful than they are. As it is, nothing much follows from the bare facts of being able to read and write. It's a bit like learning to ride a bicycle. Nothing much follows from that if a bike is not available, or if your movements are constrained, or if you have no opportunity to practise. But, if you have learned to ride and have a machine to ride you can undertake journeys that greatly increase your scope for travel. If you can read and write and have access to texts and writing materials you can undertake significant intellectual journeys that would otherwise be impossible.

It may help to make a distinction between consequences and possibilities. I think we can say that the consequences of literacy depend on the social formation to a large extent but that the possibilities of literacy do not. The principal possibility opened up by becoming literate is to increase the scope of the mind, to augment its potential. There's nothing automatic about it but it's worth learning to read and write because there are further things you can learn to do if you're literate which you can't do if you're not. Science and mathematics, for example, are not consequences of literacy in the sense that they were bound to happen once people learned to read and write, but they are parts of the augmented scope of the literate mind. Literacy is a necessary, but not a sufficient, condition for science and mathematics. It's also a necessary, but not sufficient, condition for many of the other, perhaps less obvious things, that literate minds can do.

12.2   Positive consequences for individuals

The consequences of literacy for the individual can be approached in two related but distinct ways. There are consequences flowing from access to the infinite universe of texts and there are consequences flowing from the reflective space afforded by literacy which allows for the development of thinking and for the study and composition of texts away from the whirl of everyday social interaction. These consequences can be discussed in terms of the processes of revision and interpretation described in Chapters 7 and 8. Why is revision important for the development of meanings? What kinds of semantic interpretations can be built on the syntactic foundations of universal processing capacity?

It is important at this point to address a significant limitation of the Turing machine model, and that limitation is the fact that the functional states of a Turing machine are fixed. This means that we cannot model processes of development and learning directly. This is clearly a serious limitation because much of what we achieve with literacy is generally understood in terms of learning and development. However, the limitation is not catastrophic and it can be overcome in various ways. One way would be to model development and learning via a sequence of Turing machine models. Chapter 7.3 shows that a machine with two functional states can produce the symbol sequence 010101...whereas a machine with four functional states is needed to produce the sequence 0010110111...In general, machines with larger numbers of functional states are capable of producing and interpreting more complex symbol structures. Thus we might build a sequence of models with increasing numbers of functional states to represent how learning affects the mind. Ideally, however, we would like a model in which the number and nature of functional states are changed as a result of symbol processing.

There are models of this kind which have been explored extensively by mathematicians and cognitive scientists. They are variously known as connectionist or neural network models and they have the crucial feature of being able to learn from their experience (Rumelhart and McClelland, 1986; McClelland and Rumelhart, 1986; Clark, 1989, 1993; Teuscher, 2002). For the purposes of this book, connectionist models have the disadvantage of being technically rather more complex to describe than Turing machines, although in some respects they are more realistic. However, the understanding that we get from connectionist models supports the idea that we can think of learning and development in terms of sequences of Turing machines. That being so, we can talk about the consequences of literacy in terms of changes to states of mind resulting from reading and writing texts even though we cannot model those changes directly with a single Turing machine. The best way to think about these things is as follows: we can prove with Turing machine models that particular types of engagement with texts change processing capacities fundamentally, even though the 'minds' modelled with those machines are fixed. Given this, the implication is that literacy must be at least as powerful as this for minds which can also develop as a result of their reading and writing.

12.2.1   Access to the universe of texts

The most obvious consequence of literacy is that it provides the individual with access to the universe of texts. The world which opens up to the literate is a world in which knowledge about every conceivable topic is recorded. It is also a world in which speech is captured and represented via external symbols. David Olson has argued in *The World on Paper* (1994) that writing provides a model of speech which leads to new kinds of awareness and new modes of thinking. It is the latter point that I particularly wish to stress. It is obviously an important aspect of literacy that it enables speech to be represented, but it is equally important, and perhaps more important, that literacy enables us to represent thoughts, concepts, and relations between them, such as inferences. Access to the universe of texts thus gives us access to durable representations of the thoughts of other people about matters as simple as what to eat for lunch or as complex as quantum gravity. It enables us to represent particular things, such as what I ate for lunch yesterday and general principles, such as what makes a food nutritious for humans. It is clear that access to the universe of texts is not all or nothing. We are not able to understand texts just by virtue of being able to read the words, but the possibility of understanding is there for literate people in a way that is not available to someone who cannot read and write. Moreover, the possibility of understanding things deeply as a result of studying texts is uniquely available to the literate. This is not to say that non-literate people cannot understand things deeply. It is, rather, to say that the study of texts is a particularly powerful means of gaining deep understandings. Access to the universe of texts thus implies the possibility of obtaining deep understandings of an indefinitely wide range of thought.

12.2.2   Writing the very small and the very large

Texts serve to expand our intellectual grasp in ways analogous to the extensions of perception made possible by the microscope and the telescope. We can read and write about matters which lie far beyond the limits of our unaided perception. Consider units of length as an example. In the literate epoch it has become possible for physicists to talk meaningfully about lengths as short as the Planck length. This is 16.163×10^{-36} metres. It is so short that it lies far beyond the capacities of current measurement technology, but it is meaningful because it describes the scale at which quantum effects start to dominate the structure of spacetime (http:// en.wikipedia.org/wiki/Planck_length). Towards the other end of the spectrum astronomers use the parsec as a measurement of length. It is the distance travelled by light in about 3.26 years, which is about 19 trillion miles (http://en.wikipedia.org/wiki/Parsec). Such short and long distances are physically meaningful because they describe aspects of the structure of the universe we live in, but both the means to calculate them and the means to express them concisely are consequences of literacy and the cumulative scientific knowledge that it has made possible. Measurements and concepts of duration have similarly expanded as a result of literacy. The vast time scales of evolutionary processes have been mentioned in earlier chapters as well as the tiny time scales of the electronic processes which make computers useful. Durations and lengths of the kind routinely described in contemporary science are both inexpressible and unthinkable without the resources of literacy.

Writing the very long also becomes a possibility. The length of an argument is no longer limited by what can be held in mind. Complex inferential structures, such as the incompleteness proofs of Kurt Gödel and Turing's proof of the unsolvability of the halting problem can be constructed, checked, and revised as necessary. An interesting point about inferential structures of this kind is that the accumulation of simple steps shapes the overall picture. Complex inferences do not necessarily require startling insights or extraordinary thinking. One might think of an analogy between a complex inference constructed of simple logical steps and the process whereby the passage of water over rocks, given enough time, is able to build huge canyons and river systems. Logical practice can be transformed by durable representations without concomitant transformations of the capabilities of individual minds.

12.2.3   Reflective reading and writing

Reflective literacy practices have important consequences. I like to think of them in terms of 'Slow Reading' by analogy with 'Slow Food'. The slow food movement was founded by Carlo Petrini in 1986 in northern Italy and it has more than 100,000 members. The movement argues against the industrialised pre-processing of food and its hasty consumption and in favour of what might be called a more 'ruminative' approach to all aspects of nutrition. Here is an excerpt from its manifesto:

> *We are enslaved by speed and have all succumbed to the same insidious virus: Fast Life, which disrupts our habits, pervades the privacy of our homes and forces us to eat Fast Foods.*
>
> *To be worthy of the name, Homo Sapiens should rid himself of speed before it reduces him to a species in danger of extinction.*
>
> *A firm defense of quiet material pleasure is the only way to oppose the universal folly of Fast Life.*
>
> *May suitable doses of guaranteed sensual pleasure and slow, long-lasting enjoyment preserve us from the contagion of the multitude who mistake frenzy for efficiency.*
>
> *Our defense should begin at the table with Slow Food.*
>
> *Let us rediscover the flavors and savors of regional cooking and banish the degrading effects of Fast Food.*
>
> *In the name of productivity, Fast Life has changed our way of being and threatens our environment and our landscapes. So Slow Food is now the only truly progressive answer.*
>
> *That is what real culture is all about: developing taste rather than demeaning it. And what better way to set about this than an international exchange of experiences, knowledge, projects?*
>
> *Slow Food guarantees a better future.*
>
> (Downloaded from http://www.slowfood.org.uk/Cms/Page/history, 24/6/2011)

Many of these recommendations could be carried over, more or less unchanged, into recommendations about the practices of reading and writing. 'Slow Reading guarantees a better future' could be a useful slogan. In one of his famous odes, John Keats described a Grecian urn as a 'foster-child of silence and slow time' (Keats and Stillinger, 1978, p. 372) and I think we can consider the literate mind in a somewhat similar way. Literacy, considered as a pleasurable and enduring habit of mind, as an aspect of life-long learning, rather than just as an economic or social necessity, needs time, encouragement, and suitable contexts for its development. Learning to read and to write are not, in themselves, sufficient conditions for the development of literacy as an intrinsic part of one's sense of self. This is particularly the case, perhaps, with mathematical and scientific literacy, but it is also true of the skills required to make sense of a good deal of contemporary writing in other fields. Slow reading and writing, therefore, focus on the conditions needed to foster literate careers.

A related idea emphasises the importance of close reading and rigorously structured, reflective, writing. These processes are slow because they take time to mature. Speed reading is all well and good for those who need to process large amounts of information quickly, but close reading, which pays attention to sentence structure, choice of words, figures of speech, allusion, and so forth, enables a careful reader to come to understand the multiple layers of meaning that skilled writers are able to build into their texts. Such an understanding also helps a potential writer to understand the range of possibilities, skills, and choices that can make a text more interesting, comprehensible, and stylish. Reading and writing understood and taught in this way are emancipatory practices, an idea expressed powerfully in a sonnet by Joe Winter, a poet and teacher for many years:

> *At Khelaghar*
>
> First up some steps: and then a room without walls.
> Supports for the roof – and in between, some trees.
> What is this room in which the fresh air falls?
> A place in which to work and be at ease.
> It is the loveliest classroom. To one who has been
> clamped between walls of learning; who in turn
> has caged young minds in crowded Nature-mean
> high-rise low-vision London schools – to learn
> and teach here, is a breath of what may be.
> And yet perhaps I took away the walls
> for one or two, at times, when I was able.
> Part of all making is a making-free.
> This tree-room lies inside the world's school-halls:
> a boy and girl, a teacher, and a table.
>
> (From *Guest and Host*, Winter, 2003)

A significant amount of contemporary pedagogy and educational research has focused on the need to provide ways for learners of all ages to engage more substantially with literacy. The notorious 'fourth grade slump' in the United States and continuing concerns with poor literacy achievement among both children and adults in the U.K. show that reflective reading and writing are desirable, but clearly not automatic, consequences of literacy learning. When reflective reading and writing are in place they have significant effects on their practitioners. I consider two examples.

12.2.3.1   *Literate thinking and envisionments*

Judith Langer describes literacy as 'the ability to think like a literate person, to call upon the kinds of reasoning abilities that people generally use when they read and write (such as the ability to reflect on text, symbols, and their meanings), even when reading and writing are not involved, and even in the context of electronic or graphic modes and media' (Langer 2011, p. 12). Notice the emphasis on thinking. Reading and writing are necessary, but not sufficient, conditions for literacy from this perspective. What is also needed is a sense of what has and has not been understood, and the means to find one's way in the networks of knowledge and debate which define the literate world. These ideas suggest a familiarity and confidence with written materials, a sense that they will buoy you up rather than weigh you down. Langer uses the term 'envisionment' to describe the dynamic processes of sense making that lead to literate thinking.

> Envisionments are the worlds of knowledge in our minds that are made up of what we understand and what we don't about a particular topic or experience at any point in time. They are dynamic sets of related ideas, questions, images, anticipations, agreements, arguments, and hunches that fill our minds during every reading, writing, discussion, technology interaction, or other experience where we gain or express thoughts and understandings. (Langer, 2011, p. 17)

Education, for Langer, involves processes of envisionment building and refinement. Her ideas fit very well with the Turing machine model of literacy proposed in this book. We can think of envisionments as sets of functional states. They both produce and are produced by dynamic interactions with texts. A more sophisticated, deeper envisionment is like a machine with more functional states. You can do more with it. The reference to images in the quotation is consonant with the suggestion in Chapter 1.15 that liberating the imagination may be among the most important effects of literacy. Langer discusses envisionment building in a range of academic disciplines and explains how classroom sessions can be structured to encourage disciplined but creative leaps of the imagination. Envisionment may be described as an active use of reflection to improve understanding.

Complex texts frequently require multiple readings and reflection before they are properly understood. It is often important to identify what hasn't been understood. Once one has a clear idea of what has not been understood it is possible to focus on specific problem areas for further investigation. A belief in the possibility of progress is something that supportive, communicative environments need to foster. If someone's response to challenging material is to think or say 'I'm no good at that, I just can't do it' it will naturally be difficult to make headway. An environment that encourages confidence that problems can be overcome is one in which deeper envisionments can be constructed.

12.2.3.2 *Reflective practice*

It is striking to find very close agreement with Langer's description of envisionments in the work of Gillie Bolton who uses what she calls *through-the-mirror* writing as a means to enable adult practitioners in a range of disciplines to reflect critically on themselves, their work, and its positioning in social contexts. Reflective practice, she says can enable enquiry into

- what you know but do not know you know
- what you do not know and want to know
- what you think, feel, believe, value, understand about your role and boundaries
- how your actions match up with what you believe
- how to value and take into account personal feelings

(Bolton, 2010, p. 4)

Reflective practice is clearly a close cousin of envisionment. Both have the goal of making explicit and available for examination what is otherwise implicit. The writing associated with Bolton's reflective practice methodology is called *through-the-mirror* writing to reflect the strange world Alice found herself in when she stepped through the looking glass in the sequel to her adventures in Wonderland. The looking glass world is simultaneously the same as and different from the familiar everyday world. So it is with *through-the-mirror* writing. One's experiences, hopes, and fears are seen in a new light. Bolton raises the question 'Why writing?' given that writing is often a difficult activity for those who rarely or never do it for pleasure. Her answers accord with the ideas discussed in this book. First, writing is a private activity, under the control of the writer and outside the barrage of constant social interaction and expectation that is so important for our daily lives and that has shaped our evolution as discussed in Chapter 6. Second, writing provides a durable record:

> Speech or thought can be forgotten, or shift and change like a whisper game, vanishing on the air. Interlocutors often remember conversations differently, each party certain their recollection is correct. Writing leaves clear footprints on the page, aiding progressive thought. Writing stays in the same form to be worked on later. Rewriting and redrafting, to get closer and closer to what needs to be expressed, is self-educative. (Bolton, 2010, p. 106)

It is interesting to note that the writing produced in this way may very well be written quickly. One of the recommendations for reflective practice writers is simply to get things down on paper. Don't think about grammar or spelling, don't be self-critical. Evade the inner censor by writing exactly what comes to mind. One might think that this emphasis on getting things down at speed is in conflict with the slow food analogy. However, speed can be of the essence even with slow food. We can think of a speedily written text which is subsequently studied and revised, as akin to fresh ingredients, rapidly sourced and harvested, but then prepared and savoured at leisure.

12.2.4 Reading and writing for pleasure

From the standpoint of the individual, the most important consequence of literacy may simply be the pleasure to be had from reading and writing. The instrumental consequences are important of course, and there is no doubt about the positive effect on knowledge that literacy provides, but if there were no pleasure to be derived from it, it is hardly likely that it would attract such passionate devotees as it does. The vast spaces of the universe of texts do not, themselves, mandate any particular approach to texts. Instead, the capacities to read and write open up limitless terrain for the intellectual explorer wherever she wishes to go. It is the sense of a potentially endless journey, of the satisfactions to be had from textual exploration in whichever direction one wishes which is the inspirational message to be gleaned from the possibilities of literacy. Arguments to the effect that literacy is essentially social practice seem to me to shackle the individual imagination and to tie it too closely to local contexts. Escape is what many people seek from their reading. Too much drill, of course, shackles the imagination in different ways. Literacy, once acquired, is an endless source of opportunities. The invitation offered by the universe of texts is 'Come and look for yourself. Read what you wish to read, write what you wish to write.'

Reading gives us a space where time slows down, where we can absorb the thoughts of the quick witted at our leisure. The 24-year-old Alan Turing explored places that most of us could never discover on our own. His intellect, in its spheres of expertise, was fast and brilliant. It is a thrilling journey to follow his construction of the universal machine, to understand why the details of his text are as they are. And the same is true of the journeys that people make to understand whatever domains they find of interest to them. People who read texts closely find all sorts of treasures in them. Close readings ponder choices of words, consider possible alternatives that the author might have chosen, and try to tease out the many layers of meaning that may be intended. A close reading considers the goals of the author, the genre within which a work is located. A close reading may spin off new ideas, directions suggested or implied by a work but not explored in it. A close reading may explore parallels in other works, references to them, allusions or echoes. A close reading assumes that the meaning of a text may not always be immediately available, that it may require some digging beneath the surface.

The pleasures of writing are, perhaps, a little harder to achieve and many avid readers may write little or nothing of their own. The intention to communicate which is characteristic of much writing makes the writer aware of a possible audience and that can be daunting. It is, of course, possible to write purely for oneself or for close and trusted friends which reduces the sense of exposure. Private writing has much to recommend it; it can serve as a wonderful way to clarify thinking– in fact to find out just what it is that we do think as the section on reflective practice suggests. Writing is also a means to greater enjoyment of reading. Appreciation of the effort needed to produce a pleasing turn of phrase, or to express a complex idea or feeling precisely comes in part from trying to do these things oneself. From such efforts can come pleasure, perhaps tinged with envy, with the achievements of others.

One of the great benefits of literacy is that it can be enjoyed throughout the life span even when one's physical powers are in decline. Perhaps literacy leads to greater interiority as one gets older, to a greater consciousness of the inner world or of the possibilities of the life of the mind. Sherman (2010) has written a fascinating account of the possibilities of what he calls 'contemplative aging'. His approach is based on being rather than doing, on living for the moment and what it has to offer. One might think of contemplative aging, in Langer's terms, as exploring envisionments for their intrinsic qualities rather than for their instrumental benefits. Having a private inner life is one of the universals on Brown's list. Literacy can promote, develop, and enrich this inner life.

12.3   Negative consequences for individuals

There are parts of the world today in which becoming literate is fraught with danger, and there are parts of the world in which those with highly developed literate expertise such as teachers and academics are targets for intimidation and violence. O'Malley (2010) provides a shocking and depressing catalogue of deliberate attacks on educational institutions, their staff, and their students quite apart from the euphemistic 'collateral damage' sustained in armed conflicts. The problems are multi-faceted; they include the assassination of teachers and researchers for making unwelcome discoveries, acid attacks on girls to prevent them from going to school, and the abduction of pupils for forced recruitment as child soldiers. There are particular problems in conflict areas such as Afghanistan (Glad, 2009) but O'Malley reports that educational establishments and the people in them have been attacked in at least 31 countries in Africa, Asia, Europe, and Latin America over the past three years (p. 15). The scale of the problems is significant. O'Malley lists, among others, 670 attacks on schools, staff, and students in Afghanistan in 2008, the destruction of 356 schools in Pakistan as a result of battles between the Army and the Taliban, 300 schools blown up by Maoist rebels in India between 2006 and 2009, and more than 300 kindergarten, school, and university buildings damaged during Israel's Operation Cast Lead in Gaza at the turn of 2008–9. O'Malley details 17 different categories of motive for the attacks, including the prevention of education, revenge killings, silencing of opposition views, silencing of human rights campaigns, and abduction for ransom. The physical and psychological effects of such brutal attacks are not hard to imagine. They include loss of life, injury, permanent handicapping, trauma, depression, loss of motivation, and loss of concentration.

Jarecki and Kaisth (2009) in a report on the activities of the Scholar Rescue Fund, say that 'scholar oppression is a permanent condition of life' (p. 3). They identify governments as the sole or a contributory source of persecution in almost 75 of the cases the Fund dealt with and suggest that 'Scholar persecution is a tactic that repressive governments and/or non-state actors actively and deliberately employ to achieve their objectives. And – given the results that we are reporting here – it is a tactic that is effective, strategic, and widespread' (p. 9). Instances include a Sri Lankan professor of psychiatry whose reports on the trauma suffered by victims of the civil war led to his being targeted by both separatist rebels and government troops. A Moroccan scholar who specialises in sociological research on human sexuality and reproductive health was forced to flee when his work was labelled as anti-Islamic by religious conservatives. A law professor was targeted for lecturing on human rights:

A Colombian law professor was both pleased and puzzled when he saw a new student, older than most of his classmates, vigorously making notes whenever the professor spoke of human rights. His pleasure turned to discomfort when the supposed student accosted him after class and asked to walk with him. When the new student commented on the professor's "courageous talk" then asked whether he was afraid of walking home alone at night, the professor panicked. Instead of continuing home, he spent the night with friends. And a good thing, too, because that night eight armed men came to his house and asked for him. (Jarecki and Kaisth, 2009, p. 7)

Quite apart from the consequences for the individuals directly involved, it is easy for climates of fear and intimidation to be created which muzzle free speech and enable repressive regimes to operate with minimal risks that their activities will be reported.

Clearly, then, there are circumstances in which becoming or trying to become literate has negative consequences for individuals. Extreme consequences of the kind described typically result from adverse societal contexts in which articulate people may be seen as threats. In a sense, this dark side of literacy serves to illustrate how powerful a force it is, if a regime fears its effects sufficiently to kill literate people. Other negative consequences, physically less taxing but maybe of equal psychological impact, include various forms of indoctrination. These may have religious or political roots or both. Indoctrination may be obvious and explicit, 'we're good and they're bad' but it may also be much more subtle and constant debate takes place, in peaceful as well as in conflict-riven societies, about relations between curricula and identity. The teaching of history in the British primary curriculum is a case in point:

> [P]arents at one community sounding, in common with some politicians, argued that 'Britishness' arises from a knowledge of British history. Others took a different view, believing that a condition of cultural plurality may demand if not as many histories as there are cultures, then certainly an approach to history which highlights diversity and the very different tales that can be told about the past, depending on where in the cultural mix one happens to find oneself. (Alexander, 2010, p. 229)

Perhaps what this demonstrates is not so much a negative consequence of literacy but a risk that the positive consequences may be more constrained than one might hope. From the standpoint of the universe of texts with its vast range of possibilities, the design and choice of texts for education is clearly a pressing matter. Two rather different general strategies can be identified, one focused on content and one on process. From a content point of view, it might be deemed desirable in a given society, to teach specific content with clear cultural messages. From a process point of view, content might be viewed not just as an end in itself, but also as a means to fostering and developing independent judgement. The universe of texts is so vast that it is highly desirable for individuals to be able to chart their own course through it. Thus history teaching, which highlights diversity and the possibility of giving different accounts of 'the same' events, might be thought preferable to an approach which presents a particular account of 'what happened' as canonical.

12.4   Positive consequences for society

The consequences of literacy for the maintenance and development of human societies and cultures are profound. Goody and Watt (1963) famously and controversially argued that literate societies distinguished myth from history in ways that were not possible for purely oral societies; they also proposed that literacy enabled new types of logical argument. Many other societal consequences can also be described. I shall consider only a small number of examples. Practically all the institutions of contemporary societies are dependent in one way or another on literacy, and this becomes more and more the case as reliance on the internet and cyberspace increases. Legal systems, financial systems, and educational systems in their modern forms are unthinkable without documentary evidence and organisation. The greater the dependence on documentation the more people are needed with specific skills to manage the institutions on which we all depend, and hence the increased pressure on educational institutions to produce those people.

12.4.1   Complex, durable institutions

Humans are prepared to travel to far distant places for the sake of novelty. They seek out attractions like funfairs and theme parks; they enjoy altering their states of consciousness in many ways. New experiences are often welcomed and sought out, particularly by the young. How often do we hear 'I'm bored' from children? However, novelty and change are welcome only against a background of stable and durable societal institutions. The ordinary business of living is much better carried out when the future is predictable and tolerably just. Carolyn Nordstrom has written eloquently about the disruptive effects of war on the durable societal institutions that most of us are able to take for granted. She quotes the words of a man caught up in a battle zone, making both him and the zone anonymous to guard against possible reprisals:

> Someone without hope for a better future, will they plant their fields? Will they work to develop industry? Will they devote time to helping others, work to resolve conflicts, work to repair damaged towns, and build up their societies? Will they work to staff hospitals, build new schools, open new trade routes? No. All that depends on a sense that things can be better, that these actions will have some benefit in the future. People have to have confidence, a sense of hope, in their future. Without this, people don't build up something so it will be destroyed. So people stop working, and society stops progressing. (Nordstrom, 2004, p. 68)

The point to make is not that literacy guarantees the existence of stable institutions; clearly if that were so, war and conflict would have come to an end with the invention of literacy. What can be argued, however, is that institutions promoted by literacy, such as legal systems and international diplomacy, have led to a decline in violence and to a more peaceful world for most of us. This may seem an implausible claim given the carnage of wars throughout the twentieth century and the numerous conflicts that still rage around the world, but there is evidence to support it. Using data gathered by Keeley (1995), Richard Wrangham has proposed that rates of death by warfare are much lower than in the non-literate past:

> Shockingly, death rates in the modern era tend to be lower even when periods of major war are included. During the twentieth century, for example, Germany, Russia, and Japan each experienced rates of war deaths that were less than half the average hunter-gatherer rate. The contrast reflects a difference in the practice of war between prestate and state societies. In prestate societies all men are warriors, and all women are vulnerable. In state societies, by contrast, fewer people are directly exposed to violence (even though civilians and children often suffer worse casualties than the military) because armies fight on behalf of the larger group. (Wrangham, 2004, p. 30)

Negotiations, treaties, arbitration, and conflict resolution– all these activities are fostered by literacy. Without literate records, precise details of what was agreed will most likely be remembered differently by the parties to the conflict, possibly leading to further accusations of bad faith and betrayal. Jared Diamond in *Guns, Germs and Steel*, describes the tense meetings between individuals in traditional New Guinean societies even in circumstances where neither had a particular grievance.

> In traditional New Guinea society, if a New Guinean happened to encounter an unfamiliar New Guinean while both were away from their respective villages, the two engaged in a long discussion of their relatives, in an attempt to establish some relationship and hence some reason why the two should not attempt to kill each other. (Diamond, 1997, pp. 271–2)

In the absence of all the institutional checks and balances that we take for granted in everyday life, in situations where there are no police forces or armies, strangers may quite reasonably be treated as potentially hostile. In such cases stable institutions, even under a despotic regime, may be preferable to no institutions at all.

12.4.2 Cultural ratchets

In Chapter 6, I discussed the suggestion made by Michael Tomasello and his colleagues that humans are uniquely equipped with a capacity, called collective intentionality, which enables us to create and share goals and to benefit from the cultural products of others by means of cultural ratchets. Literacy is the pre-eminent means for creating and storing cultural ratchets. Books, blueprints, plans, patents, theories, and theses are all instances of cultural ratchets. The durability of written materials means that they can be examined at leisure. The ideas they contain can be discussed, explained, explored, understood, criticised, revised, improved, and generally worked upon. The easy dissemination of written materials means that they can be shared among large numbers of people. This means that the insights of the exceptionally gifted can be deployed for the benefit of the community as a whole. Without the abiding presence of the writings of Turing and Darwin, for example, my own work would necessarily have taken a very different course. The opportunity to re-read and reflect on their works has had a strong influence on my approach to literacy, among other things. One could, of course, read them once and never return to them again, but the opportunity to revisit their writings makes it possible to rethink earlier engagements with them and to deepen one's understanding. If, as a result of reading my book, others are stimulated to read Turing and Darwin and to develop the ideas set out here further, the cultural ratchets will have moved on a further click or two.

12.4.3   Equality of opportunity

All else being equal, literacy promotes equality of opportunity. It does this partly because the universe of texts is as diverse as the people who make use of it and partly because the techniques of literacy are equally available, in principle, to young and old, to male and female, to the meek as well as the arrogant. Intellectual prowess is not dependent on physical power or on any particular set of psychological characteristics. Anyone, in short, can have useful ideas. Over the course of the literate epoch oppressed groups have time and again demonstrated facility with literate techniques in the face of scepticism and scorn. The position of women with respect to education is a particular case which continues to be relevant if only because equality of opportunity has not yet been fully achieved. Some parts of the global community continue to deny education to women and girls on religious and other grounds, although the bulk of opinion is firmly and urgently in favour of their education (Schultz, 2002; Colclough, 2007; Hausmann, Tyson and Zahidi, 2008).

Literate institutions create pressure for greater equality of educational opportunity because the contributions of women, when they can be made, stand up to scrutiny when judged impartially. Women perform at the highest levels in all academic disciplines. It is very clear that they tend not to advance to the highest levels of hierarchical, academic institutions as often as men do but it is not yet clear whether this is due solely to discrimination or whether there are average temperamental characteristics to be taken into account as well. This we would be able to discover if genuine equality of opportunity were in place for long enough to enable women to engage freely in the study of whatever subjects they chose without any artificial constraints. It can be doubted whether this will ever come about, but were it to do so we might still find sex-based differences of interest and aptitude. From the standpoint of the universe of texts that might be no bad thing. The universe is so vast and the portion of it as yet explored so vanishingly small that the widest possible range of interests should be encouraged. The immense scope of the universe of texts suggests that parochialism of every kind should be avoided in favour of wide-ranging exploration.

12.5   Negative consequences for society

The consequences of literacy that have negative effects on societies are, to some extent, the inevitable accompaniments of its positive aspects, like the shadows that are cast by bright sunlight. Excessive bureaucracy, unmanageable complexity, delays and inefficiencies of management sprout from the fertile fields of documentation needed to maintain contemporary societies. Considering only my own, rather sheltered, corner of academe the weight of paper and electronic documentation apparently needed to keep a modern university going is increasing all the time. I am ill equipped, both temperamentally and by training, to explore the labyrinthine complexities that underpin contemporary institutions, but one point of interest concerns the increase in opportunities for the construction of hierarchies and stratifications that literacy appears to offer. This is not to say that pre-literate societies were non-hierarchical or that their members were uninterested in status differences. Dietler (1996), for example, describes the potent uses of food for the production of status differences. However, the hierarchies he describes are limited in extent; they serve mainly to distinguish leaders from followers and the rich from the poor. The opportunities afforded by the simple device of differential job titles seem quite obviously to change the game in powerful ways. Literate classification, whatever its subject matter, offers the means to record and perpetuate minute differences which can then be pressed into service in the interests of marking status differences. I suppose it is a moot point whether classification should be considered a negative aspect of literacy. Clearly there are all sorts of positive classifications. However, in so far as job classification is used as the basis for differential pay and conditions and maintains or increases levels of inequality in society, it has negative connotations particularly for those whose occupations are considered to be of low status. Ganzeboom and Treiman (1996) provide an interesting insight into occupational classifications and their associated prestige.

12.6   A game of consequences

The debate about the consequences of literacy, engendered by Goody and Watt (1963) and still a live issue in contemporary discussion, has helped literacy scholars to a clearer understanding of their subject matter. However, it has also led to the postulation of dichotomies such as 'autonomous' vs. 'ideological', which really cannot be sustained on close examination of the texts involved. Moreover, the debate has, to a degree, been characterised by what has been called a 'discourse of derision' (Alexander, 2010, p. 22) in which slogans and straw men take the place of reasoned argument. This, in itself, might be considered a negative societal consequence of literacy. When we consider individuals interacting with texts from the standpoint taken in this book it is clear, beyond question, that literacy does have consequences for them. From this it also follows that literacy must have societal consequences as well, although these may be harder to understand because of the complex configuration of other factors in which literacy practices are embedded. The 'game of consequences' could, therefore, profitably take a different direction in future. It could explore the effects of literacy rather than debating their existence.

12.7   Looking to the future: the literate construction of what it means to be human

Among the numerous influences on human behaviour is the understanding of what it means to be human. This understanding differs between cultures and societies and influences the kinds of social institutions that are created and how they are valued. The question of human nature has been a fundamental concern of all literate societies. In some it has been pursued as a purely philosophical exercise, in others it has had obvious political significance as well (Rodriguez-Salgado, 2009). Some societies, for example those with strong beliefs in a creator and an afterlife, understand human life as a temporary state of preparation for an eternal hereafter. Others consider human life as one among a number of forms of life and believe in reincarnation and the possibility of moving from one form of life to another. (Given the opportunity I would like to experience life as a raven in another incarnation! They are intelligent birds [Heinrich, 2006] which appear to enjoy mountain environments as I do.) Literacy makes possible the recording of different forms of belief and enables them to be compared. Comparisons may reinforce belief in the rightness of one's own point of view but may also lead to an appreciation of the contingent nature of world views and to the complex mixture of factors that underpin their emergence. The possibility I wish to consider is that a more pervasive understanding of our current selves rooted in the evolutionary past of our species may lead to a construction of what it means to be human which will promote a better understanding of the problems we face and the nature of possible solutions to them. Such a project, a social construction of humanity derived from evolutionary biology, is essentially a literate undertaking because of the enormous range of evidence it needs to consider and because of the protracted nature of discussion and argument it can be expected to generate. It is also a forward looking project; it takes as given the possibilities of literacy and considers how they might be deployed for a better awareness and understanding of the choices we have to make.

A good deal of social science, as discussed in earlier chapters, assumes that biology builds general-purpose, language-using learning machines which are then handed over to processes of socialisation and acculturation for shaping into the various human forms that can be observed. If that is the correct view then there is little for humans to learn from biology about what kinds of social institutions might be desirable or feasible. General purpose learning machines, generalists for short, are by definition capable of learning any definable behaviour, any function from input to output. Biological versions of such machines should experience all kinds of learned behaviours as equally natural. But we humans don't, for the simple reason that we are not generalists. We are something fundamentally different: we are flexible specialists. The two can be similar enough in terms of observable behaviour for potentially disastrous confusions to arise. The fundamental difference is between a system designed to be general-purpose, and one designed to function flexibly, but for specific purposes, in a wide range of environments. The difference this makes can be described as follows: The nature of the environment in which a generalist functions is of no special interest to it because it has no purposes of its own. It can behave as flexibly as desired and it operates as easily in one environment as it does in another. That's what it means to be general-purpose. The nature of the environment in which a flexible specialist operates, by contrast, is of deep interest to it because it does have goals and purposes. If the environment offers easy fulfilment of its goals and few obstacles, the functioning of the flexible specialist is facilitated and its behaviour can be relaxed; if the environment prevents fulfilment of its goals and throws up many obstacles, its functioning is frustrated and its behaviour may become strained. Thus the qualities of the environment make the behaviour of the flexible specialist predictable to a degree, at least in terms of broad categories, whereas the behaviour of the generalist is not predictable from its environment.

Confusion is likely to arise if the goals of the flexible specialist are long term and implicitly defined; then it may be impossible to tell it apart, in any given environment, from a generalist simply by observing the behaviour of both. That, I think, is where much social science goes astray. It treats human beings as generalists, whereas in fact they are flexible specialists. It is undoubtedly true that the behaviour of a flexible specialist is malleable and may be shaped by its environment, but that does not modify its goals. The generalist by contrast has no goals of its own and is, therefore, equally amenable to all environments.

The processes of socialisation and acculturation which a flexible specialist experiences and the institutions and other environmental factors which frame its behaviour will have very different effects according to how well they align with its goals. If they align well then its behaviour will tend to be docile; if they align badly its behaviour will tend to be truculent and unruly. It follows that the design of social institutions should take account of the goals of flexible specialists, and that implies that we need to know what those goals are. We need to know that for at least two reasons: first, to be able to construct social institutions on truly rational foundations, and second to tackle the difficult problem of what to do if the goals of different flexible specialists come into conflict.

The understanding on which this book is based is that humans are flexible specialists who have learned to construct external symbolic representations and have invented literacy. This technology of the intellect stands in complex relations to the implicit goals which evolution has built into the structures of the human psyche. It makes it possible for us to behave as if we were generalists. That is what universal interpretation does for us. But it also enables us to pursue our specialist goals in new and previously unforeseen ways. Moreover, literacy increases the possibilities both for creating social institutions which are in harmony with the goals of large numbers of us, and for creating new sites of conflict between us. Developing a more accurate understanding of human nature should thus be an urgent project to be set alongside other issues, such as climate change and the threat of overpopulation, which currently challenge us. The point is not to claim that evolutionary theory tells us what to do; it does not. The point, rather, is for us to understand what the blind process of evolution has constructed, perhaps in order to limit its more negative impact. A literate, reasoned approach to human nature is very different from an assertion that the natural is necessarily good.

We have learned from evolutionary theory that the fundamental goals built into us, as into other animal species, have to do with the acquisition of resources to survive, stay healthy, find sexual partners, and rear offspring. The fundamental goals are overlain by the results of socialisation and prevailing cultural practices but still tend to influence behaviour. Influence, not determine. Where resources are plentiful and accessible, conflict will be minimised and relatively peaceful co-existence is possible. Where resources are scarce or inaccessible, more conflict is to be expected. Understanding the sources of co-operation and conflict in human nature leads to a better prospect of tackling the urgent problems of contemporary society:

> In any combat, the more you know about your opponent, the better your chances of winning. Before the present century, those who talked of combating evolution did not know what they were up against. We still have a lot to learn; but the knowledge we are now acquiring gives us, for the first time, a chance deliberately to deflect the tendencies in our genes. Understanding how our genes influence us makes it possible for us to challenge that influence. (Singer, 2011, p. 169)

Singer goes on to say that the basis of the challenge must be our capacity to reason. Literacy, by systematising and extending that capacity, is our primary tool not only for knowledge of the inanimate world but also for self-knowledge.

12.8   Conclusions

Amid the press of humanity in busy or crowded places, a book is a haven for the mind, a refuge for the weary and a source of solace. For many people a daily newspaper provides a window onto the wider world. People with hobbies, enthusiasms, and obsessions follow them via printed material in its numerous forms, across a huge range of topics. A written work can insulate the reader from the external world or may link her to other readers, fellow members of a conceptual community. A diary provides a space for reflection on the doings of the day. Such a space is private, in principle, but it may be intended at some point for wider consumption; diaries and memoirs of the famous or notorious are eagerly anticipated and read with relish. Notes, memos, formal and informal letters, invitations, and greetings cards foster communication between individuals. This book has explored the nature of literate communication and considered what different forms of literature from mathematics to poetry have in common and how they differ. Eleanor Cook has suggested that poetry is the most concentrated and highly organised form of literary output: 'It encompasses more than other verbal constructions in the way of thinking and feeling and sensation, and also in the pleasure of language. Good poems offer our most energetic – and energizing – verbal artifacts.' (Cook, 1998, p. xi) Here is a final example.

> *Sunset at Fossoli*
>
> I know what it means not to return.
> Through the barbed wire
> I saw the sun go down and die.
> I felt the words of the old poet
> Tear at my flesh:
> 'Suns can go down and return.
> For us, when the brief light is spent,
> There is an unending night to be slept.'
>
> 7 February 1946

This poem by the Italian writer Primo Levi (1988, p. 15) is a short but telling product of a highly literate mind. It is a poignant commentary on the transience of human life and its quiet tone has a powerful emotional effect. The contrast between the 'brief light' of a life and the 'unending night' that both follows and preceded it is striking. The brief light of a human life is an extraordinary flowering of consciousness when viewed from an evolutionary perspective. That there are conscious animals at all is remarkable; that there is a species, *Homo sapiens*, which, having invented literacy, understands something of its own origins and constructs theories about them is a truly startling testimony to the power and scope of the evolutionary process.

Aspects of the poem and its contents other than its reference to the brevity of the human span can illustrate and illuminate some of the principal themes with which the book has been concerned. The first point is, simply, that *Sunset at Fossoli* is a poem. Any work which hopes to do justice to the literate mind must include poetry in its scope because it is one of the pre-eminent forms of literate output. Poetry is a human universal which links literate and non-literate cultures. The first work of world literature, the epic *Gilgamesh*, is a poem which predates the more famous Homeric epics by about a thousand years. Literate cultures, without exception, have produced and continue to produce poets and poetry. Poets choose and use words carefully; they also think very carefully about how words work and about the multiplicity of purposes that they can serve simultaneously. Threads of meaning are interwoven and work together to produce the overall effect.

If poetry must be considered in a book on the literate mind then so too must mathematics because it too is a profound characteristic of literate societies. One might also say, although it is a superficial point, that poets and mathematicians have in common an interest in the details of their work that may appear obsessive to the outsider. I have mentioned that poets choose and use words carefully; mathematicians choose and use symbols, numbers, and sometimes words with equal care. That the results of mathematical and poetic activity are so different is a fact that stands in need of explanation, but it is not to be found in the care or otherwise with which mathematicians and poets practise their respective crafts.

A second point of theoretical interest for the account of the literate mind set out in the book is that Levi's poem quotes another poet. The lines at the end which struck me most forcibly on my first reading are not by Levi himself but by the Roman poet Catullus. This borrowing demonstrates in the most direct way possible that poets work within a literate tradition and that they build on the achievements of others and refer to them not just by quotation as in this case, but also by allusion, by echo, and by other literate devices (Ricks, 2002). The development of traditions, in the form of literatures, is one of the most powerful features of literate life generally, not just of poetry, and the fact that it is commonplace should not blind us to its importance. Traditions encode the collective wisdom (and possibly foolishness!) of a society and enable current limitations to be transcended. If there were no writing there would be much less in the way of tradition for us to learn from; nothing, in fact, apart from what can be communicated orally directly from one generation to the next and whatever can be preserved in artefacts.

Again, although it is also commonplace, the means by which it is known that Catullus was the poet quoted by Levi is relevant to understanding some of the possibilities of literate thinking. Pages 73–75 of the edition of Levi's collected poems which I have, consist of notes. A three-line note for page 15 gives the reference to Catullus and also says that Fossoli was the location for a prison camp. It would be hard to overestimate the importance of notes and references for the nature of literate thinking and traditions. They serve as points of contact with other works and establish networks of communication. In the age of the internet where the text of a note can easily be used as a search term via hyperlinks, this is very clear.

Mathematics and science, as well as poetry and other forms of literature, would be impossible without their literate traditions. In mathematics in particular, new developments build on existing achievements although quite how this works is not yet understood from within. 'As mathematics develops, previously complicated notions and results are assimilated and become everyday tools for the attack on yet more difficult problems. A realistic mathematical theory of this common psychological experience has yet to be provided' (Feferman and Solovay, 1990, p. 292). It may be that the common psychological experience referred to resists mathematical formulation because the complexity of any system capable of having such experiences is irreducible. A somewhat similar idea about tradition is evident in a remark made by the American poet Wallace Stevens, 'Progress in any aspect is a movement through changes of terminology' (Stevens, 1989, p. 184).

The fact that Catullus was the poet from whom Levi borrowed is itself a point of interest both for his language and for his life. Latin is not spoken by any ordinary communities anymore and it is sometimes described, quite unfairly, as a 'dead' language. Anyone who has access to the Latin text of Catullus's poetry, even if needing a translation to understand it, will very quickly find that 'dead' is a most misleading term to apply to language which is charged with life and liveliness. However, a more positive construal is possible; 'dead' simply means 'no longer spoken' rather than moribund and that serves to focus attention on another obvious but important aspect of literacy, namely the possibility of preserving languages by writing them down. The written record needs interpretation, of course, but the simple fact of writing down can preserve the lives of languages which otherwise would not just die but vanish without trace.

Thinking about Catullus the man recalls another of the principal themes of the book. As Peter Green says in the introduction to his very enjoyable bilingual edition of Catullus, little is known for certain about his life, but we learn a great deal about his passions and his psychology through the poems. His preoccupations with sex and social life are as recognisable today as they were to his contemporaries. As Green says of his work, 'Gossip, dinner parties, love-affairs, literary rivalries, libellous *feuilletons*, passion-ate moments of self-dramatization: all are here. It is one of Catullus's great skills to make his reader, almost without realizing it, an invisible eaves-dropper on this intensely alive social picture of a mere two millennia ago' (Catullus and Green, 2005, p. 11). Green perhaps intends us to read 'mere' as a litotes, but from an evolutionary perspective a millennium or two really is small beer. We recognise Catullus's preoccupations because we share them and both he and we would have recognised the preoccupations of our common ancestors 2,000 years before he was writing. A further thou-sand years back takes us to the earliest writing. Beyond that point there are, of course, no written records but there are cave paintings, and there is the archaeological record which yields some information about the likely lives of our ancient ancestors. We would, I think, have to go back a very long way before we found ancestors whose psychology was fundamentally different from our own and the point I have made about this is that liter-acy co-opts the non-literate mental processes of creatures whose passions and psychology have been formed by evolutionary processes working over geological time spans. The literate mind is not, despite its many novelties, a mind fundamentally different from that of our non-literate ancestors. The literate mind is better construed as one whose natural proclivities, for good and for ill, are amplified by reading and writing. To say this is not to deny the scale of the cultural changes that have occurred as a result of literacy. The transformation of human life since the invention of writing is one of the most striking features of human existence viewed on an evolutionary time scale and the desire to understand this transformation has been one of the principal motivations for the writing of the book.

Before leaving *Sunset at Fossoli* I would like to focus briefly on the art of the poem itself which illustrates, even in translation, some of the subtle pos-sibilities that literacy allows the reader to ponder. The poem invites us to consider a number of different time frames ranging from the momentary to the eternal. If we read the poem without its first line it records a sunset and the recollection it provoked. 'Through the barbed wire/ I saw the sun go down and die' describes, with rather chilling effect, a time of day which, for many of us, has often had rather more positive associations. The chilling effect is intensified when we understand through the quote from Catullus that Levi experienced the sunset as a metaphor for the ending of human life, and it is easy to feel a shiver as he records the effect of the words of the older poet. The impact of the poem is magnified and the possible chronologies are greatly enlarged when we read the poem in the context of the first line. The given date, 7 February 1946, suggests that the poem could have been written on a return visit to Fossoli, where Levi had been held in a prison camp at the beginning of 1944 before being transported to Auschwitz. If the poem is read this way, 'I know what it means not to return' is burdened with a sense of loss. Almost all of those who went from Fossoli to Auschwitz did not return. Thus we can imagine Levi bearing witness to the dead in thinking 'I have returned, but I know what it means not to return.' While further considering the impact that a return to Fossoli would have had on Levi, one might ask whether the sunset was watched on that return visit or whether he was recalling an occasion when he saw the sunset as a prisoner. A similar question applies to the recollection of the words of Catullus.

But it is also possible that Levi did not return to Fossoli, that the poem is an act of remembrance or imaginative creation and that the first line carries a somewhat different burden of meaning and plays on the contrast between Levi's not returning, although he might have, and the impossibility of the dead returning, either to life or to Fossoli. It may well be that the provenance of the poem is known to scholars but, as is often the case, one can appreciate it without that knowledge. While there is great value in a fully contextualised, definitive interpretation of a poem, the process of imaginative entry into the possibilities that the bare words on the page provide is an equally important feature of literate life. Finally, the lines of Catullus which Levi quoted are drawn from a lusty poem in which he exhorts his mistress, Lesbia, to live and love without fear of the scandal that might ensue. The contrast between this and the barbed wire of Fossoli is poignant indeed.

Sunset at Fossoli has served as a vehicle for reflection on some of the major themes with which the book is concerned: two of these, the Darwinian perspective and the mathematics of computation, underlie everything else. The Darwinian perspective explains how *Homo sapiens* evolved and, perhaps most importantly for this book, how we have come to have the passions and motivations that we do. It explains why we care about anything at all and predicts what things we are likely to care about the most. Evolutionary theory does many other things as well, but the light it throws on human psychology, particularly social psychology, is indispensable here. If humans were not social, literacy would not have been invented.

The account of literacy proposed in the book views reading and writing as natural extensions of a number of basic human capacities including, but not limited to, the capacity for language. Among those capacities is what Michael Tomasello calls 'shared intentionality'. Shared intentionality is seen in 'behavioral phenomena that are both intentional and irreducibly social, in the sense that the agent of the intentions and actions is the plural subject "we"' (Tomasello, 2008, p. 72). *Homo sapiens* is the most intensely social species on the planet; people are passionately interested in what other people think and feel, and everyone needs a degree of shared understanding in order to pursue both individual and common goals. Social species, in general, are powerful by virtue of their capacities to function as collectives, and humans are no exception. Profound sociality is what makes it possible for us to develop, understand, and implement co-operative ideas of global scope, such as the universal declaration of human rights, but it also exerts a more baleful form of leverage when we organise in coalitions to fight wars, defend sectional interests, or exploit weaker groups. Literacy extends and amplifies natural social impulses which have their roots in our evolutionary history. It follows that if we are to understand both the scope and the limitations of the literate mind, we have to set our literate capacities in an evolutionary framework or, to put the matter slightly differently, we have to understand that literate culture is, to a significant extent, pre-literate culture carried on by other means. The theory of evolution has, therefore, had a fundamental place in the account of the literate mind that the book presents. Evolution does not explain everything, of course, but the scope of the theory is vast and the light it casts on human social life is uniquely bright and consequently harsh at times. It may be this harshness that accounts, in part, for the reluctance that some people have to accept an evolutionary account of humanity and to appreciate the great weight of evidence that supports it.

Evolutionary theory helps us to understand the human goals and purposes, both co-operative and conflictive, that are amplified by literacy but it does not explain why literacy, per se, is such a powerful technology. One of the most powerful intellectual products of the literate era, the logico-mathematical theory of computation, provides a great deal of what is needed to explain literacy as a technology. The theory of computation is, at root, a theory about written marks and their manipulation and this means it can be used to explain the mechanics of literacy at a very basic level. It also has the curious property that it can be applied to itself and used in a form of self-examination, which yields some extremely interesting and surprising results. The reflexive capacity for thinking about the self is viewed, by some writers, as one of the principal capacities which is amplified by literacy and leads to some of its most sophisticated products. Thus, the theory of computation gives us not only an account of the basic characteristics of literacy but can also help us to appreciate many of its more advanced aspects. Moreover, because the theory of computation is a general theory of written marks, it applies not only to the alphabetic writing which we commonly associate with the term 'literacy' but also to mathematics and other symbol systems which are fundamental for the development of science.

References

Aarseth, E. J. (1997). *Cybertext: perspectives on ergodic literature*. Baltimore, MD: Johns Hopkins University Press.

Aiello, L. C. and Wheeler, P. (1995). The Expensive-Tissue Hypothesis: The Brain and the Digestive System in Human and Primate Evolution. *Current Anthropology, 36*(2), 199–221.

Ainsworth, M. D. S. (1978). *Patterns of attachment: a psychological study of the strange situation*. New Jersey; New York; London: Wiley.

Alexander, R. J. (Ed.). (2010). *Children, their world, their education: final report and recommendations of the Cambridge Primary Review*. London: Routledge.

Andersson, M. B. (1994). *Sexual selection*. Princeton, N.J.: Princeton University Press.

Aspray, W. and Burks, A. W. (Eds.). (1987). *Papers of John von Neumann on computing and computer theory*. Cambridge, Mass. Los Angeles: MIT Press; Tomash Publishers.

Astington, J. W. (Ed.). (2000). *Minds in the making: essays in honor of David R. Olson*. Oxford, UK; Malden, Mass.: Blackwell.

Badcock, C. R. (2009). *The imprinted brain: how genes set the balance between autism and psychosis*. London; Philadelphia: Jessica Kingsley Publishers.

Barber, P. (Ed.). (2005). *The map book*. London: Weidenfeld and Nicolson.

Barkow, J. H., Cosmides, L., and Tooby, J. (Eds.). (1992). *The adapted mind: evolutionary psychology and the generation of culture*. New York: Oxford University Press.

Bartlett, F. C. (1932). *Remembering: a study in experimental and social psychology*. Cambridge; New York: Cambridge University Press.

Barton, D. (2007). *Literacy: an Introduction to the ecology of written language*. Oxford, UK: Blackwell Publishing.

Barwell, R. (2009). Researchers' descriptions and the construction of mathematical thinking. *Educational Studies in Mathematics, 72*(2), 255–269.

Berger, P. L. and Luckmann, T. (1966). *The social construction of reality: a treatise in the sociology of knowledge*. Garden City, N.Y: Doubleday.

Bernardo, A. B. I. (1998). *Literacy and the mind: the contexts and cognitive consequences of literary practice*. Hamburg: UNESCO Institute for Education; Box: Luzac Oriental.

Biber, D. (2009). Are there linguistic consequences of literacy? Comparing the potentials of language use in speech and writing. In D. R. Olson and N. Torrance (Eds.), *The Cambridge handbook of literacy* (pp. 75–91). Cambridge, UK: Cambridge University Press.

Bishop, D. V. M., Adams, C. V., and Norbury, C. F. (2004). Using nonword repetition to distinguish genetic and environmental influences on early literacy development: A study of 6-year-old twins. *American Journal of Medical Genetics, 129B*(1), 94–96.

Black, R. W. (2008). Just Don't Call Them Cartoons. The New Literacy Spaces of Anime, Manga, and Fanfiction. In J. Coiro, M. Knobel, C. Lankshear and D. Leu, J (Eds.), *Handbook of research on new literacies*. New York: Routledge.

Blackmore, S. J. (1999). *The meme machine*. Oxford: Oxford University Press.

Blakemore, S.-J. and Frith, U. (2005). *The learning brain: lessons for education*. Oxford: Blackwell.

Bloch, W. G. (2008). *The unimaginable mathematics of Borges' Library of Babel*. Oxford; New York: Oxford University Press.

Boghossian, P. A. (2006). *Fear of knowledge: against relativism and constructivism*. Oxford: Clarendon.

Bolter, J. D. (2000). *Writing space: computers, hypertext, and the remediation of print* (2nd ed.). Mahwah, N.J.: Lawrence Erlbaum Associates.

Bolton, G. (2010). *Reflective practice: writing and professional development* (3rd ed.). London: SAGE.

Boolos, G. and Jeffrey, R. C. (1989). *Computability and logic* (3rd ed.). Cambridge; New York: Cambridge University Press.

Borges, J. L. (1999). *Collected fictions*. London: Allen Lane.

Boroditsky, L. (2001). Does Language Shape Thought?: Mandarin and English Speakers' Conceptions of Time. *Cognitive Psychology, 43*(1), 1–22.

Boroditsky, L. and Ramscar, M. (2002). The Roles of Body and Mind in Abstract Thought. *Psychological Science, 13*(2), 185–189.

Boyd, R. P. D. and Richerson, P. J. (1985). *Culture and the evolutionary process*. Chicago ; London: University of Chicago Press.

Brandt, D. and Clinton, K. (2002). Limits of the Local: Expanding Perspectives on Literacy as a Social Practice. *Journal of Literacy Research, 34*(3), 337–356.

Brockmeier, J. and Olson, D. R. (2009). The Literacy Episteme. From Innis to Derrida. In D. R. Olson and N. Torrance (Eds.), *The Cambridge handbook of literacy* (pp. 3–21). Cambridge, UK: Cambridge University Press.

Brown, D. E. (1991). *Human universals*. New York: McGraw-Hill.

Byrne, B., Coventry, W. L., Olson, R. K., Hulslander, J., Wadsworth, S., DeFries, J. C., et al. (2008). A behaviour-genetic analysis of orthographic learning, spelling and decoding. *Journal of Research in Reading, 31*(1), 8–21.

Byrne, R. W. and Whiten, A. (Eds.). (1988). *Machiavellian intelligence: social expertise and the evolution of intellect in monkeys, apes, and humans*. Oxford: Clarendon.

Caldwell, J. C. (1976). Toward a Restatement of Demographic Transition Theory. *Population and Development Review, 2*(3/4), 321–366.

Caldwell, J. C. and Caldwell, B. (2006). *Demographic transition theory*. Dordrecht: Springer.

Campbell, B. (Ed.). (1972). *Sexual selection and the descent of man 1871–1971*. Chicago, Ill: Aldine Publishing Company.

Carroll, J. (1995). *Evolution and literary theory*. Columbia: University of Missouri Press.

Carroll, J. (2004). *Literary Darwinism: evolution, human nature, and literature.* New York: Routledge.

Catullus, G. V. and Green, P. (2005). *The poems of Catullus* (Bilingual ed.). Berkeley: University of California Press.

Chaitin, G. J. (1987). *Algorithmic information theory.* Cambridge: Cambridge University Press.

Chaitin, G. J. (2006). *Meta maths: the quest for Omega.* London: Atlantic.

Chambers. (1993). *The Chambers dictionary.* London: Chambers.

Clark, A. (1989). *Microcognition: philosophy, cognitive science, and parallel distributed processing.* Cambridge, Mass.: MIT Press.

Clark, A. (1993). *Associative engines: connectionism, concepts, and representational change.* Cambridge, Mass. ; London: MIT Press.

Cliff Hodges, G. (2010). Reasons for reading: why literature matters. *Literacy,* 44(2), 60–68.

Cochran, G. and Harpending, H. (2009). *The 10,000 year explosion: how civilization accelerated human evolution.* New York: Basic Books.

Coiro, J., Knobel, M., Lankshear, C., and Leu, D., J (Eds.). (2008). *Handbook of research on new literacies.* Abingdon, UK: Routledge.

Colclough, C. (2007). *Global gender goals and the construction of equality: conceptual dilemmas and policy practice*: University of Cambridge. RECOUP Working Paper No. 2.

Cole, M. and Cole, J. (2006). Rethinking the Goody Myth. In D. R. Olson and M. Cole (Eds.), *Technology, literacy, and the evolution of society: implications of the work of Jack Goody* (pp. 305–324). Mahwah, NJ: Lawrence Erlbaum Associates.

Collins, F. S. et al., (2004). Finishing the euchromatic sequence of the human genome. *Nature,* 431, 931–945.

Collins, J. and Blot, R. K. (2003). *Literacy and literacies: texts, power, and identity.* Cambridge: Cambridge University Press.

Cook, E. (1998). *Against coercion: games poets play.* Stanford, Calif.: Stanford University Press.

Cook-Gumperz, J. (Ed.). (2006). *The social construction of literacy* (2nd. ed.). Cambridge, UK ; New York: Cambridge University Press.

Cope, B. and Kalantzis, M. (Eds.). (2000). *Multiliteracies: literacy learning and the design of social futures.* Abingdon, UK: Routledge.

Coulmas, F. (1996). *The Blackwell encyclopedia of writing systems.* Cambridge, MA ; Oxford: Blackwell.

Cronin, H. (1991). *The ant and the peacock: altruism and sexual selection from Darwin to today.* Cambridge, UK: Cambridge University Press.

Cunningham, A. E. and Stanovich, K. E. (2001). What Reading Does for the Mind. *Journal of Direct Instruction,* 1(2), 137–149.

Dalton, B., Proctor, C. P., Uccelli, P., Mo, E., and Snow, C. E. (2011). Designing for Diversity: The Role of Reading Strategies and Interactive Vocabulary in a Digital Reading Environment for Fifth-Grade Monolingual English and Bilingual Students. *Journal of Literacy Research,* 43(1), 68–100.

Damerow, P. (1996). Food production and social status as documented in proto-cuneiform texts. In P. Wiessner and W. Schiefenhövel (Eds.), *Food and the status quest* (pp. 149–169). Providence: Berghahn Books.

Dantzig, T. and Mazur, J. (2005). *Number: the language of science* (The Masterpiece Science ed.). New York: Pi Press.

Darwin, C. (1859). *On the origin of species ... A facsimile of the first edition, with an introduction by Ernst Mayr.*: pp. xxvii. ix. 502. Harvard University Press: Cambridge.

Darwin, C. (1871). *The descent of man, and selection in relation to sex, with an introduction by John Tyler Bonner and Robert M. May 1981.* Princeton, N.J.: Princeton University Press.

Dauben, J. W. (1979). *Georg Cantor: his mathematics and philosophy of the infinite.* Cambridge, Mass: Harvard University Press.

Dawkins, R. (1976). *The selfish gene.* Oxford: Oxford University Press.

Dawkins, R. (2005). *The ancestor's tale: a pilgrimage to the dawn of life.* London: Phoenix.

Dehaene, S. (2009). *Reading in the brain: the science and evolution of a human invention.* New York: Viking.

Dennett, D. C. (1991). *Consciousness explained.* Boston: Little, Brown and Co.

Dennett, D. C. (1995). *Darwin's dangerous idea: evolution and the meanings of life.* New York: Simon and Schuster.

Derrida, J. (1997). *Of grammatology* (Corrected ed.). Baltimore: Johns Hopkins University Press.

Derrida, J. (2002). *Without alibi* (P. Kamuf, Trans.). Stanford, CA: Stanford University Press.

Devitt, A. J. (2004). *Writing genres.* Carbondale: Southern Illinois University Press.

Dey, L. and Haque, S. K. M. (2008). *Opinion Mining From Noisy Text Data.* Paper presented at the *AND '08*, Singapore.

Diamond, J. M. (1997). *Guns, germs and steel: a short history of everybody for the last 13,000 years.* London: Vintage edition, 2005.

Diamond, J. M. (2005). *Collapse: how societies choose to fail or survive.* London: Allen Lane.

Dickins, T. E. (2004). Social Constructionism as Cognitive Science. *Journal for the Theory of Social Behaviour, 34*(4), 333–352.

Dietler, M. (1996). Feasts and Commensal Politics in the Political Economy: Food, Power, and Status in Prehistoric Europe. In P. Wiessner and W. Schiefenhövel (Eds.), *Food and the status quest. an interdisciplinary perspective.* Providence, RI: Berghahn Books.

Dobson, T. M. and Willinsky, J. (2009). Digital Literacy. In D. R. Olson and N. Torrance (Eds.), *The Cambridge handbook of literacy* (pp. 286–312). Cambridge, UK: Cambridge University Press.

Donovan, C. A. and Smolkin, L. B. (2006). Children's Understanding of Genre Writing and Development. In C. A. MacArthur, S. Graham and J. Fitzgerald (Eds.), *Handbook of writing research* (pp. 131–143). New York: The Guilford Press.

Doronila, M. L. C. (1996). *Landscapes of literacy: an ethnographic study of functional literacy in marginal Philippine communities.* Hamburg: UNESCO Institute of Education.

Doueihi, M. (2011). *Digital cultures.* Cambridge, Mass.: Harvard University Press.

Dozier, C., Jackson, P., Guo, X., Chaudhary, M., and Arumainayagam, Y. (2003). *Creation of an expert witness database through mining*. Paper presented at the *ICAIL '03*, Edinburgh.

Drèze, J. and Sen, A. (2002). *India: development and participation* (2nd ed.). Oxford: Oxford University Press.

Driver, P. M. and Humphries, D. A. (1988). *Protean behaviour: the biology of unpredictability*. Oxford: Clarendon Press.

Drouin, M. and Davis, C. (2009). R u txting? Is the Use of Text Speak Hurting Your Literacy? *Journal of Literacy Research, 41*(1), 46–67.

Duffy, T. M. and Waller, R. (1985). *Designing usable texts*. Orlando: Academic Press.

Dunbar, R. I. M. (1996). *Grooming, gossip and the evolution of language*. London: Faber and Faber.

Durham, W. H. (1991). *Coevolution: genes, culture, and human diversity*. Stanford, Calif.: Stanford University Press.

Eisenstein, E., L. (1979). *The printing press as an agent of change*. Cambridge, UK: Cambridge University Press.

Ekman, P. and Davidson, R. J. (1994). *The nature of emotion: fundamental questions*. New York: Oxford University Press.

Eliot, S. and Rose, J. (2009). *A companion to the history of the book*. Oxford: Wiley-Blackwell.

Emery, N. J., Clayton, N. S., and Frith, C. D. (2007). Introduction. Social intelligence: from brain to culture. *Philosophical Transactions of the Royal Society B: Biological Sciences, 362*(1480), 485–488.

Ensslin, A. (2007). *Canonizing hypertext: explorations and constructions*. New York: Continuum.

Evans, N. and Levinson, S. C. (2009). The myth of language universals: Language diversity and its importance for cognitive science. *Behavioral and Brain Sciences, 32*(05), 429.

Farah, I. (2005). The cultural benefits of literacy. *Paper commissioned for the EFA GLobal Monitoring Report 2006, Literacy for Life.*

Feferman, S. and Solovay, R. M. (1990). Introductory note to 1972a. In S. Feferman, J. W. Dawson Jr., S. C. KIeene, G. H. Moore, R. M. Solovay and J. Van Heijenoort (Eds.), *Kurt Gödel: collected works. volume II. publications 1938–1974*. Oxford: Oxford University Press.

Fisher, R. A. S. and Bennett, J. H. (1999). *The genetical theory of natural selection: a complete variorum edition*. Oxford: Oxford University Press.

Fodor, J. A. (1983). *The modularity of mind: an essay on faculty psychology*. Cambridge, MA: MIT Press.

Foley, R. (1995). *Humans before humanity: an evolutionary perspective*: Oxford ; Cambridge, MA : Blackwell Publishers.

Foucault, M. (2002). *The order of things: an archaeology of the human sciences*: London: Routledge Classics. First English edition by Tavistock Publications, 1970.

Frank, S. A. (1995). George Price's Contributions to Evolutionary Genetics. *Journal of Theoretical Biology, 175*, 373–388.

Frank, S. A. (1998). *Foundations of social evolution*. Princeton, NJ: Princeton University Press.

Franks, B. (2011). *Culture and cognition: evolutionary perspectives*. Basingstoke, UK: Palgrave Macmillan.

Freire, P. (1993). *Pedagogy of the oppressed* (New rev. 20th-Anniversary ed.). New York: Continuum.

Ganzeboom, H. B. G. and Treiman, D. J. (1996). Internationally Comparable Measures of Occupational Status for the 1988 International Standard Classification of Occupations. *Social Science Research, 25*, 201–239.

Geake, J. G. (2009). *The brain at school: educational neuroscience in the classroom*. Maidenhead, England ; New York: McGraw Hill/Open University Press.

Gee, J. P. (2008). *Social linguistics and literacies: ideology in discourses* (3rd ed.). London: Routledge.

Gelb, I. J. (1952). *A study of writing; the foundations of grammatology*. London, UK: Routledge and K. Paul.

Gelernter, J. and Lesk, M. (2009). *Text Mining for Indexing*. Paper presented at the *JCDL '09*, Austin, Texas.

George, A. (Ed.) (1994). *Mathematics and mind*. New York; Oxford: Oxford University Press.

Gergen, K. J. (1999). *An invitation to social construction*. London; Thousand Oaks, Calif.: Sage.

Gibson, J. J. (1966). *The senses considered as perceptual systems*. Boston: Houghton Mifflin.

Gibson, J. J. (1979). *The ecological approach to visual perception*. Boston: Houghton Mifflin.

Gingeras, T. R. (2009). Implications of chimaeric non-co-linear transcripts. *Nature, 461*(7261), 206–211.

Ginzburg, C. (1980). *The cheese and the worms: the cosmos of a sixteenth-century Miller*. London: Routledge and Kegan Paul.

Glad, M. (2009). *Knowledge on fire: attacks on education in Afghanistan*: CARE International.

Gödel, K. (1931). On formally undecidable propositions of *Principia mathematica* and related systems 1. *Monatshefte für Mathematik und Physik, 38*, 173–198.

Goldstein, R. (2005). *Incompleteness: the proof and paradox of Kurt Gödel*. New York: W.W. Norton.

Goodman, Y. M. and Martens, P. (2007). *Critical issues in early literacy: research and pedagogy*. Mahwah, NJ: Lawrence Erlbaum Associates.

Goody, J. (Ed.). (1968). *Literacy in traditional societies*. Cambridge, UK: Cambridge University Press.

Goody, J. (1977). *The domestication of the savage mind*. Cambridge, UK: Cambridge University Press.

Goody, J. (1986). *The logic of writing and the organization of society*. Cambridge: Cambridge University Press.

Goody, J. (2000). *The power of the written tradition*. Washington ; London: Smithsonian Institution Press.

Goody, J. and Watt, I. (1963). The Consequences of Literacy. *Comparative Studies in Society and History, 5*(3), 304–345.

Gordon, C. (2010). Reflecting on the EFA Global Monitoring Report's framework for understanding quality education: A teacher's perspective in Eritrea. *International Journal of Educational Development, 30*(4), 388–395.

Gottschall, J. (2008). *The rape of Troy: evolution, violence, and the world of Homer*. Cambridge: Cambridge University Press.

Gottschall, J. and Wilson, D. S. (Eds.). (2005). *The literary animal: evolution and the nature of narrative*. Evanston, Ill.: Northwestern University Press.

Graff, H. J. (1991). *The literacy myth: cultural integration and social structure in the nineteeth century*. New Brunswick, NJ: Transaction Publishers.

Graff, H. J. (1995). *The labyrinths of literacy: reflections on literacy past and present* (Rev. and expanded ed.). Pittsburgh: University of Pittsburgh Press.

Graff, H. J. (2007). *Literacy and historical development: a reader* (Rev. and expanded ed.). Carbondale: Southern Illinois University Press.

Green, C. E. and McCreery, C. (1994). *Lucid dreaming: the paradox of consciousness during sleep*. London: Routledge.

Haeri, N. (2009). The Elephant in the Room. Language and Literacy in the Arab World. In D. R. Olson and N. Torrance (Eds.), *The Cambridge handbook of literacy* (pp. 418–430). Cambridge, UK: Cambridge University Press.

Halpern, D. F. (2000). *Sex differences in cognitive abilities* (3rd ed.). Mahwah, N.J.: L. Erlbaum Associates.

Halverson, J. (1992). Goody and the Implosion of the Literacy Thesis. *Man, New Series, 27*(2), 301–317.

Hamilton, W. D. (1963). The Evolution of Altruistic Behaviour. *The American Naturalist, 97*, 354–356. Reprinted in Hamilton (1995).

Hamilton, W. D. (1964a). The Genetical Evolution of Social Behaviour, I. *Journal of Theoretical Biology, 7*, 1–16. Reprinted in Hamilton (1995).

Hamilton, W. D. (1964b). The Genetical Evolution of Social Behaviour, II. *Journal of Theoretical Biology, 7*, 17–52 Reprinted in Hamilton (1995).

Hamilton, W. D. (1975). Innate social aptitudes of man: an approach from evolutionary genetics. In R. Fox (Ed.), *ASA studies 4: biosocial anthropology* (pp. 133–153). London: Malaby Press.

Hamilton, W. D. (1995). *Narrow roads of gene land: the collected papers of W. D. Hamilton. Vol.1, evolution of social behaviour*. Oxford; New York: W.H. Freeman/Spektrum.

Hardman, D. (2009). *Judgment and decision making: psychological perspectives*. Malden, MA; Oxford: BPS Blackwell.

Harris, J. R. (1998). *The nurture assumption: why children turn out the way they do*. New York: Free Press.

Harris, R. (2000). *Rethinking writing*. London: Continuum.

Harris, R. (2009). *Rationality and the literate mind*. New York; London: Routledge.

Hausmann, R., Tyson, L. D., and Zahidi, S. (2008). *The global gender gap report 2008*. Geneva: World Economic Forum.

Havelock, E. A. (1963). *Preface to Plato*: Basil Blackwell: Oxford.

Hawkes, K. and Paine, R. R. (Eds.). (2006). *The evolution of human life history.* Santa Fe; Oxford: School of American Research; James Currey.

Heaney, S. and O'Driscoll, D. (2008). *Stepping stones: interviews with Seamus Heaney.* London: Faber.

Heath, S. B. (1983). *Ways with words: language, life, and work in communities and classrooms.* Cambridge: Cambridge University Press.

Hecht, A. (2003). *Collected later poems.* New York: Knopf.

Heinrich, B. (2006). *Mind of the raven: investigations and adventures with wolf-birds* (1st Harper Perennial ed.). New York: Harper Perennial.

Hellinga, L. (2009). The Gutenberg Revolutions. In S. Eliot and J. Rose (Eds.), *A companion to the history of the book.* Chichester, West Sussex: Wiley-Blackwell.

Hill, G. (2008). *Collected critical writings.* Oxford: Oxford University Press.

Hirschfeld, L. A. and Gelman, S. A. (Eds.). (1994). *Mapping the mind: domain specificity in cognition and culture.* Cambridge, UK: Cambridge University Press.

Hoblitzell, A., Mukhopadhyay, S., You, Q., Fang, S., Xia, Y., and Bidwell, J. (2010). *Text mining for bone biology.* Paper presented at the *HPDC'10.*

Hockett, C. F. (1973). *Man's place in nature.* New York; London: McGraw-Hill.

Hodges, A. (1983). *Alan Turing: the enigma.* London: Vintage.

Hollander, J. (2001). *Rhyme's reason: a guide to English verse* (3rd ed.). New Haven: Yale Nota Bene/Yale University Press.

Householder, F. W. (1971). *Linguistic speculations.* Cambridge: Cambridge University Press.

Houston, S. D. (Ed.). (2004). *The first writing : script invention as history and process.* Cambridge: Cambridge University Press.

Hudson, V. M. and Boer, A. M. d. (2004). *Bare branches: the security implications of Asia's surplus male population.* Cambridge, Mass.; London: MIT Press.

Humphrey, N. (1976). The social function of intellect. In P. P. G. Bateson and R. A. Hinde (Eds.), *Growing points in ethology* (pp. 303–317). Cambridge, UK: Cambridge University Press.

Humphrey, N. (2011). *Soul dust: the magic of consciousness.* London: Quercus.

Hunley, K. L., Healy, M. E., and Long, J. C. (2009). The global pattern of gene identity variation reveals a history of long-range migrations, bottlenecks, and local mate exchange: Implications for biological race. *American Journal of Physical Anthropology, 139*(1), 35–46.

Iser, W. (1978). *The act of reading: a theory of aesthetic response.* Baltimore, MD: The Johns Hopkins University Press.

Jamie, K. (2004). *The tree house.* London: Picador.

Janks, H. (2010). *Literacy and power.* New York: Routledge.

Jarecki, H. G. and Kaisth, D. Z. (2009). *Scholar rescue in the modern world.* New York: Institute of International Education.

Jayaweera, S. (1987). Editorial Introduction. *International Review of Education, 33*(4), 415–418.

Jolly, A. (1966). Lemur Social Behavior and Primate Intelligence. *Science, New Series, 153*(3735), 501–506.

Joshi, M. R. and Aaron, P. G. (Eds.). (2005). *Handbook of orthography and literacy.* New York: Routledge.

Kapranov, P., Cheng, J., Dike, S., Nix, D. A., Duttagupta, R., Willingham, A. T., et al. (2007). RNA Maps Reveal New RNA Classes and a Possible Function for Pervasive Transcription. *Science, 316*(5830), 1484–1488.

Keats, J. and Stillinger, J. (1978). *The poems of John Keats*. Cambridge, Mass.: Belknap Press of Harvard University Press.

Keeley, L. H. (1995). *War before civilization*. New York; Oxford: Oxford University Press.

Kellogg, R. T. (1994). *The psychology of writing*. New York: Oxford University Press.

Kenny, A. (2006). *Wittgenstein. Revised edition*. Oxford, UK: Blackwell Publishing.

Kintsch, W. (1998). *Comprehension: a paradigm for cognition*. Cambridge, UK: Cambridge University Press.

Kirk, D. (1996). Demographic Transition Theory. *Population Studies, 50*(3), 361–387.

Kitcher, P. (1984). *The nature of mathematical knowledge*. New York; Oxford: Oxford University Press.

Knobel, M. and Lankshear, C. (Eds.). (2007). *A new literacies sampler*. New York: NY: Peter Lang.

Kokko, H. and Jennions, M. D. (2008). Parental investment, sexual selection and sex ratios. *Journal of Evolutionary Biology, 21*(4), 919–948.

Kotsopoulos, D. and Cordy, M. (2008). Investigating imagination as a cognitive space for learning mathematics. *Educational Studies in Mathematics, 70*(3), 259–274.

Kress, G. R. (2003). *Literacy in the new media age*. London: Routledge.

Laidlaw, L. (2005). *Reinventing curriculum: a complex-perspective on literacy and writing*. Mahwah, N.J.: L. Erlbaum Associates.

Lander, E. S. et. al., (2001). Initial sequencing and analysis of the human genome. *Nature*, 409, 860-921.

Landin, P. J. (1966). The Next 700 Programming Languages. *Communications of the ACM, 9*(3), 157–166.

Landow, G. P. (2006). *Hypertext 3.0: critical theory and new media in an era of globalization* (3rd ed.). Baltimore: Johns Hopkins University Press.

Langer, J. A. (2011). *Envisioning knowledge: building literacy in the academic disciplines*. New York: Teachers College, Columbia University.

Larson, J. (Ed.). (2007). *Literacy as snake oil: beyond the quick fix* (Rev. ed.). New York: P. Lang.

Lawson, D. W. (2011). Life history theory and human reproductive behaviour. In V. Swami (Ed.), *Evolutionary psychology: a critical introduction* (pp. 183–214). Chichester, UK: BPS Blackwell.

Leu, D., J. (2000). Literacy and technology: Deictic consequences for literacy education in an information age. In M. L. Kamil, P. D. Mosenthal, P. D. Pearson and R. Barr (Eds.), *Handbook of reading research* (Vol. 3, pp. 743–770). Mahwah, NJ: Lawrence Erlbaum Associates.

Levi, P. (1979). *If this is a man and the truce*. Harmondsworth: Penguin.

Levi, P. (1988). *Collected poems*. London: Faber.

Levintova, E. (2010). Past imperfect: The construction of history in the school curriculum and mass media in post-communist Russia and Ukraine. *Communist and Post-Communist Studies, 43*(2), 125–127.

Levi-Strauss, C. (1962). *The savage mind (La pensee sauvage.)*: Weidenfeld and Nicolson.

Lewis, C., Enciso, P., and Moje, E. B. (2007). *Reframing sociocultural research on literacy: identity, agency, and power*. Mahwah, N.J.; London: Lawrence Erlbaum Associates.

Li, M. and Vitányi, P. M. B. (2008). *An introduction to Kolmogorov complexity and its applications* (3rd ed.). New York: Springer.

Lloyd, B. B. and Gay, J. (1981). *Universals of human thought : some African evidence*. Cambridge: Cambridge University Press.

Lumsden, C. J. and Wilson, E. O. (1981). *Genes, mind and culture : the coevolutionary process*. Cambridge, Mass. ; London: Harvard University Press.

Machover, M. (1996). *Set theory, logic, and their limitations*. Cambridge: Cambridge University Press.

Maddy, P. (1990). *Realism in mathematics*: Clarendon.

Maddy, P. (1997). *Naturalism in mathematics*. Oxford: Clarendon Press.

Maddox, B. (2008). What Good is Literacy? Insights and Implications of the Capabilities Approach. *Journal of Human Development, 9*(2), 185–206.

McClelland, J. L. and Rumelhart, D. E. (1986). *Parallel distributed processing : explorations in the micro-structure of cognition. Vol.2, Psychological and biological models*. Cambridge, Mass. ; London: MIT Press.

McCutchen, D. (2008). Cognitive Factors in the Development of Children's Writing. In C. A. MacArthur, S. Graham and J. Fitzgerald (Eds.), *Handbook of writing research*. New York, NY: The Guilford Press.

McElheny, V. K. (2010). *Drawing the map of life : inside the Human Genome Project*. New York, NY: Basic Books.

McLuhan, M. (1962). *The Gutenberg galaxy; the making of typographic man*. Toronto: University of Toronto Press.

McMurry, J. (1994). *Fundamentals of organic chemistry* (3rd ed.). Pacific Grove, Calif.: Brooks/Cole Pub. Co.

Mercier, H. and Sperber, D. (2011). Why do humans reason? Arguments for an argumentative theory. *Behavioral and Brain Sciences, 34*(2), 57–74.

Michel, J. B., Shen, Y. K., Aiden, A. P., Veres, A., Gray, M. K., Pickett, J. P., et al. (2011). Quantitative Analysis of Culture Using Millions of Digitized Books. *Science, 331*(6014), 176–182.

Miller, G. (2000). *The mating mind : how sexual choice shaped the evolution of human nature*. Oxford: Heinemann.

Miller, G. F. (1997). Protean primates: The evolution of adaptive unpredictability in competition and courtship. In A. Whiten and R. W. Byrne (Eds.), *Machiavellian intelligence II* (pp. 312–340). Cambridge, UK: Cambridge University Press.

Mithen, S. (1996). *The prehistory of the mind: a search for the origins of art, religion and science*. London: Thames and Hudson.

Moje, E. B. and Lewis, C. (2007). Examining Opportunities to Learn Literacy: The Role of Critical Sociocultural Literacy Research. In C. Lewis, P. Enciso and E. B. Moje (Eds.), *Reframing sociocultural research on literacy: identity, agency, and power*. Mahwah, NJ: Lawrence Erlbaum Associates.

Moll, H. and Tomasello, M. (2007). Cooperation and human cognition: the Vygotskian intelligence hypothesis. *Philosophical Transactions of the Royal Society B: Biological Sciences, 362*(1480), 639–648.

Moore, M. (1967). *The complete poems of Marianne Moore.* New York: Macmillan /
The Viking Press.

Moran, J. H., Gode, A., Rousseau, J.-J., and Herder, J. G. (1986). *On the origin of
language.* Chicago: University of Chicago Press.

Nagel, E. and Newman, J. R. (1989). *Gödel's proof.* London, UK: Routledge.

Nell, V. (1988). *Lost in a book : the psychology of reading for pleasure.* New
Haven: Yale University Press.

Nelson, N. (2008). The Reading-Writing Nexus in Discourse Research. In C.
Bazerman (Ed.), *Handbook of research on writing: history, society, school, individual, text.* (pp. 435–450). New York: Lawrence Erlbaum Associates.

Nordstrom, C. (2004). *Shadows of war : violence, power, and international prof-
iteering in the twenty-first century.* Berkeley: University of California Press.

Norris, S. P. and Phillips, L. M. (2009). Scientific Literacy. In D. R. Olson and
N. Torrance (Eds.), *The Cambridge handbook of literacy* (pp. 271–285).
Cambridge, UK: Cambridge University Press.

Nussbaum, M. C. (2000). *Women and human development: the capabilities
approach.* Cambridge: Cambridge University Press.

Nussbaum, M. C. (2003). Women's Education: A Global Challenge. *Signs: Journal
of Women in Culture and Society,* 29(2), 325–355.

Nussbaum, M. C. (2006). *Frontiers of justice: disability, nationality, species membership.* Cambridge, Mass: The Belknap Press: Harvard University Press.

Olson, D. R. (1994). *The world on paper: the conceptual and cognitive implications
of writing and reading.* Cambridge, UK: Cambridge University Press.

Olson, D. R. and Torrance, N. (Eds.). (2009). *The Cambridge handbook of literacy.*
Cambridge, UK: Cambridge University Press.

O'Malley, B. (2010). *Education under Attack 2010.* Paris: Unesco.

Ong, W. J. (1982). *Orality and literacy: the technologizing of the word.* London:
Methuen.

Padel, R. (2009). *Darwin: a life in poems.* London: Chatto and Windus.

Pahl, K. and Rowsell, J. (2005). *Literacy and education: understanding the new
literacy studies in the classroom.* London: Sage Publications.

Pais, A. (1982). *'Subtle is the Lord': the science and the life of Albert Einstein.*
Oxford: Clarendon.

Penrose, R. (1989). *The emperor's new mind: concerning computers, minds, and
the laws of physics.* London: Vintage, 1990.

Penrose, R. (1994). *Shadows of the mind: a search for the missing science of consciousness.* Oxford: Oxford University Press.

Penrose, R. (2004). *The road to reality: a complete guide to the laws of the universe.*
London: Jonathan Cape.

Petersson, K. M., Ingvar, M., and Reis, A. (2009). Language and Literacy from a
Cognitive Neuroscience Perspective. In D. R. Olson and N. Torrance (Eds.), *The
Cambridge Handbook of Literacy* (pp. 152–181). Cambridge, UK: Cambridge
University Press.

Pierce, M., Katzir, T., Wolf, M., and Noam, G. G. (2010). Examining the Construct
of Reading Among Dysfluent Urban Children: A Factor Analysis Approach.
Journal of Literacy Research, 42(2), 124–158.

Pinker, S. (1994). *The language instinct: the new science of language and mind*. London: Allen Lane. The Penguin Press.

Pinker, S. (1997). *How the mind works*. London: Allen Lane. The Penguin Press.

Pinker, S. (2002). *The blank slate: the modern denial of human nature*. London: Allen Lane.

Plaisant, C., Rose, J., Yu, B., Auvil, L., Kirschenbaum, M. G., Smith, M. N., et al. (2006). *Exploring erotics in Emily Dickinson's correspondence with text mining and visual interfaces*. Paper presented at the 6th ACM/IEEE-CS joint conference on Digital libraries

Price, G. (1970). Selection and covariance. *Nature, 227*, 520–521.

Price, G. (1972). Extension of covariance selection mathematics. *Annals of Human Genetics, 35*, 485–490.

Price, G. (1995). The Nature of Selection. *Journal of Theoretical Biology, 175*, 389–396.

Pring, R., Hayward, G., Hodgson, A., Johnson, J., Keep, E., Oancea, A., et al. (2009). *Education for all: the future of education and training for 14–19 year olds*. London: Routledge.

Purcell-Gates, V., Jacobson, E., and Degener, S. (2004). *Print literacy development: uniting cognitive and social practice theories*. Cambridge, Mass.: Harvard University Press.

Quine, W. V. (1974). *Methods of logic* (3rd ed.). London: Routledge and Kegan Paul.

Reder, S. and Davila, E. (2005). Context and Literacy Practices. *Annual Review of Applied Linguistics, 25*, 170–187.

Richerson, P. J. and Boyd, R. (2005). *Not by genes alone: how culture transformed human evolution*. Chicago: The University of Chicago Press.

Ricks, C. (2002). *Allusion to the poets*. Oxford: Oxford University Press.

Robeyns, I. (2005). The Capability Approach: a theoretical survey. *Journal of Human Development, 6*(1), 93–114.

Robinson-Pant, A. (2005). The social benefits of literacy. *Paper commissioned for the EFA GLobal Monitoring Report 2006, Literacy for Life*.

Robinson-Pant, A. (2008). 'Why Literacy Matters': Exploring A Policy Perspective on Literacies, Identities and Social Change. *Journal of Development Studies, 44*(6), 779–796.

Robson, E. (2009). The Clay Tablet Book in Sumer, Assyria, and Babylonia. In S. Eliot and J. Rose (Eds.), *A companion the the history of the book* (pp. 67–83). Chichester: Wiley-Blackwell.

Rodriguez-Salgado, M. J. (2009). 'How oppression thrives where truth is not allowed a voice': The Spanish Polemic about the American Indians. In G. K. Bhambra and R. Shilliam (Eds.), *Silencing human rights: critical engagements with a contested project*. Basingstoke, UK: Palgrave Macmillan.

Roff, D. A. (1992). *The evolution of life histories: theory and analysis*. London: Chapman and Hall.

Rosenblatt, L. M. (1994). *The reader, the text, the poem: the transactional theory of the literary work* (Paperback ed.). Carbondale: Southern Illinois University Press.

Rucker, R. v. B. (1995). *Infinity and the mind: the science and philosophy of the infinite*. Princeton, NJ: Princeton University Press.

Rumelhart, D. E. and McClelland, J. L. (1986). *Parallel distributed processing: explorations in the microstructure of cognition. Vol.1, Foundations*. Cambridge, Mass.; London: MIT Press.

Saito, M. (2003). Amartya Sen's Capability Approach to Education: A Critical Exploration. *Journal of Philosophy of Education, 37*(1), 17–33.

Salem, R. (2004). *Men's surveys: new findings*. Baltimore: Johns Hopkins Bloomberg School of Public Health.

Schimmel, S. (2008). *The tenacity of unreasonable beliefs: fundamentalism and the fear of truth*. Oxford; New York: Oxford University Press.

Schultz, T. P. (2002). Why Governments Should Invest More to Educate Girls. *World Development, 30*(2), 207–225.

Scribner, S. and Cole, M. (1981). *The psychology of literacy*. Cambridge, Mass. ; London: Harvard University Press.

Sear, R. (2011). Parenting and families. In V. Swami (Ed.), *Evolutionary psychology: a critical introduction*. (pp. 215–249). Chichester, UK: BPS Blackwell.

Searle, J. R. (1983). *Intentionality: an essay in the philosophy of mind*. Cambridge: Cambridge University Press.

Searle, J. R. (1992). *The rediscovery of the mind*. Cambridge, Mass.: MIT Press.

Searle, J. R. (1995). *The construction of social reality*. London: Allen Lane.

Sen, A. (1999). *Development as freedom*. Oxford: Oxford University Press.

Seymour-Smith, M. (1998). *The 100 most influential books ever written: the history of thought from ancient times to today*. Secaucus, N.J.: Carol Pub. Group.

Sheridan, D., Street, B. V., and Bloome, D. (2000). *Writing ourselves: mass-observation and literacy practices*. Cresskill, N.J.: Hampton Press.

Sheridan, M. P. and Rowsell, J. (2010). *Design literacies: learning and innovation in the digital age*. Abingdon: UK: Routledge.

Sherman, E. A. (2010). *Contemplative aging: a way of being in later life*. New York: Gordian Knot Books.

Shiohata, M. (2009). Exploring literacy and growth: An analysis of three communities of readers in urban Senegal. *International Journal of Educational Development, 29*(1), 65–72.

Shriver, L. (2003). *We need to talk about Kevin*. Washington, D.C.: Counterpoint; Oxford: Oxford Publicity Partnership.

Singer, P. (2011). *The expanding circle: ethics, evolution, and moral progress: with a new afterword by the author*. Princeton, NJ: Princeton University Press. First published 1981.

Skelton, C. and Francis, B. (2009). *Feminism and 'The Schooling Scandal'*. Abingdon, UK: Routledge.

Skinner, B. F. (1974). *About behaviourism*. London: Jonathan Cape Ltd.

Snell, B. (1953). *The discovery of the mind: the Greek origins of European thought ... translated by T. G. Rosenmeyer*: pp. xii. 323. Basil Blackwell: Oxford.

Snow, C. E. and Uccelli, P. (2009). The Challenge of Academic Language. In D. R. Olson and N. Torrance (Eds.), *The Cambridge handbook of literacy* (pp. 112–133). Cambridge, UK: Cambridge University Press.

Snowling, M. J. and Hulme, C. (Eds.). (2005). *The science of reading: a handbook*. Oxford: Blackwell.

Sober, E. and Wilson, D. S. (1998). *Unto other: the evolution and psychology of unselfish behavior*. Cambridge, Mass. ; London: Harvard University Press.

Sozou, P. D. (2009). Individual and social discounting in a viscous population. *Proceedings of the Royal Society B: Biological Sciences, 276*(1669), 2955–2962.

Staal, F. (1988). *Universals: studies in Indian logic and linguistics*. Chicago: University of Chicago Press.

Stanovich, K. E. (2000). *Progress in understanding reading: scientific foundations and new frontiers*. New York; London: Guilford Press.

Stanovich, K. E. (2003). Understanding the Styles of Science in the Study of Reading. *Scientific Studies of Reading, 7*(2), 105–126.

Stanovich, K. E. (2004). *The robot's rebellion: finding meaning in the age of Darwin*. Chicago: University of Chicago Press.

Stanovich, K. E. and Cunningham, A. E. (1993). Where does knowledge come from? Specific associations between print exposure and information acquisition. *Journal of Educational Psychology, 85*(2), 211–229.

Stanovich, K. E., West, R. F., and Harrison, M. R. (1995). Knowledge Growth and Maintenance Across the Life Span: The Role of Print Exposure. *Developmental Psychology, 31*(5), 811–826.

Steele, C. (2010). *Whistling Vivaldi: and other clues to how stereotypes affect us*. New York: W.W. Norton and Company.

Stevens, W. (1989). *Opus posthumous* (Revised, enlarged and corrected by Milton Bates ed.). New York: Knopf.

Street, B. V. (1984). *Literacy in theory and practice*. Cambridge, UK: Cambridge University Press.

Street, B. V. (1993). The new literacy studies, guest editorial. *Journal of Research in Reading, 16*(2), 81–97.

Street, B. (1998). New Literacies in Theory and Practice: What are the Implications for Language in Education? *Linguistics and Education, 10*(1), 1–24.

Street, B. V. (Ed.). (2001). *Literacy and development: ethnographic perspectives*. London; New York: Routledge.

Street, B. V. (2005). Understanding and Defining Literacy. *Paper commissioned for the EFA Global Monitoring Report 2006, Literacy for Life*.

Street, B. V. and Lefstein, A. (2007). *Literacy: an advanced resource book*. London: Routledge.

Stringer, C. (2011). *The origin of our species*. London: Allen Lane, Penguin Group.

Stromquist, N. (2006). Women's rights to adult education as a means to citizenship. *International Journal of Educational Development, 26*(2), 140–152.

Swanson, D. R. and Smalheiser, N. R. (1997). An interactive system for finding complementary literatures: a stimulus to scientific discovery. *Artificial Intelligence, 91*, 183–203.

Tardy, C. M. and Swales, J. M. (2008). Form, Text Organization, Genre, Coherence, and Cohesion. In C. Bazerman (Ed.), *Handbook of research on writing* (pp. 565–581). New York: Lawrence Erlbaum Associates.

Teuscher, C. (2002). *Turing's connectionism: an investigation of neural network architectures*. London: Springer.

Teuscher, C. (2004). *Alan Turing : life and legacy of a great thinker*. Berlin; New York: Springer.

Tishkoff, S. A. and Kidd, K. K. (2004). Implications of biogeography of human populations for 'race' and medicine. *Nature Genetics, 36*(11s), S21–S27.

Tolchinsky, L. (2009). The Configuration of Literacy as a Domain of Knowledge. In D. R. Olson and N. Torrance (eds.), *The Cambridge handbook of literacy* (pp. 468–486). Cambridge, UK: Cambridge University Press.

Tomasello, M. (1999). *The cultural origins of human cognition*. Cambridge, Mass.; London: Harvard University Press.

Tomasello, M. (2008). *Origins of human communication*. Cambridge, Mass.; London: MIT.

Tomasello, M. (2009). *Why we cooperate*. Cambridge, Mass.: MIT Press.

Tomasello, M., Carpenter, M., Call, J., Behne, T., and Moll, H. (2005). Understanding and sharing intentions: The origins of cultural cognition. *Behavioral and Brain Sciences, 28*, 675–735.

Tomasello, M., Kruger, A. C., and Ratner, H. H. (1993). Cultural learning. *Behavioral and Brain Sciences, 16*, 495–552.

Traulsen, A. and Nowak, M. A. (2006). Evolution of cooperation by multi-level selection. *Proceedings of the National Academy of Sciences, 103*(29), 10952–10955.

Trivers, R. L. (1971). The evolution of reciprocal altruism. *Quarterly Review of Biology, 46*, 35–57.

Trivers, R. L. (1972). Parental Investment and Sexual Selection. In B. Campbell (Ed.), *Sexual selection and the descent of man 1871–1971* (pp. 136–179). Chicago, Ill: Aldine Publishing Company.

Turing, A. M. (1936). On Computable Numbers with an application to the Entscheidungsproblem. *Proceedings of the London Mathematical Society, ser.2, 42*, 230–265.

Turing, A. M. (1992). *Collected works of A.M. Turing: mechanical intelligence: edited by Darrell Ince*. Amsterdam; London: North-Holland.

Tymoczko, T. (Ed.). (1998). *New directions in the philosophy of mathematics: an anthology* (Rev. and expanded ed.). Princeton, N.J.: Princeton University Press.

UN. (2010). *The Millennium Development Goals Report 2010*. New York: United Nations.

UNESCO. (2002). *EFA Global Monitoring Report: education for all: is the world on track?* Paris: UNESCO Publishing.

UNESCO. (2003–4). *EFA Global Monitoring Report: gender and education for all: the leap to equality*. Paris: UNESCO Publishing.

UNESCO. (2005). *EFA Global Monitoring Report: education for all: the quality imperative*. Paris: UNESCO Publishing.

UNESCO. (2006). *Education for All Global Monitoring Report: literacy for life*. Paris: UNESCO Publishing.

UNESCO. (2007). *EFA Global Monitoring Report: strong foundations: early childhood care and education*. Paris: UNESCO Publishing.

UNESCO. (2008). *EFA Global Monitoring Report: education for all by 2015: will we make it?* Oxford, UK: Oxford University Press.

UNESCO. (2009). *EFA Global Monitoring Report: overcoming inequality: why governance matters.* Oxford: Oxford University Press.

UNESCO. (2010). *EFA Global Monitoring Report: reaching the marginalized.* Paris, Oxford: UNESCO; Oxford University Press.

UNESCO. (2011). *EFA Global Monitoring Report: the hidden crisis: armed conflict and education:* UNESCO Publishing.

Unterhalter, E. (2003). The Capabilities Approach and Gendered Education: An Examination of South African Complexities. *Theory and Research in Education,* *1*(1), 7–22.

Unterhalter, E. (2005). Global inequality, capabilities, social justice: The millennium development goal for gender equality in education. *International Journal of Educational Development, 25*(2), 111–122.

Urton, G. (2003). *Signs of the Inka Khipu: binary coding in the Andean knotted-string records.* Austin: University of Texas Press.

Van Heijenoort, J. (Ed.). (1967). *From Frege to Gödel: a source book in mathematical logic, 1879–1931.* Cambridge, Mass.: Harvard University Press.

Vendler, H. (1995). *The given and the made: strategies of poetic redefinition.* Cambridge, Mass.: Harvard University Press.

Vendler, H. (2004). *Poets thinking: Pope, Whitman, Dickinson, Yeats.* Cambridge, Mass.: Harvard University Press.

Venter, J. C. (2001). The Sequence of the Human Genome. *Science, 291*(5507), 1304–1351.

Von Neumann, J. (1948). The General and Logical Theory of Automata. In W. Aspray and A. W. Burks (Eds.), *Papers of John von Neumann on computing and computer theory.* Cambridge, Mass.: MIT Press.

Waage, J. K. (1997). Parental Investment–Minding the Kids or Keeping Control? In P. A. Gowaty (Ed.), *Feminism and evolutionary biology* (pp. 527–553). London: Chapman and Hall.

Wagner, C. S. (2008). *The new invisible college: science for development.* Washington, D.C.: Brookings Institution Press.

Walker, M. and Unterhalter, E. (Eds.). (2007). *Amartya Sen's capability approach and social justice in education.* Basingstoke: Palgrave Macmillan.

Watson, J. B. (1913). Psychology as the Behaviorist Views It. *Psychological Review, 20*, 158–177.

Wells, A. J. (2006). *Rethinking cognitive computation: Turing and the science of the mind.* Basingstoke: Palgrave Macmillan.

Wells, A. J. (2002). Gibson's Affordances and Turing's Theory of Computation. *Ecological Psychology, 14*(3), 141–180.

Whiten, A. and Byrne, R. W. (Eds.). (1997). *Machiavellian intelligence II: extensions and evaluations.* Cambridge: Cambridge University Press.

Wilkinson, R. G. and Pickett, K. (2009). *The spirit level: why more equal societies almost always do better.* London: Allen Lane.

Williams, G. C. (1966). *Adaptation and natural selection: a critique of some current evolutionary thought.* Princeton, NJ: Princeton University Press.

Wilson, D. S. and Wilson, E. O. (2007). Survival of the selfless. *New Scientist, 3 November*, 42–46.

Winter, J. (2000). *To do with freedom*. Calcutta: Writers Workshop.

Winter, J. (2003). *Guest and host: poems from Calcutta*. London: Anvil Press Poetry.

Witherspoon, D. J., Wooding, S., Rogers, A. R., Marchani, E. E., Watkins, W. S., Batzer, M. A., et al. (2007). Genetic Similarities Within and Between Human Populations. *Genetics, 176*(1), 351–359.

Wittgenstein, L. (1953). *Philosophical investigations*. Oxford, UK: Basil Blackwell.

Wrangham, R. (2004). Killer species. *Daedalus, 133*(4), 25–35.

Wynne-Edwards, V. C. (1962). *Animal dispersion: in relation to social behaviour*. Edinburgh; London: Oliver and Boyd.

Young, M. (2009). Basic Capabilities, Basic Learning Outcomes and Thresholds of Learning. *Journal of Human Development and Capabilities, 10*(2), 259–277.

Zammit, K. (2011). Moves in hypertext: The resource of negotiation as a means to describe the way students navigate a pathway through hypertext. *Linguistics and Education, 22*(2), 168–181.

Zjada, J. and Zjada, R. (2003). The Politics of Rewriting History: New History Textbooks and Curriculum Materials in Russia. *International Review of Education, 49*(3–4), 363–384.

Zlidar, V. M., Gardner, R., Rutstein, S. O., Morris, L., Goldberg, H., and Johnson, K. (2003). *New survey findings: the reproductive revolution continues*. Baltimore: Johns Hopkins Bloomberg School of Public Health.

Index